Student Study Guide to Accompany Psychology: An Introduction, Eighth Edition

Gerow/Bordens

Printed in the United States of America

ISBN 1-58316-142-2

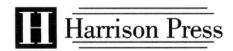 Harrison Press

465 South Meadows Parkway, Suite 20-49 • Reno NV 89521 • 1-800-970-1883

Table of Contents

1. The Science That Is Psychology 1

2. The Biological Basis of Psychological Functioning 21

3. Sensation and Perception 39

4. Varieties of Consciousness 59

5. Learning 75

6. Memory 93

7. "Higher" Cognitive Processes 108

8. Human Development 126

9. Personality 144

10. Motivation and Emotion 159

11. Psychology, Stress, and Physical Health 173

12. The Psychological Disorders 187

13. Treatment and Therapy for Psychological Disorders 203

14. Social Psychology 218

15. Industrial/Organizational, Environmental, and Sport Psychology 234

Chapter 1

The Science That Is Psychology

STUDY TIP #1

<u>Now's The Time</u>

Welcome to psychology! I hope that you find this course (and this textbook and study guide) to be all that you expect it to be. At the beginning of each chapter in the Study Guide, I will share some thoughts on how to maximize your performance in this course. The suggestions and advice that I'll make come directly from psychology itself and have been tested over generations of college students.

You are about to begin a new course, and a new semester. It's all rather exciting, really. In many ways, the beginning of a new semester is nearly magical—filled with promise, high hopes, and good intentions. There are new people to meet, new experiences to be relished, new things to be learned.

What I would like you to start thinking about right now is that <u>right now</u> is the very best time to get started with your studying. The points you earn on your first classroom test are just as valuable as the points you'll earn on your final exam. As I am writing this study tip, it is final exam week on my campus. Several of my students are now wishing that they had done better on our classroom quizzes earlier in the semester because <u>now</u> they find that they must do a truly superior job on the final exam. That's putting unnecessary pressure on one's self at finals time.

There is recent research that demonstrates that procrastinators—people who tend to put things off until "later"—are healthy and happy people at the beginning of a semester. Toward the end of the semester, however, because they have neglected so much work, they are unhappy, stressed, and suffer an abnormally high incidence of physical ailments and illnesses.

So get to it—not this weekend, or tomorrow, or the day after, but right now, today. As the semester goes by, you'll be glad you got off to a good start. I wish you well. If at any time during this course you have any questions at all, please feel free to contact me at **TheCyProf@aol.com**.

Josh R. Gerow

Outline ~ Chapter 1: The Science That Is Psychology

Topic 1A: What Is Psychology?

I. What Is Psychology?
   A. **Psychology** is the science of behavior and mental processes.
   B. Psychology is a science.
       1. Psychologists use scientific techniques to build a body of knowledge.
       2. Psychologists have an interest in animals as well as humans.
       3. Psychologists study mental processes.

II. The Subject Matter of Psychology
   A. **Behavior** is what organisms do—their actions and responses.
       1. The behaviors of organisms are observable and potentially measurable.
       2. Observable behaviors are *publicly verifiable.*
   B. Psychologists also study two types of mental processes: cognitions and affects.
       1. **Cognitions** are mental events, such as perceptions, beliefs, thoughts, ideas, and memories.
       2. **Affect** refers to mental processes that involve one's feelings, mood, or emotional state.
   C. The ABCs of psychology refer to the science of affect, behavior, and cognition.
   D. An **operational definition** defines concepts in terms of the procedures used to measure or create them.

III. Psychology: Science and Practice
   A. A **science** is an organized body of knowledge gained through application of scientific methods.
       1. The **scientific method** is a method of acquiring knowledge by observing a phenomenon, formulating hypotheses, further observing and experimenting, and refining and re-testing hypotheses.
       2. A **hypothesis** is a tentative explanation of some phenomenon that can be tested and either supported or rejected.
       3. A scientific hypothesis may be rejected or supported, but it cannot be "proven" as true.
   B. The goal of many psychologists is to apply what is known to their work.
       1. All psychologists are scientists.
       2. *Science-practitioners* include clinical or counseling psychologists, I/O psychologists, sports psychologists, etc.
       3. We may say that psychology has two interrelated goals.
           a. One goal is to use scientific methods to better understand the behaviors and mental processes of organisms.
           b. The second goal is to apply that understanding to help solve problems in the real world.

IV. Psychological Approaches Past and Present
   A. No two psychologists approach their subject matter exactly the same way.
   B. Each psychologist brings unique experiences, expertise, values, and prejudices to the study of behavior and mental processes. This is true today, and always has been.

V. Psychology's Roots in Philosophy and Science
   A. René Descartes (1596-1650) viewed the human body as a machine, subject to physical laws.
       1. This doctrine is known as **mechanism**.
       2. **Dualism** refers to the idea that a human possesses a mind as well as a body.

3. Descartes proposed *interactive dualism* to explain how the mind and body influence each other.
   B. John Locke (1632-1704) and his British followers developed the doctrine of **empiricism**.
      1. Like Aristotle in the third century B.C., Locke and his followers believed the mind of a newborn was like a blank slate, or *tabula rasa.*
      2. They believed that the mind became filled with ideas and memories due to experience and observation.
   C. Charles Darwin (1809-1882) had a profound effect on psychology by confirming that the human species was part of the natural world of animal life.
      1. *The Origin of the Species* was published in 1859.
      2. Darwin emphasized that *adaptation* to one's environment was often a mental as well as a physical process.
   D. Gustav Fechner (1801-1887), a German physicist, applied his training in the methods of physics to the psychological process of sensation.
   E. Hermann von Helmholtz (1821-1894) performed experiments and developed theories in the physiology laboratory to explain how long it takes the nervous system to respond to stimuli, how information is processed through the senses, and how we experience color.

VI. The Early Years: Structuralism and Functionalism
   A. Wilhelm Wundt (1832-1920) is often credited as the founder of psychology for opening his laboratory at the University of Leipzig in 1879.
      1. For Wundt, psychology was the scientific study of the mind and of consciousness.
      2. His approach is known as **structuralism.**
      3. **Introspection** was the primary method used to dissect mental activity into its component parts.
   B. William James (1842-1910) thought consciousness was continuous.
      1. He did not believe that it could be broken into elements.
      2. He believed that psychology should not be concerned with the structure of the mind, but rather its function: How does the mind *function* to help the organism adapt to its environment?
      3. This approach is called **functionalism**.
   C. Margaret Floy Washburn (1871-1939), the first woman to be awarded a Ph.D. in psychology, addressed questions of animal consciousness and intelligence in a textbook she wrote, *The Animal Mind.*
   D. Mary Calkins (1863-1930) was the first woman elected president of the American Psychological Association in 1905, even though Harvard would not award her a Ph.D. for which she had met all academic requirements.
   E. Christine Ladd-Franklin (1847-1930) received her Ph.D. 40 years after it was earned, and authored an influential theory on how humans perceive color.

VII. Behaviorism
   A. John B. Watson (1878-1958) believed that psychology had to focus on events that can be observed and measured, an approach known as **behaviorism.**
      1. He banished the study of the mind form psychology.
      2. Watson essentially changed the definition of psychology.
   B. B.F. Skinner (1904-1990) studied relationships between responses and the circumstances under which those responses occur.
      1. He believed that psychology should be defined as "the science of behavior."
      2. What mattered for Skinner is how behaviors are modified by events in the environment.

VIII. Psychoanalytic Psychology
    A. Sigmund Freud (1856-1939), a Viennese physician, was interested in "nervous disorders."
    B. His insights came from observations of patients and himself.
    C. His approach emphasized the influence of instincts and the unconscious mind, a school of psychology called **psychoanalytic psychology.**
    D. His approach was the beginning of modern clinical psychology.

IX. Humanistic Psychology
    A. The leaders of this approach were Carl Rogers (1902-1987) and Abraham Maslow (1908-1970).
    B. **Humanistic psychology** posits that the individual, or self, is the central concern of psychology.
    C. This approach emphasizes individuals being in control of their destinies.
    D. Rogers developed a system of psychotherapy and Maslow developed a theory of human motivation.

X. Gestalt Psychology
    A. This approach was championed by Max Wertheimer (1880-1943).
    B. Gestalt is a German word that roughly means "whole" or "totality."
    C. This approach emphasized the notion of the "whole being more that the sum of its parts."
    D. **Gestalt psychology** focuses on perception and how we select and organize information from the outside world.

XI. Contemporary Approaches to Psychology
    A. There are over 500,000 psychologists in the world today.
    B. The American Psychological Association has more than 155,000 members, and has over 50 divisions to which its members belong.
    C. The American Psychological Society, formed in 1988, has about 15,000 members.
    D. **The Biological Approach** emphasizes biochemistry to explain psychological functioning in terms of genetics and the operation of the nervous system.
    E. **The Evolutionary Approach** focuses on how behaviors and mental processes promote the species' survival and adaptation to the environment.
    F. **The Psychodynamic, or Psychoanalytic Approach** suggests that behaviors and mental processes reflect an interaction or conflict among unconscious urges, drives, instincts, and the perceptions of societal pressures.
    G. **The Behavioral Approach** focuses on learning, and observable behaviors.
    H. **The Cognitive Approach** focuses on how an organism processes information about itself and the world in which it lives.
    I. **The Cross-Cultural Approach** appreciates that what an individual finds reinforcing or motivating and how mental illness is defined, varies enormously from culture to culture.
    J. **An Emerging Approach: Positive Psychology** focuses on mental health.
        1. Martin Seligman and Mihaly Csikszentmihayi introduced this approach.
        2. Seligman says that there are three pillars to positive psychology: the study of subjective well-being, positive individual traits, and positive institutions.

TOPIC 1B: The Research Methods of Psychology

I. Making Observations
    A. All of science begins with observation.
    B. Before we can explain what organisms do, we must observe what it is that they do.
    C. **Naturalistic observation** involves carefully and systematically watching behaviors as they occur naturally, with a minimum of involvement by the observer.
        1. It is important that observed organisms do not realize they are being observed.

2. One must overcome the **observer bias** of having one's expectations, motives, experiences, etc. interfere with one's observations.
3. Naturalistic observation often takes great patience because the behaviors of interest may not occur very often.

D. **Surveys** amount to systematically asking a large number of persons the same question or questions.
1. A **sample** is a subset of a larger population that has been chosen for study.
2. To be useful one's sample for a survey needs to be relatively large and representative of the population of interest.

E. In a **case history approach**, a single person, or a small group of persons, is studied in considerable depth.
1. The method is retrospective, reviewing what has happened in the past.
2. It was the method most often used by Sigmund Freud.

II. Looking For Relationships Among Observations
A. **Correlational research** is a process in which variables are not manipulated, but relationships between two or more variables are measured and investigated.
B. In **experimental research**, one or more variables are manipulated, and scientists look for a relationship between manipulation and changes in behavior.

III. Correlational Research
A. Correlational research involves measuring two or more variables and looking for a relationship or association between them.
B. No variables are manipulated.
C. If it is not proper or possible to manipulate a variable of interest, then this method is warranted.
D. Any research involving the age of a person as a variable is correlational, because a person's age is fixed, although it may be associated with many other variables.

IV. The Correlation Coefficient
A. A **correlation coefficient** (r) is a statistic that yields a number between -1.00 and +1.00.
B. A **positive correlation** tells us that two responses are related to each other.
1. As the value of one variable increases (or decreases), the value of the second also increases (or decreases).
2. The direction for change for each variable is in the same.
C. A negative sign indicates a **negative correlation** or inverse relationship between variables.
1. As the value of one variable increases, the value of the second decreases.
2. Here, the direction of change for each variable is opposite.
D. If the correlation coefficient is near zero, there is no relationship between the two measures.
1. As correlations approach zero, predictability decreases.
2. The closer to the extreme of +1.00 or -1.00, the stronger the relationship between the measured responses, and the more confidence we can have predicting the value of one knowing the other.
E. One cannot infer a causal relationship between variables based on a correlational study.
F. Even when two responses are highly correlated, one cannot make predictions for individual cases.

V. Looking for Cause and Effect Among Observations
A. An **experiment** is a series of operations used to investigate relationships between manipulated events and measured events, while other events are controlled or eliminated.
B. Experiments are designed to discover cause-and-effect relationships among variables.

VI. Doing Experiments: The Basic Process
A. An **independent variable** is the variable that is manipulated by the experimenter, and its value is determined by the experimenter.

B. A **dependent variable** provides the measure of a participant's behavior, and its value depends on what the participant does.

C. The **experimental group** receives a nonzero level of the independent variable.

D. The **control group** receives a zero level of the independent variable and provides a baseline of behavior to which performance of subjects in the experimental group is compared.

E. A **placebo** is something given to research participants that has no identifiable effect on performance.

F. An **extraneous variable** is any factor—other than the independent variable—that might affect the value of the dependent variable.
   1. These variables need to be controlled or eliminated.
   2. The quality or value of an experiment is often a reflection of the extent to which extraneous variables have been successfully controlled.

VII. Doing Experiments: Exercising Control
   A. Extraneous variables need to be considered and controlled for before an experiment begins.
   B. **Random assignment** insures that participants have an equal chance of being assigned to any one of the groups used in the experiment.
   C. A **baseline design** allows participants to serve in both experimental and control group conditions while their behavior is observed.

VIII. The Generality of Psychological Research
   A. **Generalization** (in the context of doing scientific research) refers to the ability to apply results of one's research beyond the restricted conditions of the experiment.
   B. **Field experiments** are conducted in the real world.
   C. A balance must be struck between experimental control and generality.

IX. Using a Meta-analysis
   A. A **meta-analysis** is a statistical procedure of combining the results of many studies to more clearly see the relationship, if any, between independent and dependent variables.
   B. A meta-analysis minimizes the errors that can plague single, smaller studies.

X. Ethics in Psychological Research
   A. Psychologists have long been concerned with the ethical implications of their work.
   B. Psychologists need to be concerned not only with the application of their research but also with the gathering of information.

XI. Ethics and Research with Human Participants
   A. The **APA ethical guidelines** specifies ethical treatment of human and animal subjects used in psychological research.
   B. Participants' confidentially must be guaranteed.
   C. Participation in research must be voluntary.
   D. Persons should be included in experiments only after they have given their consent.
   E. All participants should be debriefed after the experiment has been completed.
   F. There are additional guidelines if children or other specialized populations are used.

XII. Ethics and the Use of Animal Subjects in Research
   A. APA ethical guidelines for using animals in research are quite stringent.
   B. Government regulations also must be followed.
   C. All these guidelines and regulations protect the safety and well-being of animals used in research.

Practice Test Questions

TOPIC 1A: WHAT IS PSYCHOLOGY?

Multiple Choice

1. If you feel queasy, apprehensive, or nervous at the sight of exam papers, you are experiencing
   ___a. cognition.   ___c. placebo.
   ___b. affect.   ___d. conflict.

2. Which of the following best describes psychology's subject matter?
   ___a. what people do, normally and abnormally
   ___b. the actions of people when they are stimulated
   ___c. the mental activities and behaviors of organisms
   ___d. what people think about the things that affect them

3. Which of the following is the best example of an operational definition?
   ___a. Hypotheses are educated guesses that can be confirmed or rejected by evidence.
   ___b. Class participation is the number of times a student raises his or her hand in class.
   ___c. Cognitive processes include perception, remembering, problem solving, and understanding.
   ___d. Reading ability can be used to predict success in introductory psychology classes.

4. When a researcher develops a tentative explanation for some phenomenon that can be tested and then either rejected or supported, that researcher has developed
   ___a. a scientific method.   ___c. a hypothesis.
   ___b. empirical evidence.   ___d. an operational definition.

5. Clinical psychologists and industrial/organizational psychologists are sometimes referred to as "scientist-practitioners" because they
   ___a. seldom have a Ph.D. in psychology.
   ___b. work in clinics and hospitals.
   ___c. usually do not use the scientific method in their work.
   ___d. work to apply psychological knowledge in the real world.

6. When psychology emerged as a separate discipline, it did so because it had combined
   ___a. energy with matter.
   ___b. scientific methods with philosophical questions.
   ___c. cognitive processes with affective reactions.
   ___d. mental process with behavior.

7. René Descartes and John Locke deserve mention in any discussion of the history of psychology because they
   ___a. predicted that the science of psychology would be successful and popular.
   ___b. believed that human actions could be explained in their own right, without relying on God or religion.
   ___c. realized the importance of the pineal gland in human behavior.
   ___d. applied scientific methods to issues of human nature and understanding.

8. Which of these psychologists placed the LEAST emphasis on human consciousness?
   ___a. Wilhelm Wundt   ___c. John Locke
   ___b. John Watson   ___d. William James

9. In psychology's development, those psychologists most concerned with the basic processes underlying our perception of the world were the _____ psychologists.
   ___a. behaviorist   ___c. psychoanalytic
   ___b. humanist   ___d. gestalt

10. Which of these psychologists is best associated with the study of animal behaviors?
   ___a. Max Wertheimer   ___c. Margaret Floy Washburn
   ___b. Christine Ladd-Franklin   ___d. Abraham Maslow

11. Who is most likely to have made the statement, "Psychology should focus on the person, the self, in all its aspects as it interacts with the fabric of experience"?
   ___a. a behaviorist psychologist   ___c. a functionalist psychologist
   ___b. a cognitive psychologist   ___d. a humanistic psychologist

12. Which contemporary approach to psychology owes the greatest debt to the work of Sigmund Freud?
   ___a. the behavioral approach   ___c. the psychoanalytic approach
   ___b. the psycho-physiological approach   ___d. the evolutionary approach

13. Among other things, the newly emerging field of "positive psychology" focuses on
   ___a. one's genetic constitution and how it influences behaviors and mental processes.
   ___b. the study of subjective well-being, satisfaction, optimism, hope, and faith.
   ___c. the reinforcement and punishment contingencies that follow one's behaviors.
   ___d. the growth and development of the individual from the stage of the embryo until death.

True/False

1. ____True ____False   Science is the only way to gain insight into the nature of human behavior.

2. ____True ____False   Psychologists study the ABCs; Affect, Behavior, and Cognition.

3. ____True ____False   The first psychology laboratory was opened in the late 1900s by Sigmund Freud in Vienna.

4. ____True ____False   Psychology began as "the science of the mind, or of consciousness."

5. ____True ____False   Clinical and counseling psychologists may be referred to as "scientist-practitioners."

TOPIC 1B: THE RESEARCH METHODS OF PSYCHOLOGY

Multiple Choice

1. The basic, or first step, of all of the specific research methods in psychology is
   ___a. the formation of correct hypotheses.
   ___b. knowing ahead of time if one's theory is accurate.
   ___c. making careful observations of one's subject matter.
   ___d. choosing to use people rather than animals in one's research.

2. Although there are many varieties and types of research in psychology, research methods tend to fall into one of which two categories?
   ___a. experimental and correlational
   ___b. meta-analyses and baseline designs
   ___c. unilateral and factorial
   ___d. physical or social

3. Of these techniques of observation, which is likely to engage the greatest number of subjects or participants?
   ___a. role-playing   ___c. surveys
   ___b. naturalistic observation ___d. case studies

4. Observer bias is a problem in all psychological methods, but is particularly problematic when using
   ___a. laboratory experiments.   ___c. correlational studies.
   ___b. naturalistic observation.   ___d field experiments.

5. Which of these correlation coefficients indicates the presence of a relationship between two variables such that we can most confidently predict one response knowing the other?
   ___a. + .56   ___c. - .71
   ___b. + .0002   ___d. - 2.34

6. A correlation between which pair of variables is most likely to be NEGATIVE?
   ___a. high school GPAs and college GPAs
   ___b. scores on a typing test and actual typing skills
   ___c. number of cigarettes smoked and the likelihood of developing lung cancer
   ___d. the brightness of the lighting in a restaurant and the quality of food there

7. The quality or value of the results of an experiment mostly depend upon
   ___a. the extent to which extraneous variables have been controlled or eliminated.
   ___b. the number of independent variables that have been manipulated.
   ___c. the extent to which the independent and the dependent variables are correlated with each other.
   ___d. whether humans or nonhumans were used as participants in the experiment.

8. If you want to experimentally test the usefulness of a new drug for treating some psychological disorder, the independent variable in your experiment will be
   ___a. the extent to which patients show improvement after taking the drug.
   ___b. the amount of the drug administered to the patients.
   ___c. the type of psychological disorder being treated.
   ___d. other forms of treatment or therapy that the patients are receiving.

9. If one is used, a placebo is usually given to
      ___a. confederates or associates of the experimenter.
      ___b. members of the experimental group.
      ___c. only those participants who know that they are getting a placebo.
      ___d. members of the control group.

10. A major advantage of the baseline experimental design is that
      ___a. participants serve in both the experimental and control conditions.
      ___b. it tends to take significantly less time than do standard experimental methods.
      ___c. more participants can take part in the experiment.
      ___d. participants will not need to be debriefed when the experiment is over.

11. In what way are ethical issues in psychology different (at least by degree) from ethical issues in other sciences?
      ___a. Psychologists use living organisms in their research.
      ___b. Psychology is such a young science, just what is ethical is difficult to determine.
      ___c. Ethics matter as much in the collection of information as in the application of information.
      ___d. Issues studied by psychologists tend to have an impact on the daily lives of so many people.

True/False

1. ____True ____False   Surveys provide more useful information than do either case history studies or naturalistic observation.

2. ____True ____False   Positive correlations are more useful than negative correlations.

3. ____True ____False   Experiments are the only scientific methods used by psychologists.

4. ____True ____False   An experiment should involve only two groups, one experimental and one control group.

5. ____True ____False   A meta-analysis involves the re-examination of previously collected data.

Key Terms and Concepts
Topic 1A

psychology_____

_____

behavior_____

_____

cognitions_____

_____

affect_____

_____

operational definition_____

_____

science_____

_____

scientific methods_____

_____

hypothesis_____

_____

mechanism_____

_____

dualism_____

_____

empiricism_____

_____

structuralism_____

_____

functionalism_____

_____

behaviorism_____

_____

psychoanalytic psychology_____

_____

humanistic psychology_____

_____

Topic 1B

gestalt psychology_____

_____

naturalistic observation_____

_____

observer bias_____

_____

survey_____

_____

sample_____

_____

case history_____

_____

correlational research_____

_____

experimental research_____

_____

correlation coefficient_____

_____

positive correlation coefficient_____

_____

negative correlation coefficient_____

_____

experiment_____

_____

independent variable_____

_____

dependent variable_____

_____

experimental group_____

_____

control group_____

_____

placebo_____

_____

extraneous variables_____

_____

random assignment_____

_____

baseline design_____

_____

generalization (in research)_____

_____

field experiments_____

_____

meta-analysis_____

_____

APA ethical guidelines_____

_____

Answers to Practice Test Questions

TOPIC 1A: WHAT IS PSYCHOLOGY?

Multiple Choice

1. **b**   If you <u>feel</u> anything, you are having, or experiencing affect. Remember: cognitions are thoughts or ideas. Conflicts often give rise to affect.
2. **c**   Psychologists study all of these things, but the only answer that is general enough not to exclude a part of psychology's subject matter is alternative **c**.
3. **b**   Operational definitions tell us how we are to measure something, not what that thing <u>is</u>. Here we have four correct statements (or reasonable definitions), but alternative **b** is the only one that provides an operational definition.
4. **c**   All you need to do here is recognize the definition of the term "hypothesis."
5. **d**   What makes psychologists "scientist-practitioners" is that they spend most of their time trying to apply psychological knowledge to problems in the real world. That is, they "practice" the "science" of psychology.
6. **b**   Alternatives **c** and **d** tell us about psychology's subject matter. When psychology began, the focus was on applying scientific methods to deal with old philosophical questions about the nature of the mind.
7. **b**   What both these men did—as philosophers, not as scientists—was to focus on understanding human nature without reference to deity or to religious beliefs.
8. **b**   Wundt, James, and Locke would have been comfortable defining psychology as the study of human consciousness. It was John B. Watson who had a problem with a science of consciousness and preferred to define psychology as the science of behavior.
9. **d**   Perception is a basic process that has been a concern of every variety of psychology over the years, but it was the German gestalt psychologists who made perception their central concern.
10. **c**   In fact she wrote the first text on animal behaviors. Christine Ladd-Franklin focused on color vision. Wertheimer was a gestalt psychologist, and Maslow a humanistic psychologist.
11. **d**   Although no psychologist would actually disagree with such a statement, it is most likely to have been made by a humanistic psychologist. [What sort of statement would be best associated with each of the other types of psychologist?]
12. **c**   The most common association with Freud is "psychoanalytic" and we shall encounter the term often in the study of psychology.
13. **b**   This alternative goes a long way toward defining just what the new, emerging approach of "positive psychology" is all about.

True/False

1. **F**   There are many ways of gaining insight into the nature of the world and the organisms that populate it. As it happens, psychology values science above the others, but there *are* others.
2. **T**   There are lots of different ABCs, but in psychology, our ABCs are indeed, affect, behavior, and cognition.
3. **F**   The first laboratory was opened in the late 1800s (1879) in Leipzig, Germany, by Wilhelm Wundt.
4. **T**   Yes, it did. Then it became "the science of behavior." Now it is the "science of behavior <u>and</u> mental processes.
5. **T**   Clinical and counseling psychologists are among those scientist-practitioners who apply psychological information in the real world.

TOPIC 1B: THE RESEARCH METHODS OF PSYCHOLOGY

Multiple Choice

1. **c**   No matter which of the scientific methods one uses in psychology, all of them flow from first making careful observations of one's subject matter.
2. **a**   Yes, there are many specific methods, but ultimately they will yield either a correlation or a cause-and-effect statement resulting from experimentation.
3. **c**   The advantage of surveys is that it generally gathers observations form large numbers of persons. Its analysis is seldom very deep, but it can be very broad.
4. **b**   The whole point of naturalistic observation is to view behaviors as they actually occur in nature with as little influence of the observer as possible.
5. **c**   Actually, this is a rather "standard" test item. Alternative **d** is wrong because correlation coefficients cannot exceed +1.00 or –1.00. Useful predictions hinge on how close the coefficient is to either extreme of +1.00 or –1.00, where the sign (+ or -) is irrelevant.
6. **d**   With a negative correlation, high scores on one variable are associated with low scores on the other. It is our experience, at least, that as the lighting in a restaurant goes up (think "fast food"), the quality goes down.
7. **a**   When doing an experiment, the most important—and often the most difficult—thing is to be sure that one has adequately controlled all extraneous variables.
8. **b**   The independent variable is the one that you manipulate; here, the amount or dosage of the drug. Degree of improvement might be your dependent variable, while the type of disorder being treated and other concurrent therapies would be extraneous variables.
9. **d**   Actually, the most proper name for this group is "placebo control."
10. **a**   Baseline designs use subjects as their own controls, where each participant gets both the experimental treatment and the control condition. None of the statements, **b**, **c**, or **d** is correct.
11. **c**   All sciences have ethical concerns about how (or if) to apply what they have learned. The unique problem for psychology—because it uses living organisms as the focus of its study—is that ethical issues are important in the collection of information as well as in its application.

True/False

1. **F**   The type of information afforded by these three techniques is different, to be sure, but to say that one is any more useful than the others depends entirely upon the use to which the observations are to be put. That is, they are just different, not better or worse.
2. **F**   The usefulness of a correlation is not determined by whether it is positive or negative, but by its magnitude.
3. **F**   Probably most of what we know in psychology we have learned by doing experiments, but it is not correct to argue that experimentation is the only scientific method that psychologists use.
4. **F**   Although there is seldom a need for more than one control group, there is considerable good sense for having more than one independent variable—as in factorial experiments.
5. **T**   By definition, one does not (or does not need to) collect new data to perform a meta-analysis; it is a statistical analysis of existing data.

Flash Cards In Psychology

As students, nearly all of us have had some experience using flash cards. For one purpose or another, most of us were first introduced to flash cards in elementary school. I can recall simple arithmetic flash cards that my second-grade teacher used. There was a simple problem on one side (8 + 3) and the answer (11) on the other side. Over and over she drilled us on simple addition and subtraction problems. My other clear recollection of flash cards is of those I made for myself as I struggled with French vocabulary in high school. Do you have any memories of having used flash cards?

What I am proposing here is that this (very "low tech") method can be useful in learning many of the terms and concepts of general psychology. College students sometimes feel that flash cards are too elementary to be truly helpful. And I agree that there <u>are</u> many learning situations for which flash cards may not be advisable. For learning basic vocabulary and for memorizing basic ideas and facts, however, flash cards have much to recommend them. Here I will do three things: (1) I'll explain why—or how—flash cards can be useful, (2) I'll provide some guidelines for making and using flash cards, and (3) I'll provide a sample of a few flash cards for each of the first five chapters of <u>Psychology: An Introduction, Seventh Edition,</u> just to get you started. I am reluctant to provide too many, because the process of making flash cards can be as much of a learning experience as using them.

The Nature and Advantages of Flash Cards

Flash cards are simple cards—3x5 inch index cards work very well—which are used to rehearse associative learning. Whenever you have two pieces of information, say a term and its definition, and you are required to learn to associate one with the other, you will find flash cards useful. One piece of information (the term) is written on one side of the card and the associated information (the definition) is written on the other side.

Flash cards help you learn basic facts and vocabulary. It is important for you to realize that learning about psychology and preparing for exams involves more than just memorizing facts and the definitions of terms. Good exams will also test on conceptual understanding, relationships, the "big picture," and the application of facts. (This is why we ask, "Before You Go On" questions throughout the text and why we've provided "Practice Tests" in this study guide.). What flash cards <u>can</u> do is ensure that you know the foundations for the higher level thinking that will be required on exams.

Flash cards have several advantages, most of which are quite self-evident:
1. They are portable. When carrying your textbook or your notebook is not convenient, you can always find a place for a few 3x5 index cards.
2. They help you practice retrieval skills. Exams require that you locate and retrieve information that you have stored in your memory. Yes, you do have to get that information into memory—which is what learning is all about. But on an exam, you will also have to get that information out of memory storage—which is what retrieval is all about. By using flash cards, you not only will be learning new information, you will be practicing retrieval as well.
3. Flash cards help to inform you about what you know and where trouble spots may be. Self-testing with flash cards can help you avoid surprises at exam time.

Making and Using Flash Cards

On the face of it, making useful flash cards should be a simple matter, and it is. There are, however, a few guidelines that you might want to keep in mind.
1. Place only one concept, term, or phrase on each card. Index cards are relatively inexpensive, and it defeats the purpose of the cards to overload them.
2. At the same time, use only one card for each term, concept, or phrase. If you need more than one card to describe a concept or define a term, you're probably dealing with the sort of information for which flash cards are unsuitable.

3. You have to be careful with technical terminology, but whenever possible, use your own words. Remember, these cards are to help you—to provide you with cues for retrieving information from your own memory.
4. Be creative. Cards easily can accommodate simple drawings, pictures, diagrams, flow charts, and the like, just as easily as they can accommodate words.
5. Don't feel bound to the textbook. Flash cards can help you learn material from class as well as from the text.
6. Guard against "busy work." Attend to what you are doing, and don't spend a lot of time simply copying information (particularly information you already know) directly from the textbook onto cards just for the sake of making flash cards.

Procedures for using your flash cards are also reasonably self-evident. Again, however, there are a few guidelines I'd like you to keep in mind.
1. Once you have written a short pile of cards for a chapter or a topic, shuffle them. Shuffle them again each time you go through the stack. You want to learn about the concepts of general psychology no matter the order in which they appear.
2. Test yourself on both sides of each card. That is, for a vocabulary item, for example, if you were to read the definition first, could you identify the term or concept being defined?
3. After you have gone through a pile of cards a few times, begin to sort them into shorter piles. You might start with two: "I know this for sure" and "I'm totally clueless." Obviously, a "I'm really not sure of these" pile can be useful as well. Once sorted into shorter piles, you'll know where you'll need to spend most of your flash card study time.

Please remember that the points I've listed here are guidelines, not hard-and-fast rules. Flash cards will help only if you make and use them. They are for you. Because there is benefit to be derived from creating flash cards as well as from using them, I've provided only a sample of possible cards for the first five chapters of Psychology: An introduction. The rest is up to you. Good luck!

I want to acknowledge the generous help of two of my colleagues at Indiana University-Purdue University at Fort Wayne. Drs. Carol Lawton and Craig Hill helped to convince me of the value of a flash card approach to study, and provided most of the hints provided here.

A Few Flash Card Possibilities for Chapter 1
(Remember: These are just suggestions. The best flash cards are those you make yourself.)

SCIENCE	1. organized body of knowledge 2. uses scientific methods
ABCs of PSYCHOLOGY	Affect, Behavior, Cognition; i.e., how one feels, what one does, and thinks
OPERATIONAL DEFINITION	defines concepts in terms of how concept will be measured or created (e.g., intelligence = IQ test score)
RENÉ DESCARTES	philosopher – explained humans without ref. to god – mind & body separate but interact (interactive dualism)
WILHELM WUNDT	Leipzig – first psych. lab (1879) – science of mind (consciousness) – structuralism
SAMPLE	a set or portion of a larger group (population) chosen for study
VALUE OF CORRELATION	+1.00 (strongest positive—high w/ high) 0.00 (no relationship) -1.00 (strongest negative—high w/ low)
VARIABLES in an EXPERIMENT	manipulate INDEPENDENT variable measure DEPENDENT variable control EXTRANEOUS variables
RANDOM ASSIGNMENT	making sure that every member of a population has an equal chance of being included in a sample
META-ANALYSIS	statistical combination of results of several previous studies to look for relationships between variables

EXPERIENCING PSYCHOLOGY

Defining Right- and Left-Handedness

Approximately 90 percent of the population of North America is right-handed. One fact revealed in the research on handedness is that most people are not as strongly right-handed or left-handed as they may think.

Here's a project you can try yourself. Ask friends and relatives whether they use their right hand or left hand to complete each of the following tasks. They are to indicate frequency on a 5-point scale:

    (1)   ALWAYS LEFT
    (2)   USUALLY LEFT
    (3)   EQUALLY RIGHT AND LEFT
    (4)   USUALLY RIGHT, and
    (5)   ALWAYS RIGHT

The items to be judged are:

1. *Write a letter.*
2. *Throw a ball at a target.*
3. *Hold scissors to cut paper.*
4. *Deal playing cards.*
5. *Hold a toothbrush while cleaning teeth.*
6. *Unscrew the lid of a jar.*

Now have the same participants in your project actually try the following task, first using one hand, then using the other. You'll need a standard, 81/2 x 11 inch sheet of paper on which you have printed 100 little circles (something like,

□ □ □ □ □ □ □ □ □ □ □ □ □ □ □ □ □ □ □ □
□ □ □ □ □ □ □ □ □ □ □ □ □ □ □ □ □ □ □ □
□ □ □ □ □ □ □ □ □ □ □ □ □ □ □ □ □ □ □ □
□ □ □ □ □ □ □ □ □ □ □ □ □ □ □ □ □ □ □ □
□ □ □ □ □ □ □ □ □ □ □ □ □ □ □ □ □ □ □ □

When you say "go," your subject, using his or her right hand, is to tap on each circle once with a pencil, leaving a mark inside. They are to work as rapidly and as accurately as possible. Allow 30 seconds, then call "stop." After a 30-second rest, have them do the same thing, but now using their left hand. Add up the number of "hits" for each hand (where a "hit" is a mark within the circle—on the line does not count). The hand that earns the higher score may be operationally defined as the dominant hand. Did the results match the participants' self-report? Which measure (self-report or "test") provides the most accurate assessment of handedness?

Chapter 2

The Biological Basis of Psychological Functioning

STUDY TIP #2

"How Much Should I Study?"

One of the main reasons that some students do not do as well in their college courses as they would like is that they simply do not have—or do not make—enough time for studying. If you were to ask Ken Bordens or me (we wrote your text) how much time you should spend studying psychology, we're likely to say something like, "You should be studying every waking minute of every day." As it happens, of course, we know better. We know that you have other classes that require your time, and we realize that you have a multitude of commitments pulling at you for your attention. Nonetheless, if you are going to succeed at this business of being a college student, it is important to understand that being successful is going to be time-consuming. Almost certainly, the amount of time you spent studying in high school will be inadequate now that you are in college.

My students chuckle—or laugh out loud—when I tell them that the standard rule of thumb regarding study time is to schedule three hours outside of class for every hour spent in class. Note what that means: If yours is a 3-credit hour psychology class (most are), you should set aside **9 hours a week** to study psychology! That's right: 9 hours studying psychology in addition to the time you spend in class.

This rule of thumb is valid at the beginning of the semester. A few weeks' experience may suggest that more or less time will be needed depending on the difficulty of the classes you are taking. Some classes may require even more time, while a few may take less. The implications here are significant. If you are taking a full-time load, or nearly so, let's say 15-18 credit hours, I'm suggesting that as an average student, you will need 45 to 54 hours each week for study time. Yes. That's like a full-time job, and thinking about your college experience as a full-time job is a reasonable thing to do. Again: You will be in class or studying from 60 to 72 hours each week. Additionally, you will need time for sleeping, relationships, eating, dressing, driving, a part-time job, perhaps, and—I would hope—some fun! And there are only 168 hours in each week. Time management is clearly an important issue for college students.

Outline ~ Chapter 2: The Biological Basis of Psychological Functioning

TOPIC 2A: NERVE CELLS AND HOW THEY COMMUNICATE

I. Neurons: The Basic Building Blocks of the Nervous System
    A. A **neuron** is a nerve cell that transmits information from one part of the body to another via neural impulses.
    B. No two neurons are exactly alike, but they have structures in common.
        1. The **cell body** contains the cell's nucleus.
        2. **Dendrites,** tentacle-like structures, receive neural impulses from neurons.
        3. An **axon** is a long tail-like extension of a neuron that carries impulses away from the cell body to other cells.
            a. About half of all axons contain **myelin**, which is a white substance made up of fat and protein, that insulates and protects them and speeds impulses along.
            b. Myelin tends to be found on axons that carry impulses relatively long distances.
            c. A loss of myelin is the cause of **multiple sclerosis.**
            d. **Axon terminals** are where axons end in a branching series of bare end points and communicate with adjacent neurons.
    C. In most cases, dead neurons are not replaced with new ones.
        1. Functions of lost neurons can be taken over by surviving neurons.
        2. New research suggests that the growth of new neurons occurs in the adult human brain—although at nowhere near the rate of growth observed before and right after birth.

II. The Function of Neurons
    A. The function of a neuron is to transmit neural impulses from one place in the nervous system to another.
    B. A **neural impulse** is a rapid and reversible change in the electrical charges inside and outside a neuron.
    C. **Chemical ions** are particles that carry a small, measurable electrical charge that is either positive or negative.
        1. When it is "at rest," there are more negative ions than positive ions inside the axon.
        2. Electrical tension results from the attraction between the negative ions and positive ions.
            a. This tension is called the **resting potential.**
            b. The resting potential of a neuron is about -70mV.
            c. At rest the neuron is said to be in a polarized state.
            d. The resting potential is released when a neuron is stimulated to fire.
        3. When it is stimulated, the polarity of the nerve cell changes and the process is called depolarization.
            a. The **action potential** is the short-lived electrical burst caused by the sudden reversal of electric charges inside and outside a neuron in which the inside becomes positive (about +40 mV).
            b. The neuron becomes hyperpolarized during the refractory period and cannot fire.
            c. Eventually, the membrane returns to normal restoring the normal distribution of ions across the cell membrane.
    D. A neuron either fires or it does not—an observation called the **all-or-none principle.**
    E. The **neural threshold** is the minimum amount of stimulation needed to fire a neuron.

III. From One Neuron to Another: The Synapse
   A. The **synapse** is where one neuron communicates with other cells.
   B. The **synaptic cleft** is the space between a neuron and the next cell at a synapse.

IV. Synaptic Transmission
   A. **Vesicles** are small containers concentrated in a neuron's axon terminals that hold neurotransmitter molecules.
   B. **Neurotransmitters** are chemical molecules released at the synapse that, in general, will either excite or inhibit a reaction in the cell on the other side of the synapse.
   C. **Receptor sites** are places on a neuron where neurotransmitters can be received.
      1. It is the interaction of neurotransmitter and receptor site that causes inhibition or excitation.
      2. Once released form their receptor sites, neurotransmitter are either destroyed by enzymes, or taken back up into the neuron from which they came, a process called **reuptake**.

V. Neurotransmitters
   A. Today, we know of nearly 60 neurotransmitters, and there are many yet to be discovered.
   B. There are probably more than 1,000 kinds of neurotransmitter receptors.
      1. There are subtypes of receptor sites for brain chemicals.
      2. The search for and identification of these receptor sites has become one of the hottest areas of brain research.
   C. There are many neurotransmitters, including:
      1. Acetylcholine (Ch) is found throughout the nervous system, where it acts as either an excitatory or inhibitory neurotransmitter, both within the brain and between neurons and muscle cells.
      2. Norepinephrine is involved in activation, vigilance, and mood regulation.
      3. Dopamine has been associated with the thought and mood disturbances of some psychological disorders, and impairment of movement.
      4. Serotonin is related to various behaviors such as the sleep/wake cycle, and plays a role in depression and aggression.
      5. Endorphins are natural pain suppressors.
   D. Any neuron can have hundreds or thousands of axon terminals and synapses, and has the potential for exciting or inhibiting many other neurons.

VI. The Human Nervous Systems: The Big Picture
   A. The **central nervous system** **(CNS)** includes all neurons and supporting cells in the spinal cord and brain.
   B. The **peripheral nervous system (PNS)** consists of all neurons *not* found in the brain and spinal cord but in the periphery of the body.
   C. The PNS is divided into two parts.
      1. The **somatic nervous system (SNS)** includes sensory and motor neurons outside the CNS that serve the sense receptors and the skeletal muscles.
      2. The **autonomic nervous system (ANS)** involves neurons in the peripheral nervous system that activate smooth muscles, such as the stomach, intestines, and glands.
         a. The ANS consists of the sympathetic and the parasympathetic divisions.
         b. The sympathetic division is active when we are in states of emotional excitement or under stress.
         c. The parasympathetic division is active when we are relaxed.

VII. The **endocrine system** is a network of glands that affects behaviors through the secretion of chemicals called hormones.
   A. Its function is to transmit information from one part of the body to another.
   B. Hormones can exert a direct influence over behavior.
   C. There are several endocrine glands throughout our bodies.

1. The **pituitary gland**, nestled under the brain, is the master gland, and secretes many different hormones.
    a. This gland controls such processes as body growth rate, water retention, and the release of milk from the mammary glands.
    b. It also regulates the output of the thyroid and adrenal glands, as well as the sex glands.
2. The **thyroid gland** releases thyroxine, the hormone that regulates the pace of the body's functioning.
3. The **adrenal glands**, located on the kidneys, release adrenaline, or epinephrine, into the bloodstream to activate the body in times of stress or danger.

TOPIC 2B: THE CENTRAL NERVOUS SYSTEM

I. The Structure of the Spinal Cord
   A. **The spinal cord** is a mass of interconnected neurons within the spinal column that transmits impulses to and from the brain and is involved in spinal reflex behaviors; it reaches from the lower back to high in the neck, just below the brain.
   B. **Sensory neurons** carry impulses from the sense receptors to the central nervous system.
   C. **Motor neurons** carry impulses away from the central nervous system to muscles and glands.
   D. **Interneurons** are neurons within the CNS.

II. The Functions of the Spinal Cord
   A. The communication function of the spinal cord involves the transmission of information to and from the brain.
   B. The second function of the spinal cord involves the control of spinal reflexes.
      1. **Spinal reflexes** are simple, involuntary responses to a stimulus that involve sensory neurons, the spinal cord, and motor neurons.
      2. With a simple spinal reflex, impulses travel in on sensory neurons, within on interneurons, and out on motor neurons.
      3. Some spinal reflexes require only sensory neurons, motor neurons, and synapses connecting, and do not require interneurons within the spinal cord itself.

III. The "Lower Brain Centers"
   A. The lower brain centers are physically located beneath the cerebral cortex.
   B. The lower brain centers develop first, both in an evolutionary sense and within the developing brain.
   C. The **brain stem** is the lowest part of the brain, just about the spinal cord, and consists of the medulla and the pons.
      1. The **medulla** is the structure in the brain stem that contains centers that monitor reflex functions such as heart rate and respiration.
         a. **Cross laterality** is the arrangement of nerve fibers crossing from the left side of the body to the right side of the brain, and from the right side of the body to the left side of the brain.
         b. Cross laterality begins in the medulla and also occurs in the pons.
      2. The **pons** is a brain stem structure that forms a bridge that organizes fibers from the spinal cord to the brain and vice versa.
   D. The **cerebellum** is a spherical structure at the rear, base of the brain that coordinates fine and rapid muscular movements.
      1. Damage to the outer region of the cerebellum results in intention **tremors**, which are involuntary trembling movements.
      2. Damage to inner areas of the cerebellum results in tremors at rest.
   E. The **reticular formation** is a network of nerve fibers extending from the base of the brain to the cerebrum; it controls one's level of activation of arousal.

F. The **basal ganglia** are collections of structures in the center of the brain that are involved in the control of large, slow movements; a source of much of the brain's dopamine.
    1. Dopamine, created and usually found in great quantity in the basal ganglia, is insufficient in those persons with Parkinson's disease.
    2. L-dopa is a drug that increases dopamine availability in the basal ganglia.
    3. Transplanting brain cells from aborted human fetuses into the brains of persons with Parkinson's can reverse the course of the disease.
G. The **limbic system** is a collection of structures near the middle of the brain involved in emotionality and long-term memory storage.
    1. The *amygdala* produces reactions of rage or aggression when stimulated.
    2. The *septum* reduces the intensity of emotional responses.
    3. The *hippocampus* is involved with the formation of memories for experiences.
    4. The **hypothalamus** is a structure made up of several nuclei involved in feeding, drinking, temperature regulation, sex, and aggression.
H. The **thalamus** is located just below the cerebral cortex; it projects sensory impulses to the appropriate areas of the cerebral cortex.
    1. While it also acts like a relay station, its major function involves the processing of information from the senses.
    2. Like the pons, nuclei in the thalamus may have a role in establishing normal patterns of sleep and wakefulness.

IV. The Cerebral Cortex
    A. The **cerebral cortex** is the large, convoluted outer covering of the brain that is the seat of voluntary action and cognitive functioning.
    B. A crevice runs down the middle of the cortex dividing it into the left and right cerebral hemispheres.
    C. There are four major divisions of each hemisphere, called lobes.
        1. The *frontal lobes* (left and right) are largest, and are defined by two crevices called the central fissure and the lateral fissure.
        2. The *temporal lobes* are located at the temples, below the lateral fissure, with one on each side of the brain.
        3. The *occipital* lobes are at the back of the brain.
        4. The *parietal lobes* are wedged in behind the frontal lobes and above the occipital and temporal lobes.
    D. In terms of *function*, there are three major areas of the cerebral cortex.
        1. **Sensory areas** receive and process impulses from sense receptors.
        2. **Motor areas** are where most voluntary muscular movements originate.
        3. **Association areas** are in the frontal, temporal, and parietal lobes where incoming sensory input is integrated with motor responses, and where higher mental processes are thought to occur.
            a. Broca's area controls the production of speech.
            b. Wernicke's area is involved in speech comprehension and organizing ideas.
            c. Planning ahead and forethought in general seem to be localized in the very front of the frontal lobes.

V. The Two Cerebral Hemispheres: Splitting the Brain
    A. The two hemispheres are connected by the **corpus callosum**, a network of fibers.
    B. The **split-brain procedure** involves surgical lesioning (or removal) of the corpus callosum, the structure that separates the functions of the left and right hemispheres of the cerebral cortex and is a treatment of last resort for epilepsy.
    C. Virtually no behavior or mental process is the product of one hemisphere alone, but one hemisphere may be dominant with respect to a given task or processing certain types of information, the left hemisphere usually associated with linguistic and serial processing while the right hemisphere is associated with visual/spatial processing and seems more involved in emotionality.

VIII. The Two Sexes: Male and Female Brains
- A. Except for differences that are directly related to reproductive function, there are very few differences that are of real consequence between male and female brains.
- B. There is a difference in the lateralization of the brains of left-handed persons compared to right-handed persons, but no differences in cognitive abilities.
    1. Similar findings for male/female differences have proven difficult to replicate.
    2. Women are more likely than men to show signs of recovery from a stroke because the unaffected side of the brain is better able to compensate for losses in the affected side.

Practice Test Questions

TOPIC 2A: NERVE CELLS AND HOW THEY COMMUNICATE

Multiple Choice

1. Which of the following lists the major structures of the neuron in the correct order?
   ___a. cell body, dendrite, axon
   ___b. axon, dendrite, cell body
   ___c. dendrite, cell body, axon
   ___d. Any of these may be correct, depending upon the particular neuron involved.

2. Of the following structures, which is likely to occur in neurons in the greatest number?
   ___a. dendrites   ___c. axons
   ___b. nuclei   ___d. cell bodies

3. Myelin sheaths serve several different functions. Which of these is NOT something that myelin normally does?
   ___a. insulates axons from other nearby axons
   ___b. helps to speed up impulse transmission
   ___c. produces and stores the neuron's neurotransmitters
   ___d. protects the delicate axon against physical damage

4. When a neuron is "at rest,"
   ___a. it has no electrical charge.
   ___b. the inside of the neuron has a negative charge compared to the outside.
   ___c. it is in the process of "firing," or transmitting an impulse.
   ___d. chemical ions are racing in and out of the neuron.

5. When an impulse moves down or along a neuron, what physically moves from one end of the neuron to the other?
   ___a. the chemical ions involved   ___c. the fluids within the neuron
   ___b. the neural membrane itself   ___d. nothing

6. The "all-or-none principle" states that
   ___a. a neuron will either fire or it won't.
   ___b. neural impulses always travel in one direction.
   ___c. some neurons always fire; some neurons never fire.
   ___d. neurons either have a threshold or they don't.

7. Although there are many specific neurotransmitters, we can classify them in terms of their actions as being either
   ___a. central or peripheral.   ___c. excitatory or inhibitory.
   ___b. sensory or motor.   ___d. axonic or dendritic.

8. The action of neurotransmitters at the synapse is basically a(n) _____ process.
   ___a. electrical   ___c. chemical
   ___b. mechanical   ___d. psychological

9. Of these, which neurotransmitter is said to act like a natural pain suppressant, influencing our experience of pain?
   ___a. serotonin   ___c. acetylcholine
   ___b. endorphin   ___d. dopamine

10. The first major division of the human nervous system is into the _____ nervous system and the _____ nervous system.
    ___a. motor; sensory
    ___b. affective; cognitive
    ___c. central; peripheral
    ___d. somatic; automatic

11. Of the following, which "nervous system" is most intimately involved in our experience of emotion?
    ___a. peripheral nervous system
    ___b. parasympathetic nervous system
    ___c. automatic nervous system
    ___d. sympathetic nervous system

12. The endocrine system operates mostly on the basis of
    ___a. neurons in the spinal cord.
    ___b. hormones in the bloodstream.
    ___c. neurotransmitters in the brain.
    ___d. ions in the neuron.

13. The endocrine gland most intimately involved in metabolism (the body's rate of oxygen use, and growth) is the _____ gland.
    ___a. pituitary
    ___b. execrine
    ___c. thyroid
    ___d. adrenal

True/False

1. ____True ____False   Myelinated neurons carry impulses faster than do unmyelinated neurons.

2. ____True ____False   The number of neurons in your body gradually increases from birth until they begin to die off in old age.

3. ____True ____False   Every neuron has its own threshold—the minimal amount of stimulation required to get it to "fire."

4. ____True ____False   Neurotransmitters move across a synapse to either excite a new impulse in the next neuron or to inhibit that neuron from firing.

5. ____True ____False   Because it uses the bloodstream instead of the neurons, information travels faster in the endocrine system than it does in the nervous system.

TOPIC 2B: THE CENTRAL NERVOUS SYSTEM

Multiple Choice

1. Conscious, voluntary actions originate in the
   ___a. cerebral cortex.   ___c. brain stem.
   ___b. spinal cord.   ___d. muscles and glands.

2. When we look at a cross-section of the spinal cord, we clearly see areas that are made up of white matter. In this white matter we have
   ___a. the area where reflex action takes place.
   ___b. fibers going to and from the brain.
   ___c. nerve fibers entering and leaving the spinal cord itself.
   ___d. the part of the CNS that controls emotions.

3. In a spinal reflex, neural impulses enter the spinal cord on
   ___a. motor neurons.   ___c. sensory neurons.
   ___c. ascending tracts or fibers. ___d. descending tracts or fibers.

4. As one travels up through the brain from the spinal cord, the first brain structure to be encountered would be the
   ___a. corpus callosum.   ___c. medulla.
   ___b. basal ganglia.   ___d. thalamus.

5. Which of the following is best associated with the medulla?
   ___a. thinking or problem solving ___c. sensory projections to the cerebral cortex
   ___b. breathing reflexes   ___d. muscle coordination

6. Cross laterality occurs (mostly) in the
   ___a. spinal cord.   ___c. limbic system.
   ___b. brain stem.   ___d. basal ganglia.

7. If I were to electrically stimulate the reticular formation of a sleeping cat, the result would be that the cat would
   ___a. no longer demonstrate normal emotional responses.
   ___b. die.
   ___c. begin to make small twitching motions, indicative of dreaming.
   ___d. wake up.

8. Which lower brain center is most clearly involved in the experience of being thirsty?
   ___a. the hypothalamus   ___c. the amygdala
   ___c. the hippocampus   ___d. the septum

9. The brain structure that sends, or "projects," sensory impulses to the appropriate area of the cerebral cortex is the
   ___a. thalamus.   ___c. basal ganglia.
   ___b. projectorator.   ___d. body sense area of the parietal lobe.

10. The small structure in the limbic system that seems to be involved in the formation of long-term memories is the
   ___a. amygdala.   ___c. ganglion.
   ___b. hippocampus.   ___d. septum.

11. Our body senses (touch, pressure, and the like) are largely processed at the front of the _____ lobe of the cerebral cortex.

    ___a. occipital   ___c. temporal
    ___b. parietal   ___d. frontal

12. The two hemispheres of the cerebral cortex are richly interconnected by the

    ___a. white matter of the spinal cord.   ___c. corpus callosum.
    ___c. frontal lobe.   ___d. left and right ventricles.

13. A person who has had a split-brain operation is blindfolded. A paper clip is placed in her LEFT hand and we ask her to tell us what we have placed there. She is most likely to

    ___a. tell us that the object is a paper clip and be able to point to it when it is placed on a table with other objects.
    ___b. have no idea of what is in her hand.
    ___c be unable to tell us what we put in her hand, but be able to point to the paper clip when it is on a table with other objects.
    ___d. respond just as if we had placed the paper clip in her RIGHT hand.

14. The difference between male and female brains for which there is the greatest amount of evidence is that

    ___a. the brains of females are significantly larger than those of males.
    ___b. female brains have no hypothalamus.
    ___c. the brains of females are more likely to recover from traumas, such as a stroke.
    ___d. men tend to use their frontal lobes for the storage of long-term memories, whereas women use their parietal lobes.

True/False

1. ____True ____False   The correct sequence of impulses involved in a spinal reflex may be summarized as: in on sensory neurons, within on interneurons, and out on motor neurons.

2. ____True ____False   The basal ganglia are involved in the movement of large skeletal muscles, such as those that are involved in walking.

3. ____True ____False   Visual information is processed in the occipital lobe of the cerebral cortex.

4. ____True ____False   Someone whose corpus callosum has been severed in a split-brain operation will probably need to be hospitalized or closely supervised for the rest of his or her life.

5. ____True ____False   There are simply no structural differences—in general—between the brains of men and the brains of women.

Key Terms and Concepts
Topic 2A

neuron_____

_____

cell body_____

_____

dendrites_____

_____

axon_____

_____

myelin_____

_____

multiple sclerosis (MS)_____

_____

axon terminals_____

_____

neural impulse_____

_____

chemical ions_____

_____

resting potential_____

_____

action potential_____

_____

neural threshold_____

_____

synapse_____

_____

synaptic cleft_____

_____

vesicles_____

_____

neurotransmitters_____

_____

receptor sites_____

_____

reuptake_____

_____

central nervous system (CNS)_____

_____

peripheral nervous system (PNS)_____

_____

somatic nervous system_____

_____

autonomic nervous system_____

_____

endocrine system_____

_____

pituitary gland_____

_____

thyroid gland_____

_____

adrenal glands_____

_____

Topic 2B

spinal cord_____

_____

sensory neurons_____

_____

motor neurons_____

_____

interneurons_____

_____

spinal reflexes_____

_____

brainstem_____

_____

medulla_____

_____

cross laterality_____

_____

pons_____

_____

cerebellum_____

_____

tremors_____

_____

reticular formation_____

_____

basal ganglia_____

_____

limbic system_____

_____

hypothalamus_____

_____

thalamus_____

_____

cerebral cortex_____

_____

sensory areas_____

_____

motor areas_____

_____

association areas_____

_____

corpus callosum_____

_____

split-brain procedure_____

_____

Answers to Practice Test Questions

TOPIC 2A: NERVE CELLS AND HOW THEY COMMUNICATE

Multiple Choice

1. **c**   Within a neuron, impulses travel (typically) from dendrite to cell body to axon. Here's a good example of an item for which "all of the above" is not the correct choice.
2. **a**   A neuron will have only one cell body and one nucleus. As it happens, some may have two axons, but the structure most likely to occur in great numbers is the dendrite.
3. **c**   Myelin serves each of the functions named in alternatives **a**, **b**, and **d**. Be careful to note the "not" in this item. Neurotransmitters are manufactured within the neuron and stored in vesicles.
4. **b**   At rest, a neuron is in position to fire, with many more negative ions inside and positive ions outside, which makes the second alternative correct.
5. **d**   Nothing physically moves down a neuron when it fires. Physical movement is of ions going in and out of the neuron. What moves "down" a neuron is where this ion movement takes place.
6. **a**   This one is straightforward. Alternative **a** is correct by definition.
7. **c**   Watch out for this item! An important phrase in this item is "in terms of their actions," which means we're looking for what they do—which is to either excite or inhibit neural impulse transmission.
8. **c**   Within a neuron, impulse transmission is electrochemical, but at the synapse, given the action of the neurotransmitters, it is basically a chemical process.
9. **b**   Actually, there are several different endorphins, but each is involved in moderating our experience of pain.
10. **c**   The major division of the human nervous system is into central and peripheral systems. Each of these, in turn, has its own divisions.
11. **d**   It is important to know how the various nervous systems are interrelated, and the major functions of each. While the parasympathetic division is active when we are relaxed and calm, the sympathetic division is involved in emotionality. Note the spelling of alternative **c**; there is no such thing as an "automatic" nervous system.
12. **b**   The endocrine system influences behaviors and mental processes, but does so through hormones transmitted through the bloodstream.
13. **c**   The thyroid gland secretes thyroxin—the growth hormone—and is, thus, the best choice here. Yes, the pituitary does influence this gland, as it influences them all, but this item is more specific than that.

True/False

1. **T**   Indeed, one of the important functions of myelin is to speed impulses along.
2. **F**   This may sound logical, but it is not true. We are born with more neurons than we'll ever have again.
3. **T**   The threshold of one neuron may be different from that of other neurons, but every neuron does have its own threshold value of stimulation required to get it to fire.
4. **T**   This is a simple, but accurate, statement of what neurotransmitters do.
5. **F**   Actually, because it uses the bloodstream rather than neurons, the action of the endocrine system is significantly slower than the action of the central nervous system.

TOPIC 2B: THE CENTRAL NERVOUS SYSTEM

Multiple Choice

1. **a**   Conscious, voluntary actions originate in the cerebral cortex, even though other CNS structures may be involved.
2. **b**   The white matter looks white because of the myelin that surrounds the axons of the fibers going up and down the spinal cord, to and from the brain.

3. **c**   This is a straightforward terminology item. For the spinal reflex we have: in on sensory neurons, within on interneurons, and out to muscles or glands on motor neurons.
4. **c**   Although it is difficult to tell exactly where the spinal cord leaves off and the brain begins, the first brain structure to be encountered would be the medulla.
5. **b**   The medulla contains centers (nuclei) that control several important reflexes, including respiration, or breathing.
6. **b**   Cross laterality occurs in the medulla and in the pons. Because these two structures make up the brain stem, this is the best answer.
7. **d**   The reticular activating system, as the name implies, controls levels of arousal. All that would happen in this scenario is that the cat would wake up.
8. **a**   The hypothalamus is not only involved in the thirst drive, but it is also implicated in the hunger drive, temperature regulation drive, sex drive, and others.
9. **a**   This item describes very succinctly the function of the thalamus.
10. **b**   Although the septum and the amygdala are considered to be parts of the limbic system, there is no evidence that they have anything to do with memory directly. The structure that does is the hippocampus.
11. **b**   This gets a bit technical. But you should know the major features of cerebral localization (vision, hearing, movement, etc.), and you should know that the body senses are processed in the front of the parietal lobe.
12. **c**   It is the corpus callosum that normally interconnects the two hemispheres of the cerebral cortex so that as soon as one side "knows" what is going on, the other side "knows" as well.
13. **c**   Don't panic just because this item is wordy. Remember the basics of the split-brain procedure, and remember that speech is a left-hemisphere activity, and that information from the left hand would be processed in the right hemisphere. These details make alternative **c** the correct one.
14. **c**   As a rule of thumb, there are very few differences between the brains of females and males—either structurally or functionally. For reasons not yet fully understood, however, the brains of females do recover more quickly from cerebral accidents or traumas, such as strokes.

True/False

1. **T**   This is basically a repeat of item #16 in true-false form. This sequence is correct.
2. **T**   This statement is true, reinforcing the notion that the basal ganglia are implicated in Parkinson's disease.
3. **T**   Again, you should know the localization of the major functions of the cerebral cortex, including the fact that vision is processed in the occipital lobe.
4. **F**   No, as it happens, it is often very difficult to tell if someone has had this procedure, except when certain brain functions are tested in the laboratory. Split-brain patients can, and do, lead relatively normal lives.
5. **F**   Granted, as I said above, there are very few differences between the brains of females and males, but to claim that there are NO structural differences is silly.

A Few Flash Card Possibilities for Chapter 2

(Remember: These are just suggestions. The best flash cards are those you make yourself.)

PARTS of a NEURON	**cell body (& cell's nucleus), dendrites, and axon with bare endings**
MYELIN	**white, fatty covering on some axons; insulates, protects, speeds impulses**
CHEMICAL ION	**electrically charged (+ or -) chemical particle**
NEURAL THRESHOLD	**minimum amount of stimulation required to get a neuron to fire**
COMPONENTS of the ANS	**autonomic nervous system = sympathetic + parasympathetic divisions**
ENDOCRINE SYSTEM	**glands that release hormones into the bloodstream (slower than nervous system)**
SYNAPTIC SPACE	**tiny space between the axon of one neuron and dendrite of the next—where neurotransmitters go**
2 FUNCTIONS of SPINAL CORD	**1. spinal reflex behaviors 2. speed impulses to and from brain**
2 PARTS of BRAIN STEM	**the medulla and the pons**
PARTS OF LIMBIC SYSTEM	**1. amydala (emotion) 2. septum (emotion) 3. hippocampus (memory)**
CORPUS CALLOSUM	**fibers that connect left and right hemispheres of cerebral cortex—severed in split brain operation**
LOBES OF CEREBRAL CORTEX	**frontal, temporal, occipital, & parietal**

EXPERIENCING PSYCHOLOGY

How Fast Do Neural Impulses Travel?

As neural impulses speed from one part of your body to another, they travel at incredibly high rates of speed. You step on a tack, and the experience of pain is nearly immediate. Can you measure the speed of impulse transmission without the use of sophisticated equipment? Yes, you can, with the help of a few friends, if you don't mind being a little imprecise.

Ask ten people to stand next to each other with their eyes closed and holding hands. At your signal, the first person is to squeeze the hand of the next person who will, in turn, squeeze the hand of the next person, and so on, until the last person's hand is squeezed and signals so by raising his or her free hand. As you give the signal to begin, you start a stopwatch and stop it when that last person signals that he or she has received a squeeze. Repeat the procedure until the time becomes reasonably stable. Divide that time by 10.

Now have the people in the same group put their left hands on the right shoulders of the person standing next to them. At your signal, the first person squeezes the shoulder of whomever is standing to the left. The second person then squeezes the should of the person to his or her left and so on, until the last person signals being squeezed. Again, repeat the procedure until the time interval stabilizes, and again divide by 10.

Although it is a crude measure, the difference between the two time intervals, once each has been divided by 10, represents the time it takes for the neural impulses to travel between the hands and the shoulders of your volunteers. If you get an average of the length of their arms, you could convert your measurements into inches per second.

[This project is adapted from: Rozin, P. & Jonides, J. (1977). Mass reaction time: Measurement of the speed of the nerve impulse and the duration of mental processes in class. *Teaching of Psychology*, **4**, 91-94.]

Chapter 3

Sensation and Perception

STUDY TIP #3

"When Should I Study?"

I've already made the point that doing well in college is going to require a lot of study time. I also have acknowledged that there are other things for you to do each week in addition to studying. How do you best schedule study time? Fortunately, many decades of research on this issue provides some guidance.

As you will see when we discuss memory, "distributed practice is superior to massed practice." What that means is that cramming doesn't work. It means that there is an optimal balance between study and rest, study and rest. It means that you should not even think about sitting down to study anything for three hours on a Sunday afternoon, or for four hours on a Wednesday evening. That's too much time "massed" together to be truly effective.

For most college students and most course work, a concentrated, focused study effort of about 45 minutes duration is best. Then there should be a rest, a "break," of 15-20 minutes before resuming one's study. In fact, what the data show us is that just 10-15 minute episodes of good, solid study can be very useful. Another—nearly obvious—point about scheduling study time is that (usually) daylight study is superior to studying in the evenings or night time when you are more likely to be tired and unable to focus attention. Now put those two ideas together. An excellent time to study is during short periods of opportunity throughout the day. If a class gets out a little early, what a great chance to review some notes or go over some vocabulary, or start to think about what will happen in your next class.

Perhaps you got by in high school with studying on the weekends and an occasional evening or two. Unless you're awfully lucky or awfully bright, that's not likely to be the case in college.

Outline ~ Chapter 3: Sensation and Perception

TOPIC 3A: SENSATION

I. A Preliminary Distinction
- A. **Sensation** is the process of detecting external stimuli and changing those stimuli into nervous system activity.
    1. Sense receptors are specialized neural cells that change physical energy into neural impulses.
    2. Each sense receptor is a **transducer**, a mechanism that converts energy from one form to another.
- B. **Perception** is a cognitive process that involves the selection, organization and interpretation of stimuli.
- C. We say that our senses present us with information about the world, whereas perception represents that information and is affected by motivation, expectations and past experiences.

II. Concepts Related to All Sensory Processes
- A. A **sensory threshold** is the minimum intensity of a stimulus that will cause sense organs to operate.
- B. **Psychophysics** is the study of relationships between the physical attributes of stimuli and the psychological experiences they produce.
- C. An **absolute threshold** is the physical intensity of a stimulus that a person reports detecting 50% of the time.
    1. Absolute threshold levels are used to determine if one's senses are operating properly.
    2. These psychophysical questions are relevant to everyday experiences outside of the classroom.
- D. **Signal detection theory** states that stimulus detection is a decision-making process of determining if a signal exists against a background of noise.
- E. A **difference threshold** is the smallest difference between stimulus attributes that can be detected.
- F. A **just noticeable difference (jnd)** is the amount of change in a stimulus that makes it just noticeably different from what it was.
- G. **Sensory adaptation** occurs when our sensory experience decreases with continued exposure to a stimulus.
    1. **Dark adaptation** refers to the process in which the visual receptors become more sensitive to light as we spend time in the dark.
    2. **Light adaptation** is the process by which our eyes become more sensitive to dark as we spend time in the light.

III. The Stimulus for Vision: Light
- A. Light, in the form of electromagnetic energy, is the stimulus for vision.
- B. **Light** may be thought of as a wave form of radiant energy.
    1. Light waves have three important physical characteristics related to psychological experience: wave amplitude, wavelength, and wave purity.
    2. *Wave amplitude* refers to the intensity or brightness of light.
    3. *Wavelength* is the distance between any point in a wave and the corresponding point on the next cycle from peak to peak.
    4. The unit of measurement is the nanometer (nm), which is equal to one-billionth of a meter, or one-millionth of a millimeter.
    5. Wavelength determines the hue, or color, of light we perceive
    6. The human eye responds to radiant energy between roughly 380 nm and 760 nm.
    7. *Wave purity* refers to the characteristic of saturation.
    8. Monochromatic refers to light waves of all one length or hue.
    9. White light consists of a random mixture of wavelengths.

IV. The Receptor for Vision: The Eye
   A. The **cornea** is the tough, round, virtually transparent outer shell of the eye that has two functions.
      1. It protects the delicate structures at the front of the eye.
      2. It is the first point where light rays are bent.
   B. The **pupil** is an opening through which light enters the eye.
   C. The **iris** (the colored part of the eye) can expand or contract depending upon the intensity of light that hits the eye.
   D. The lens is a flexible structure whose shape is controlled by powerful **ciliary muscles** that expand or contract to change the shape of the lens.
      1. This process brings an image into focus.
      2. This changing of shape is called **accommodation**.
      3. With age, lenses tend to harden and ciliary muscles weaken.
   E. The eye is filled with two fluids.
      1. The **aqueous humor** provides nourishment to the cornea and the other structures at the front of the eye.
      2. The **vitreous humor** fills the interior of the eye (behind the lens) where it functions to keep the eyeball spherical.
   F. Vision begins to take place at the **retina**, where light energy is transduced into neural energy.
   G. There are two types of photoreceptor cells for vision, the rods and the cones.
      1. **Rods** are photosensitive cells of the retina that are most active in low levels of illumination and do not respond differentially to various wavelengths of light.
      2. **Cones** are photosensitive cells of the retina that operate best at high levels of illumination and that are responsible for color vision.
   H. Fibers from ganglion cells form the **optic nerve**, the collection of neurons that leaves the eye and starts back toward other parts of the brain.
   I. The **fovea** is a small area of the retina where there are few layers of cells between the entering light and the cone cells that pack the area.
      1. There are no rods in the fovea, only cones.
      2. Visual acuity is best at the fovea.
   J. The **blind spot** is where the nerve impulses from the rods and cones leave the eye.

V. More on Rods and Cones and What They Do
   A. There are about 120 million rods in each eye.
      1. Rods are concentrated in a ring around the fovea, out toward the periphery.
      2. Rods operate best under low levels of illumination.
      3. Rods do not contribute to our appreciation of color.
   B. There are about six million cones in each eye.
      1. Cones are concentrated in the center of the retina, in the fovea.
      2. Cones function best in medium to high levels of illumination.
      3. Cones are primarily responsible for our experience of color.
   C. The dark-adaptation curve is not smooth and regular.
      1. At the 8 to 10 minute mark, the shape of the curve changes.
      2. This is called the rod-cone break.
      3. Initially, the cones increase their sensitivity; then they drop out.
      4. The rods lower their threshold, becoming more sensitive.

VI. The Visual Pathway After the Retina
   A. When you look at your world, everything off to your left is said to be in your left visual field.
   B. Everything you see off to your right is said to be in your right visual field.
      1. Stimuli in the left visual field end up in our right occipital lobe.
      2. Stimuli from our right visual field end up in our left occipital lobe.
   C. The sorting of which fibers in the optic nerve get directed where largely occurs in the **optic chiasma**.

D. Each eye receives light energy from both visual fields.
   1. Light that enters our left eye from the left visual field initiates neural impulses that cross at the optic chiasma and go over to the right side of the brain.
   2. Light that enters the left eye from the right visual field initiates neural impulses that go straight back to the left hemisphere.
   3. From the optic chiasma, nerve fibers pass through other centers in the brain, including the lateral geniculate nucleus.
E. Nerve fibers also pass through a cluster of cells on each side of the brain called the superior colliculus that controls the movement of the eyes over a patterned stimulus.
F. Nerve cells then form synapses with neurons in the thalamus, which project neural impulses to the layers of cells in the visual cortex of the occipital lobe.
G. Vision doesn't happen in the eyes: it happens in the brain.
H. The detection and interpretation of patterns of light, shade, color and motion are functions of the cerebral cortex.

VII. Color Vision and Color Blindness
A. One theory of color vision is the **trichromatic theory**, first proposed by Thomas Young and revised by Hermann von Helmholtz.
B. The theory proposes that the eye contains three distinct receptors for color.
   1. Each receptor responds best to one of three primary hues of light: red, blue and green.
   2. By the careful combination of all three, all other colors can be produced.
C. Ewald Hering proposed the **opponent-process theory** in 1870.
   1. He proposed three pairs of visual mechanisms that respond to different wavelengths of light.
   2. These include a blue-yellow processor, a red-green processor, and a third dealing with black-white differences or brightness.
   3. Each is capable of responding to either of the two hues that give it its name, but not both.
D. There is support of Hering's theory.
   1. Excitatory-inhibitory mechanisms have been discovered at the layer of the ganglion cells and in a small area of the thalamus.
   2. The theory also is supported by the experience of negative afterimages.
E. Defective color vision occurs in about 8 percent of males and slightly less than 0.5 percent in females.
   1. Most cases are genetic in origin.
   2. In dichromatism, there is a lack of one type of cone, which supports the Young-Helmholtz theory.
   3. Color vision defects higher in the visual pathway support the opponent-process theory.
F. Both theories are probably correct, each in its own way.

VIII. The Stimulus for Hearing: Sound
A. Sound consists of a series of pressures of air (or some other medium) beating against our ear.
B. This pressure can be presented as waves, which have three major characteristics.
   1. The amplitude of a sound wave depicts its intensity—the force with which air strikes the ear.
      a. The intensity of a sound determines the psychological experience we call loudness.
      b. The higher the amplitude, the louder the sound.
      c. The *decibel scale* of sound intensity reflects perceived loudness.
      d. Zero point on the decibel scale is the lowest intensity of sound that can be detected—the absolute threshold.

2. Wave frequency refers to the number of times a wave repeats itself within a given period.
   a. Frequency is measured in terms of how many wares are exerted every second.
   b. The unit of sound frequency is the hertz (Hz).
   c. Pitch is the psychological experience produced by sound wave frequency.
   d. Pitch refers to how high or low a tone is.
   e. A healthy human ear responds to sound wave frequencies between 20 Hz and 20,000 Hz.
3. A third characteristic is wave purity or complexity.
   a. Timbre is the psychological quality or character of a sound that reflects its degree of purity.
   b. White noise is a random mixture of sound frequencies.

IX. The Receptor for Hearing: The Ear
   A. The outer ear is called the pinna.
   B. Sound waves leave the pinna and go through the auditory canal.
   C. Airwaves push against the **eardrum** (tympanic membrane) so that it vibrates at the same rate as the sound source.
   D. The eardrum transmits vibrations to three small bones: the **malleus, incus** and **stapes**, collectively known as the ossicles.
   E. These bones amplify and pass sound vibrations to the oval window.
   F. Beyond the oval window, sound vibrations are in the inner ear.
   G. The major structure of the inner ear is the **cochlea.**
      1. The receptor cells—the transducers for hearing—are here.
      2. When fluid inside the cochlea moves, the basilar membrane is bent up and down.
   H. Hearing takes place when the vibrations of the **basilar membrane** stimulate the receptors, called hair cells.
   I. The **hair cells** bend, starting the neural impulses that leave the ear, traveling on the auditory nerve toward the temporal lobe.

X. The Chemical Senses
   A. The technical term for taste is **gustation**.
      1. Taste has four psychological qualities: sweet, salty, sour and bitter.
      2. The receptor cells for taste are located in the tongue and are called taste buds.
      3. We have about 10,000 taste buds.
      4. When parts die, new segments are regenerated.
      5. All four qualities of taste can be detected at all locations of the tongue, but some may be more distinct or discernable in specific locations.
   B. Smell (**Olfaction**)
      1. The sense of smell originates in hair cells high in the nasal cavity.
      2. Many animals emit **pheromones**, chemicals that produce distinctive odors that are used as a method of communication between organisms.
      3. The primary organ involved in the detection of pheromones is the vomeronasal organ (VNO).
      4. The VNO appears to be involved in mating, territoriality and aggressiveness in animals.
      5. The VNO also can be found in humans.

XI. The Skin, or Cutaneous, Senses
   A. A square inch of skin contains nearly 20 million cells.
   B. Some skin receptor cells have free nerve endings, while others have encapsulated nerve endings.
   C. Our ability to discriminate among types of cutaneous sensation is due to the unique combination of responses the receptor cells have to various types of stimulation.

XII. The Position Senses
    A. The **vestibular sense** tells us about balance, about where we are in relation to gravity, and about acceleration or deceleration.
        1. Receptors are located on either side of the head, near the inner ears.
        2. Five chambers are located there.
        3. Over stimulation of receptor cells in these chambers can lead to motion sickness.
    B. The **kinesthetic sense** tells us about the position of various parts of our bodies and what our muscles and joints are doing.
        1. Receptors are located primarily in our joints, but some information also comes from muscles and tendons.
        2. Information from these receptors travels to the brain through pathways in the spinal cord.
        3. They provide examples of reflex reactions.

XIII. Pain: A Special Sense
    A. The experience of pain prompts more than 80% of all visits to the doctor.
    B. Many stimuli can cause pain.
    C. One theory of pain proposes that a gate control mechanism (high in the spinal cord) opens to let pain messages race to the brain or blocks messages by closing the gate.
    D. A cognitive-behavioral theory of pain also suggests that pain is influenced by attitudes, expectations and behaviors.
    E. Various techniques are used to manage pain.
        1. Drug therapy is one choice.
        2. Hypnosis and cognitive self-control also can be effective.
        3. The psychological process involved with a **placebo** (a substance a person believes will be useful in treating some symptom) is another technique.
        4. Counterirritation refers to stimulating an area of the body near the location of the pain.
        5. Acupuncture can be effective.
    F. There is some evidence that one's sensitivity to pain is genetically based.
    G. Gender and cultural issues can influence individual responses.
    H. Newborns do experience pain.

TOPIC 3B: PERCEPTION

I. Paying Attention: A Process of Selection
    A. A **salient detail** is one that captures our attention.
        1. It is remembered better than peripheral details.
        2. Peripheral details make up the perceptual background.
    B. Stimulus factors are those that make some stimuli more compelling than others.
    C. Personal factors are characteristics of a perceiver that influence which stimuli get attended to.

II. Stimulus Factors in Perceptual Selectivity
    A. The most important factor is **contrast**, the extent to which a stimulus is physically different from the other stimuli around it.
    B. Generally, the more intense a stimulus, the more likely we are to attend to it.
    C. Generally, the bigger the stimulus, the more likely we are to attend to it.
    D. Motion is another dimension for which contrast is important.
    E. Repetition can influence attention.

III. Personal Factors in Perceptual Selectivity
    A. When we are psychologically predisposed to perceive something, we have formed a mental set.

B. What we perceive is influenced by our past experiences.

C. When we attend to a stimulus, organize and identify it, and then store it in memory, we are referring to **bottom-up processing.**

D. When motivation, mental set, and past experience influence perceptual selectivity, we label it as **top-down processing.**

IV. Organizing Our Perceptual World

    A. A **gestalt** forms when one sees the overall scheme of things: the whole, totality or configuration.

    B. A basic principle of Gestalt psychology is the figure-ground relationship.

        1. Of all the stimuli in your environment, those you attend to and group together are "figures."

        2. The other stimuli become "ground."

V. Grouping Stimuli with Bottom-Up Processing

    A. **Proximity** or contiguity refers to events occurring close together in space or time and being perceived as belonging together as part of the same figure.

    B. **Similarity** refers to stimuli that have properties in common and tend to be perceived together.

    C. **Continuity,** or good continuation, is operating when we see things ending up consistently with the way they started off.

    D. **Common fate** describes our tendency to group together in the same figure those elements of a scene that appear to move together in the same direction and at the same speed.

    E. **Closure** is the tendency to fill in gaps in our perceptual world.

        1. A special case of this refers to **subjective contours**.

        2. Here, arrangements of lines and patterns enable us to see figures that are not actually there.

VI. Grouping Stimuli with Top-Down Processing

    A. This refers to perceiving stimuli because we want to, expect to, or have experienced them together in the past.

    B. How we ultimately organize our experiences of the world seems to depend on both types of processing.

VII. Perceiving Depth and Distance

    A. Ocular cues are built into our visual systems and tell us about depth and distance.

        1. Cues that involve both eyes are called binocular cues.

        2. **Retinal disparity** refers to each eye getting a somewhat different view of a three-dimensional object.

        3. **Convergence** refers to the eyes turning in, toward each other, when something is viewed up close.

    B. Monocular cues require only one eye to have their influence.

        1. Accommodation refers to the changing of the shape of the lens, by the ciliary muscles, to focus images on the retina.

        2. Physical cues to depth and distance are those we get from the structure of our environment.

            a. **Linear perspective** describes the fact that parallel lines seem to come together in the distance.

            b. **Interposition** refers to the fact that objects in the foreground tend to cover, or partially hide from view, objects in the background.

            c. **Relative size** refers to the judgment of distance; an object that produces the larger retinal image will be close to us.

            d. **Texture gradient** refers to a surface of individual pieces blending into a smooth surface as distance increases.

        e.   **Patterns of shading** tell us a great deal about an object's shape and
             solidity.

        f.   **Motion parallax** refers to the apparent difference in motion between
             objects that are closer to us and those that are farther away.

  C. The role of culture in the development of depth perception suggests that with training, most
      cultural differences in the perception of depth disappear.

VIII. The Constancy of Visual Perception

  A. **Perceptual constancies** help us organize and interpret the stimulus input we get from our
      senses.

      1. **Size constancy** is the tendency to see objects as being of constant size regardless of
         the size of the retinal image.

      2. **Shape constancy** refers to the perception that objects maintain their shape even
         though the retinal image they cast may change.

      3. **Brightness constancy** causes the apparent brightness of objects to be perceived as
         being the same regardless of the actual amount or type of light under which they are
         viewed.

      4. **Color constancy** allows you to perceive the color of a familiar object as constant,
         despite changing conditions.

IX. When Constancy Fails: Geometric Illusions and Impossible Figures

  A. **Illusions** are experiences in which our perceptions are at odds with what we know as physical
      reality.

  B. Illusions remind us that perception is a higher-level process than sensation.

Practice Test Questions

TOPIC 3A: SENSATION

Multiple Choice

1. Which term is most descriptive of the process of sensation?
    ___a. transportation   ___c. selection
    ___b. interpretation   ___d. transduction

2. Which terms are most descriptive of the process of perception?
    ___a. selecting and organizing   ___c. learning and memory
    ___b. seeing and hearing   ___d. detecting and feeling

3. The major thrust of psychophysics is the search for
    ___a. lawful relationships between events in our world and our experiences of those events.
    ___b. the elemental particles of thought and experience that make up consciousness.
    ___c. logical ways to relate how we feel (affect) to the way we think (cognition) and behave.
    ___d. the physiological or biological bases that allow us to experience the world as we do.

4. If a sound is below your absolute threshold
    ___a. you will never hear that sound.
    ___b. that sound will only enter your subconscious mind.
    ___c. you will hear that sound less than 50 percent of the time.
    ___d. you cannot tell if it is any different from any other sound.

5. Signal detection theory suggests that determining one's sensory threshold values (e.g., for brightness)
    ___a. is virtually impossible.
    ___b. is largely a matter recognizing detection to be a decision-making process.
    ___c. requires a subject to detect whether signals are different from each other.
    ___d. can only be done in a very dark room.

6. The notion of sensory adaptation suggests that what we tend to experience most readily are
    ___a. lights and sounds, not smells and tastes.
    ___b. stimuli that have remained the same for a very long time.
    ___c. objects or events that we are used to, or have adapted to.
    ___d. changes in level or type of stimulation.

7. Wavelength is to hue as wave amplitude is to
    ___a. color.   ___b. purity.
    ___b. brightness.   ___d. saturation.

8. If I were to show you all of the lights of the visible spectrum (a rainbow of light), and if I had adjusted
    the amplitudes of all the light waves in that spectrum so that they were all exactly equal, which light
    would appear to be the brightest?
    ___a. a white light
    ___b. a red light
    ___c. a yellow-green light
    ___d. They would all appear equally bright.

9. Where does the transduction of light take place in the eye?
    ___a. the lens and the ciliary muscles
    ___b. the blind spot and optic nerve
    ___c. the rods and cones
    ___d. the aqueous and vitreous humors

10. If we want to identify some small object at night, in low levels of illumination, the most sensible thing to do (other than to make more light available) is to have the image of the object fall on the

     ___a. fovea.   ___c. periphery of the retina.

     ___b. blind spot.   ___d. optic nerve.

11. When we plot a curve that shows how our eyes become sensitive as we spend time in the dark, the curve is not a smooth one, but shows a "break" at about the 7-minute mark. This break in the curve occurs because

     ___a. the cones have stopped adapting to the dark.

     ___b. the retina changes its orientation after about 7 minutes in the dark.

     ___c. at that point, our ability to see decreases markedly.

     ___d. the rods have reached a point where they no longer continue to become more sensitive.

12. The Young-Helmholtz theory of color vision proposes that there are specifically sensitive receptors for the wavelengths of light that correspond to the primary colors of light,

     ___a. red, green, and yellow.

     ___b. black and white.

     ___c. red, orange, yellow, green, blue, and violet.

     ___d. blue, green, and red.

13. The stimulus for audition is

     ___a. electromagnetic energy in wave form.

     ___b. pressures of a medium vibrating against a membrane.

     ___c. chemicals that are dissolved in the air or in a liquid.

     ___d. the cochlea of the inner ear.

14. If we can tell the difference between two people singing the very same note at the very same loudness, it is because

     ___a. of our experience of the saturation of the sounds.

     ___b. we know who the people are and recognize their voices.

     ___c. both sounds are at or above our difference thresholds for loudness.

     ___d. we can detect a difference in the timbre of the two voices.

15. Wave amplitude of light is to brightness as wave amplitude of sound is to

     ___a. loudness.   ___c. hue or color.

     ___b. pitch.   ___d. timbre.

16. The transducers for sound are

     ___a. waves of air pressure.   ___c. cochleas.

     ___b. ossicles.   ___d. hair cells.

17. The best name for one's sense of taste is

     ___a. flavor.   ___c. biochemical transduction.

     ___b. gustation.   ___d. olfaction.

18. In what way are taste buds different from other sense receptor cells?

     ___a. They conduct, or transmit, nerve impulses.

     ___b. They are really specialized neurons.

     ___c. They transduce physical energy into neural energy.

     ___d. They are replaced by new cells when they die.

19. Which sense informs us about the position of our bodies with respect to gravity?

     ___a. the vestibular sense   ___c. the cutaneous sense

     ___b. the kinesthetic sense   ___d. the gravitational sense

20. If there is such a thing as a "gate" in Melzack and Moore's gate-control theory, that gate is said to control our experience of

    ___a. arousal or excitement.   ___c. temperature and other skin senses.

    ___b. pain.   ___d. balance.

True/False

1. ____True ____False   If a stimulus is above your absolute threshold, you will detect it every time it is presented.

2. ____True ____False   As one's sensory threshold goes up, one's sensitivity in that sense goes down.

3. ____True ____False   When their amplitudes are equal, a yellow-green light and a red light will appear to be the same hue.

4. ____True ____False   Because they operate best at low levels of illumination, our rods give us more information about the colors of objects in our environments.

5. ____True ____False   Because hearing is so important in language acquisition, psychologists believe that hearing is the most important of all the human senses.

6. ____True ____False   The decibel scale provides a measure of the perceived loudness of sounds.

7. ____True ____False   Receptors for pain are found only in—or near—the skin.

TOPIC 3B: PERCEPTION

Multiple Choice

1. Factors that direct our attention to some stimuli and not to others are classified in the text as being either
    ___a. stimulus or personal.   ___c. primary or secondary.
    ___b. learned or inherited.   ___d. sensory or perceptual.

2. When we say that someone is likely to perceive something that he or she expects to perceive, we are saying that
    ___a. figures and grounds are often confused.
    ___b. some stimuli are inherently more attention-grabbing than others.
    ___c. our motivational states often direct our attention.
    ___d. we can form a mental set that influences attention.

3. We tend to hear the individual speech sounds of a word organized together and separate from other words largely because of the Gestalt organizational principle of
    ___a. proximity.   ___c. continuity.
    ___b. novelty or familiarity.   ___d. similarity.

4. What makes our perception of the world as being three-dimensional remarkable is that
    ___a. it is a skill or ability found only in humans.
    ___b. it is a perception with no particular survival function.
    ___c. images of the world are inverted by the lens of the eye to appear upside-down.
    ___d. the retina records visual experiences in only two dimensions.

5. Research from cross-cultural psychology would suggest that persons with the best ability to discern great distances would be people who spent most of their lives in
    ___a. downtown New York City.   ___c. the African Congo.
    ___b. the Sahara Desert.   ___d. the Amazon River Valley.

6. The perceptual constancies serve as reminders of the
    ___a. fact that the world is an orderly and predictable place.
    ___b. influence of motivation on psychological processes.
    ___c. differences between what is sensed and what is perceived.
    ___d. similarities that exist in the way that people of all cultures perceive the world.

True/False

1. ___True ___False   Novelty and familiarity are both stimulus factors AND personal factors that influence attention.

2. ___True ___False   Common fate is a Gestalt organizational principle that is applicable only to objects in motion.

3. ___True ___False   Motion parallax is an example of a common illusion of motion—seeing motion when there is really none there to be seen.

Key Terms and Concepts
Topic 3A

sensation_____

_____

transducer_____

_____

perception_____

_____

sensory threshold_____

_____

psychophysics_____

_____

absolute threshold_____

_____

signal detection theory_____

_____

difference threshold_____

_____

just noticeable difference (jnd)_____

_____

sensory adaptation_____

_____

dark adaptation_____

_____

light adaptation_____

_____

cornea_____

_____

pupil_____

_____

iris_____

_____

lens_____

_____

accommodation_____

_____

aqueous humor_____

_____

vitreous humor_____

_____

retina_____

_____

rods_____

_____

cones_____

_____

optic nerve_____

_____

fovea_____

_____

blind spot_____

_____

optic chiasma_____

_____

trichromatic theory_____

_____

opponent-process theory_____

_____

eardrum_____

_____

malleus, incus, stapes_____

_____

cochlea_____

_____

basilar membrane_____

_____

hair cells_____

_____

taste buds_____

_____

pheromones_____

_____

vomeronasal organ (VNO)_____

_____

vestibular sense_____

_____

kinesthetic sense_____

_____

placebo_____

_____

Topic 3B

salient detail_____

_____

contrast_____

_____

mental set_____

_____

bottom-up processing_____

_____

top-down processing_____

_____

gestalt _____

_____

figure-ground relationship _____

_____

subjective contours _____

_____

retinal disparity _____

_____

convergence _____

_____

perceptual constancies _____

_____

size constancy _____

_____

shape constancy _____

_____

brightness constancy _____

_____

color constancy _____

_____

illusions _____

_____

Multiple Choice

1. **d**   Alternative **a** is rather meaningless. Alternatives **b** and **c** are more related to perception than to sensation, but alternative **d**, transduction, is nearly synonymous with sensation.

2. **a**   Perception may involve all of the terms in all of the alternatives, but, by definition, it is a cognitive process involving the selection and organization of incoming sensory information.

3. **a**   Alternative **a** gives as simple a statement of what psychophysics is about as we can manage.

4. **c**   By definition (have you noticed already how many items seek knowledge of definitions?), stimuli that are below one's threshold will be detected less than 50 percent of the time.

5. **b**   The complete statement that signal detection is essentially a decision-making process (is it there, or isn't it?) is almost a direct quote from the text.

6. **d**   You might get this one by elimination. The first alternative is downright silly. The second and third both say virtually the same thing, which makes **d** the best choice.

7. **b**   Here's another analogy item—and a simple one at that. What is the issue here? Wavelength determines hue; wave amplitude determines what? Right! brightness.

8. **c**   As illogical as it sounds at first, when all amplitudes are adjusted to be equal, a yellow-green light (about 550 nm—right in the middle of the spectrum) will appear brighter than the others.

9. **c**   The cells that change the physical energy of light into neural impulses are the rods and cones of the retina.

10. **c**   Because it is where our rods are located, and because our rods function best "in the dark," or in low levels of illumination, we would want the object to fall on the periphery of the retina.

11. **a**   The dark adaptation curve has a "break" in it because at about the 7-minute mark, the cones are no longer becoming more sensitive, while the rods continue to adapt.

12. **d**   The major problem here for some of us is remembering that although red, blue, and yellow are the primary colors for paints or pigments, this item is asking about light, where the primary hues are red, blue, and green.

13. **b**   The stimulus for audition is sound, of course, and alternative **b** gives a reasonable definition or description of sound.

14. **d**   You really should have expected this item—or one very much like it. Everything else being equal, we rely on timbre.

15. **a**   Another analogy. Wave amplitude of sound determines loudness.

16. **d**   Located within the cochlea, or inner ear, the actual transducers for hearing are called hair cells.

17. **b**   We think that it is important for college students to know the actual ("technical") names for the various senses. Smell is olfaction; taste, gustation.

18. **d**   The first three alternatives are statements that could be made about any of the senses. Only taste buds, however, are replaced when they die.

19. **a**   Again, this is a matter of definition. Vestibular senses tell us about position relative to gravity; cutaneous senses about touch and pressure, and kinesthetic senses about the movement of muscles and joints. There is no such thing as a gravitational sense.

20. **b**   The gate-control theory is one meant to describe the important features involved in our experience of pain.

True/False

1. **F**   Not in actuality; only in theory. If it is above threshold, all we can say is that it will be detected more than 50 percent of the time.

2. **T**   This correctly states the inverse relationship between one's threshold and one's sensitivity—as one increases, the other decreases.

3. **F**   They would not appear equally bright, and they certainly would not appear to be the same hue, because hue is determined by wavelength.

4. **F**   In fact, our rods are colorblind. Don't let the fact that this item starts off with a correct assertion (rods operate best at low levels of illumination) confuse you.

5. **F**   I hope you got this one correct. Hearing is involved in language acquisition, but psychologists are not going to try to rank order the senses in terms of which is most important.

6. **T**   This statement is a true, straightforward definition.

7. **F**   Here's one of those key words in true/false items: "only." Yes, pain receptors are found in the skin, but not only in the skin, as you'll realize after a moment's reflection on all those non-skin parts of your body in which you have experienced pain.

TOPIC 3B: PERCEPTION
Multiple Choice

1. **a**   Attentional factors can be classified in many ways, of course, but of these alternatives, the choice would be the scheme used in your text, referring to them as stimulus or personal factors.
2. **d**   To say that some stimuli are attended to because of an expectation to perceive them is to say that one has developed a mental set.
3. **a**   Speech sounds within a word are perceived and organized together because they are close together, which reflects the Gestalt factor of proximity—which means "nearness" in space or time.
4. **d**   Alternatives **a** and **b** are quite absurd. Alternative **c** is a correct statement, but relevant to 3-dimensionality. The retina is 2-dimensional, making the last statement the best choice.
5. **b**   The logic here—extrapolating from research cited in the text—is that persons in environments that are cramped and cluttered are less often required (or able) to view things (such as approaching camel caravans) over great distances.
6. **c**   Perceptual constancies allow us to perceive familiar objects as unchanged, even though our sensory experience may change—making alternative **c** the best choice.

True/False

1. **T**   We tend to see familiar things in novel settings and novel things in familiar settings. What is novel and what is familiar reflects the stimuli involved and may also reflect one's personal experience.
2. **T**   This is true by definition. If you're not convinced, maybe you should go back and check.
3. **F**   This one is almost tricky. The name is deceiving. In fact, motion parallax has little to do with our perception of motion, real or illusionary. It is a cue to depth and distance.

A Few Flash Card Possibilities for Chapter 3

(And please don't forget: These are just suggestions. The best flash cards are those you make yourself!)

A TRANSDUCER	something that changes energy from one form to another, e.g. sense receptor
PSYCHOPHYSICS	the study of the relationships between the physical qualities of a stimulus and our psychological experience of them
ABSOLUTE THRESHOLD	the intensity of a stimulus that is just barely detected; below 50%, above 50%
RELATION OF LIGHT TO VISION	wave amplitude—brightness wavelength—hue (color) wave purity—saturation
ACCOMMODATION	changing of the shape of the lens to focus an image on the retina
PRIMARY HUES/ PRIMARY COLORS	light: Red, Blue, & Green pigment: Red, Yellow, & Blue
HAIR CELLS	transducers for both audition & olfaction
MENTAL SET	predisposed, expected way of perceiving; we perceive what we expect to perceive
FIGURE/GROUND	in any one sense we perceive only one stimulus (the figure) against the ground (background) of others
RETINAL DISPARITY	the cue to depth related to the fact that each eye gets a different (disparate) view of the same 3-D object

EXPERIENCING PSYCHOLOGY

How Many Pennies Make a Difference?

Here's a simple demonstration of the nature of difference thresholds. All you need for this project are two small boxes (boxes about the size that bandages come in work just fine) and two dollars worth of pennies. You can either make the called-for judgments yourself, or use a volunteer to make the judgments for you. For now, we'll assume that you have found a willing volunteer.

Begin with 10 pennies in each box. Have your volunteer compare the weights of the two boxes. (Of course, he or she should say that they seem equally heavy.) Now, without your volunteer seeing what you are doing, add one penny to one box. Have your friend judge the relative weights of the boxes. Keep adding pennies (to the same box each time) until your volunteer detects a difference (a "just noticeable difference," right?) between the two boxes. How many pennies did it take to just notice a difference?

Now start with 50 pennies in each box, and repeat the same procedure. First judge the boxes as they are, then add one penny to a box and ask for another judgment. Add another penny and then another until the volunteer detects a difference in the weight of the two boxes. How many pennies were needed this time?

Because you are starting with a heavier weight, it will take more pennies added to the box than it did before to reach a *just noticeable difference* (or jnd) for the 50-penny boxes than for the 10-penny boxes. You might weigh all the boxes involved to see if the difference (in weight—not in the number of pennies) is 5 times as great for the 50-penny boxes as for the 10-penny boxes.

Chapter 4

Varieties of Consciousness

STUDY TIP #4

"Where Should I Study?"

There's a good chance that this topic may strike you as too silly to bother with. Bear with me. It's not as silly as it sounds—and there's good psychology to back me up.

A lot of research tells us that the best place to study is the very location where you will be tested. Scuba divers learn some material at poolside. They learn different material while sitting on the bottom of the pool in their scuba gear. Some time later, they are tested on what they can remember. Material learned at poolside is remembered significantly better there than when it is tested under water. Materials learned under water are recalled better there than at poolside. So then, where is the best place to study for a psychology exam? In the classroom in which the exam is to be given.

It's not likely that you'll be able to spend a great deal of time studying in the psychology classroom (but every minute or two would help). So then where do you go? A designated place. There should be someplace at home, on campus, in the public library, that you can set aside, designate as the main place where you will do your studying. Do nothing else there but study. Make it your special "study place." The problem with trying to study at the kitchen table is that the kitchen table is associated with other non-study activities like eating.

If you are living at home, getting your own designated study area may cause a bit of family friction. You're going to need some cooperation in this regard. You can't be expected to study successfully if you are sitting in the living room, watching TV, and looking after a younger brother or sister at the same time.

Outline ~ Chapter 4: Varieties of Consciousness

TOPIC 4A: CONSCIOUSNESS AWAKE AND ASLEEP

I.   Toward a Definition
    A. Consciousness is a commonly-used term that is difficult to define with precision.
    B. It may be best to avoid a precise definition.
    C. Consciousness has two aspects:
        1. a *perceptual* aspect—an awareness of the external environment, and
        2. an *introspective* aspect—an awareness of one's own mental processes

II. Normal Waking Consciousness
    A. **Consciousness** is the awareness of the environment and of one's own mental processes.
    B. William James provided a definition of consciousness over a hundred years ago.
    C. James characterized consciousness as
        1. always changing.
        2. a very personal experience.
        3. sensibly continuous.
        4. selective.

III. The Freudian View of Levels of Consciousness
    A. Freud's vision of consciousness often is depicted as an iceberg nearly totally submerged.
        1. Ideas, memories, feelings, or motives of which we are actively aware are said to be *conscious*.
        2. Aspects of our experience that are not conscious, but can easily be brought to awareness, are stored at a *preconscious level*.
        3. Cognitions, feelings, or motives of which we are not aware are said to be in the *unconscious*.
    B. Freud theorized that the unconscious mind can and does influence us.
    C. Contents of the unconscious mind can be found in dreams, slips of the tongue, or humor.

IV. Contemporary Investigations of the Unconscious
    A. Currently, researchers are investigating if and how the unconscious mind can process information.
    B. **Subliminal perception** is the process of perceiving and responding to stimuli presented at levels of intensity that are below our absolute threshold—below our level of conscious processing.
        1. There is little scientific evidence for the power of subliminal messages.
        2. Subliminal messages that are complex and meaningful cannot be processed subliminally; however, more simple stimuli can.
    C. **Blindsight** is a phenomenon that occurs in individuals with damage to the primary visual areas of the brain but who can still see simple stimuli.
        1. That is, persons without direct vision can be aware of some visually-presented stimuli.
        2.   There may be intact lower brain centers that can account for blindsight.

V.   The Stages of a "Good Night's Sleep"
    A. We spend nearly 200,000 hours of our lives sleeping..
    B. Our best indicators of sleep are measurements of brain electrical activity with EEG, and of muscle tone, with the EMG.
    C. EEG tracings indicate that sleep can be divided into stages.

1. Stage 1 sleep is very light sleep, developing from the waking state.
    a. This stage is characterized by theta waves of 4-7 cycles per second.
    b. This stage usually lasts less than ten minutes.
2. In Stage 2 sleep, you can still be easily awakened.
    a. The EEG pattern is similar to Stage 1 sleep but sleep spindles, brief, high-amplitude bursts of electrical activity, occur about every 15 seconds.
    b. K-complexes also are noted in the EEG.
3. Stage 3 sleep is characterized by high, slow, delta wave activity of 0.5 to 4 cycles per second.
    a. In this stage, delta waves constitute between 20 and 50 percent of one's EEG pattern.
    b. Internal functions are lowering and slowing.
4. Stage 4 is deep sleep.
    a. The EEG is filled with slow, recurring delta waves.
    b. Muscles are totally relaxed.
    c. About 15 percent of sleep is in this stage.
    d. Infants spend a great deal of their sleep time in this "restorative" stage.
    e. Adults increase Stage 4 sleep time after exertion or physical exercise.

VI. REM and NREM Sleep
    A. Discovered in the early 1950s, there are periods of sleep during which the eyes dart around under closed eyelids.
        1. This stage of sleep is called **rapid eye movement**, or **REM** sleep.
        2. People awakened during REM sleep often (about 85 percent of the time) report vivid, clear dreams.
        3. During REM sleep there is considerable brain activity—EEG patterns are much like wakefulness.
        4. During REM there is *atonia*—a total relaxation of the muscles.
        5. People who thrash about during REM and do not remain motionless are said to have *REM sleep disorder*.
        6. REM also produces increased sexual arousal.
    B. Periods of sleep during which the eyes do not move are called non-REM, or NREM periods.
        1. Persons awakened during NREM sleep may report dreaming, but not vivid dreams.
        2. NREM sleep accounts for about 75 percent of the sleep of adults.

VII. Dreaming
    A. The question of what the content of a dream means has been a topic of interest for humans dating back to the ancient Greek philosophers.
    B. The most influential view of the nature of dreams was provided by Freud in his book, *Interpretation of Dreams.*
        1. Freud suggested that many dreams serve a wish-fulfillment purpose.
        2. **Manifest content** is the content of which the dreamer is consciously aware.
        3. **Latent content** is the true, underlying meaning of the dream that resides in a person's unconscious mind.
        4. Through a process called dream work, latent content shows itself in a highly disguised form that comprised several processes:
            a. The condensation process
            b. The dramatization process
            c. Dream displacement.
    C. Carl Jung suggested that dreams were more transparent or obvious than did Freud and argued that the symbolism inherent in dreams was related to universal human concerns.
    D. The **activation-synthesis theory** of dreaming suggests that dreams are activated via physiological mechanisms in the brainstem.
        1. It's a matter of the brainstem generating neural activity, and
        2. the cerebral cortex synthesizing, that activity into meaningful "stories."

VIII. Sleep Deprivation
- A. On average, Americans get about 1.5 hours less sleep each night than they need.
- B. A good night's sleep is the amount of sleep that will allow a person to awaken without the use of an alarm clock.
- C. Sleep loss accumulates as "sleep debt."
- D. Microsleeps, or short episodes of sleep, increase when normal sleep is disrupted.
- E. When deprived of REM sleep, people will spend long periods REMing during the first night after deprivation.
- F. There is some evidence that NREM sleep also rebounds.
- G. There is evidence that sleep loss may affect crucial endocrine functions related to some chronic diseases.

IX. Sleep Disorders
- A. A good night's sleep is apparently a necessary thing.
- B. Millions of persons, however, have difficulty either getting to sleep, or staying asleep, while others fall asleep unexpectedly and without intent.

X. Insomnia
- A. **Insomnia** is the inability to fall asleep or stay asleep.
    1. Chronic insomnia afflicts nearly 30 million Americans.
    2. It is more common in the elderly than in younger adults.
- B. It is often difficult to determine what causes insomnia.
- C. Pseudoinsomnia is when a person believes he or she is not getting enough sleep, and is sleeping more than he or she realizes.
- D. Seldom do medications work for the long term in treating insomnia.
    1. Although regulating melatonin may help some, research suggests its effectiveness is very limited.
    2. Many cases of insomnia are rooted in learning poor sleep habits.
    3. Cognitive and behavioral treatments are often successful in breaking the cycle of insomnia.

XI. Narcolepsy
- A. **Narcolepsy** involves going to sleep without any intention to do so.
- B. Narcolepsy is associated with the loss of specific types of neurons in the hypothalamus.
- C. There are several other symptoms that accompany narcolepsy:
    1. A sudden decrease in muscle tone
    2. Paralysis upon falling asleep
    3. Dreamlike images that occur as soon as one goes to sleep or awakens.
- D. It is estimated that nearly 350,000 Americans suffer from narcolepsy, but only 50,000 cases have been diagnosed.
- E. Narcolepsy has long been treated with prescribed stimulants, but this approach has serious side effects.
- F. A new drug, modafinil, has been approved for the treatment of narcolepsy and seems to be having good results.

XII. Sleep Apnea
- A. **Sleep apnea** involves patterns of sleep, usually short, during which breathing stops entirely.
- B. As many as 12 million Americans suffer form sleep apnea.
- C. Sleep apnea is a partial cause of hypertension, heart disease, impotence, and memory loss.
- D. The disorder may be root cause of as many as 38,000 cardiovascular deaths each year.
- C. This condition occurs most among men over age 40 who are overweight.
- D. Sleep apnea is a suspect in the cause of Sudden Infant Death Syndrome.

TOPIC 4B: VOLUNTARY ALTERATIONS OF CONSCIOUSNESS

I. Hypnosis
  A. **Hypnosis** is a state of consciousness characterized by:
     1. A marked increase in suggestibility
     2. A focusing of attention
     3. An exaggerated use of imagination
     4. An unwillingness or inability to act on one's own
     5. An unquestioning acceptance of distortions of reality.
  B. Hypnosis is a state of consciousness that typically requires the voluntary cooperation of the person being hypnotized.
  C. What are the common issues concerning hypnosis?
     1. The susceptibility to hypnosis varies from person to person.
        a. Some people resist and cannot be hypnotized.
        b. Entering the hypnotic state is entirely voluntary.
        c. The subject must have the ability to engage easily in daydreaming and fantasy.
        d. Suggestibility and a degree of passivity or willingness to cooperate is important.
     2. It is unlikely that one will do anything under hypnosis that he or she would not do otherwise.
     3. The issue of whether hypnosis represents a unique state of consciousness is in dispute.
     4. Hypnosis can be used to alleviate physical pain.
     5. Whether one can remember things under hypnosis that could not otherwise be remembered is a hotly contested issue.
     6. Age-regression hypnotic sessions have not proved valid.
     7. Using hypnosis to refresh the memory of a witness can lead to the potential of the creation of pseudomemories, or false memories.

II. Meditation
  A. **Meditation** is a self-induced state of altered consciousness characterized by a focusing of attention and relaxation.
  B. *Transcendental meditation* requires mental focusing and concentration.
  C. Once a person is in a meditative state, measurable physiological changes do take place that allow us to claim meditation to be an altered state of consciousness.
  D. David Holmes has concluded that there are no differences between meditating persons and people who are simply resting or relaxing, but others have challenged Holmes' conclusions.

III. Altering Consciousness With Drugs
  A. Chemicals that can alter psychological processes are referred to as psychoactive drugs.
  B. The use of drugs that alter mood, perception and behaviors can have negative outcomes:
     1. Dependence—the use of a drug is required to reach and maintain a level of functioning
     2. Tolerance—the state in which more and more of a drug is required to attain the same desired effect
     3. Withdrawal—a strongly negative reaction (often including vomiting, cramps, and headaches) that occurs when one stops taking a drug
     4. Addiction—an extreme dependence, with signs of tolerance and withdrawal in which long-term costs are ignored in favor of short-term pleasures.
  C. We are dealing with drug abuse when we find:
     1. Lack of control
     2. Disruption of interpersonal relationships or difficulties at work

3. Indications that drug use has continued for at least one month.
D. There is a continuum from total abstinence through heavy social use to addiction, with no clear dividing line between drug use and abuse.

IV. Stimulants
   A. **Stimulants** activate an organism, producing a heightened sense of arousal and elevation of mood.
   B. Caffeine is a widely used stimulant, commonly found in coffee, tea, chocolate and painkillers.
      1. In moderate amounts, it seems to have no life-threatening effects on the user.
      2. A mild dependency can develop, and sudden stoppage can produce headaches.
   C. Nicotine usually is ingested by smoking, and activates excitatory synapses in the central and peripheral nervous system.
      1. Nicotine is an addictive drug, results in more than 440,000 deaths in the U.S., and its use is the single most preventable cause of death.
      2. Smokeless tobacco is used by many as an alternative to smoking.
   D. Cocaine and its derivative "crack" produce pleasure and energy when first entering the bloodstream, either via smoking (free basing), inhaling (snorting), or injection.
      1. Cocaine is so addictive that a person can become dependent after one or two experiences with it.
      2. It is estimated that there are 1.7 million people in the U.S. over the age of 12 who are cocaine users.
   E. Amphetamines are manufactured stimulants with a range of different street names
      1. The drugs mask fatigue.
      2. They can cause an irregular heartbeat and increased blood pressure.

V. Depressants
   A. **Depressants** are chemicals that reduce one's awareness of external stimuli, slow bodily functioning, and decrease levels of overt behavior.
   B. Alcohol is the most commonly used of all depressants.
      1. Over 50 percent of alcohol consumption in the U.S. is by persons age 12-20.
      2. That means that these people are using the drug illegally.
      3. Over 100,000 deaths a year are attributed to alcohol use.
   C. Alcohol use by pregnant women results in a myriad of problems for a newborn.
   D. Blood alcohol level (BAL) is affected by how much one drinks and by how fast the alcohol gets into the bloodstream.
      1. The amount of food in the stomach and a person's gender affects how quickly alcohol is absorbed.
      2. Females absorb alcohol more quickly than males.
      3. One-tenth of one percent (0.1%) alcohol in the bloodstream is enough to declare someone legally drunk in most states.
   F. Alcohol use and abuse are related to sociocultural factors.
      1. Europeans constitute about one-eighth of the world's population, but consume nearly half of all alcohol produced.
      2. The use of alcohol is nearly nonexistent by Muslims and Mormons.
      3. Generally, alcohol is used sparingly by the Chinese and Orthodox Jews.
      4. In the U.S., Irish Americans are six times more likely to suffer alcoholism than are Greek Americans, in general.
      5. Adolescent Native Americans have the highest rate of alcohol use and abuse.
      6. Alcohol abuse tends to be higher among the poor.
   G. Opiates, such as morphine and codeine, are called analgesics because they can be used to reduce or eliminate sensations of pain.
      1. They seem to have little effect on motor behavior.
      2. They produce dependence and addiction, and their removal results in pain and depression.

H. Heroin is an opiate derived from morphine.
    1. Strong addiction and dependency occur rapidly.
    2. Tolerance builds as increased amounts are needed to produce the desired emotional states.
    3. Increased amounts can cause breathing to stop and lead to death.
I. Barbiturates are synthetically produced sedatives.
    1. They slow nervous system activity by blocking receptor sites of excitatory synapses or by enhancing the effects of inhibitory neurotransmitters.
    2. All produce dependency if used regularly, and some are addictive.

VI. Hallucinogens
    A. **Hallucinogens** are chemicals that lead to the formation of hallucinations, usually visual.
    B. LSD (lysergic acid diethylamide) is a potent and popular hallucinogen in most Western cultures.
        1. LSD acts on serotonin receptor sites *and* causes serotonin levels to increase.
        2. Small doses can produce major behavioral effects.
        3. Changes in mood tend to be exaggerations of one's present mood.
        4. Hallucinations involve exaggerations of some actual perception.

VII. Marijuana
    A. Marijuana is a consciousness-altering drug produced from the cannabis or hemp plant.
        1. In low doses, it can act as a depressant; in larger doses it acts as a hallucinogenic.
        2. It 1998, 72 million Americans over the age of 12 indicated that they had tried marijuana at least once.
    B. The active ingredient in marijuana is THC.
    C. Marijuana can be used to reduce the nausea associated with chemotherapy treatments for cancer.
    D. Marijuana can cause cancer, lung disease, respiratory problems, impair judgment and memory, and physical coordination.
        1. Heavy users show lower verbal IQs than light users.
        2. Long-term use may have genetic implications.
        3. It can contribute to a lower sperm count, and can have negative effects on the unborn, resulting in smaller babies, and an increased number of miscarriages.
        4. There is much variability in potency, quality, and purity of marijuana.

VIII. Ecstacy
    A. **Ecstasy (MDMA)** is a drug that is classified as a psychedelic amphetamine.
        1. This has become a popular drug over the last 20 years for adolescents and young adults; effects can be felt in as little as 30 minutes, and euphoria can last for as long as 3 to 4 hours.
    B. Tolerance can develop, and unpleasant physical symptoms can appear after use.
        1. Confusion, sleep problems, depression, severe anxiety, and paranoia can result, and may be felt immediately or weeks after the drug was taken.
        2. There is emerging evidence that brain damage in those parts of the brain associated with thought and memory may occur; the seriousness of side effects is tied to the dose taken.
        3. The interaction of ecstasy with alcohol or antidepressant drugs is particularly dangerous.

Practice Test Questions

TOPIC 4A: CONSCIOUSNESS AWAKE AND ASLEEP

Multiple Choice

1. Which psychologist was LEAST interested in matters related to consciousness?
   ___a. John Locke   ___c. John B. Watson
   ___b. William James   ___d. Wilhelm Wundt

2. James claimed that normal waking consciousness has four characteristics. Which of the following is NOT one of those characteristics? Consciousness is always
   ___a. selective.   ___c. sensibly continuous.
   ___b. stable.   ___d. personal.

3. To enter an "altered state of consciousness"
   ___a. is to change one's perception of one's self and of the environment.
   ___b. is to have weird, strange, or bizarre experiences.
   ___c. is something that one cannot do voluntarily, or on purpose.
   ___d. requires that one remain awake and aware.

4. The notion that there might be an unconscious level of awareness
   ___a. is a very old one, dating back to early philosophers.
   ___b. began with the writings of Sigmund Freud.
   ___c. was the centerpiece of early behaviorism.
   ___d. is a fairly new one in psychology, i.e., less than 20 years old.

5. Which of these is NOT a level of consciousness proposed by Freud?
   ___a. preconscious   ___c. postconscious
   ___b. unconscious   ___d. conscious

6. Research on subliminal perception tells us that
   ___a. we learn subliminal information all the time.
   ___b. there is no way that subliminal messages can have any effect on behaviors.
   ___c. one really can improve oneself by using subliminal video and audio tapes.
   ___d. subliminal messages need to be very simple if they are to have any effect at all.

7. In addition to an EEG record, the next best indicator of real sleeping is
   ___a. snoring sounds.   ___c. muscle tension.
   ___b. blood pressure.   ___d. self-report.

8. The stage of consciousness just before one goes to sleep, when one is quiet and relaxed, with eyes closed, produces a pattern of brain wave activity that is
   ___a. rapid and irregular.   ___c. made up of sleep spindles.
   ___b. called alpha wave activity.   ___d. like the pattern when one is dreaming.

9. Delta waves are most common and most evident in an EEG record when a person is
   ___a. relaxed, but not quite asleep.
   ___b. in the middle of a dream.
   ___c. thinking about something, perhaps a problem.
   ___d. in the deepest stage of sleep.

10. Which of the following is most certainly true?
      ___a. People only remember "nightmares" and not "regular" dreams.
      ___b. Everybody goes through three stages of sleep three times each night.
      ___c. We must be aware of the fact that we are dreaming when we are dreaming.
      ___d. To some extent, everybody dreams, and probably every night.

11. We know that your eyes move when you are in REM sleep. What happens to your EEG record?
      ___a. It shows that your muscles are tense and immobile.
      ___b. It appears that you might be awake.
      ___c. It is filled with cyclical alpha patterns.
      ___d. It shows a preponderance of slow theta waves.

12. Which of the following is most likely to occur during REM sleep?
      ___a. Your muscles will become totally relaxed.
      ___b. You will be dreaming about some sexual fantasy.
      ___c. You will wake up as soon as the REM episode is over.
      ___d. Your heart rate and blood pressure will decrease significantly.

13. If I were to interrupt your REM sleep episodes for two nights in a row, what would be the most likely effect?
      ___a. You would become anxious and paranoid the next day.
      ___b. You would compensate by engaging in an extra NREM period on the third night.
      ___c. The next night you would show REM rebound, REMing more than usual.
      ___d. It would take about two or three weeks for you to return to your normal sleep patterns.

14. For which of the following is there the best evidence?
      ___a. The more one exercises, the longer one will sleep.
      ___b. There are significant changes in blood chemistry that occur during sleep.
      ___c. The older we get, the more sleep we need.
      ___d. There are changes in the brain during sleep that are indicative of memory formation.

15. The chronic inability to get a "good night's sleep" is called
      ___a. insomnia.   ___c. narcolepsy.
      ___b. sleep apnea.   ___d. SIDs.

16. When one experiences sleep apnea, what happens?
      ___a. One is unable to REM and/or dream.
      ___b. One's breathing stops during sleeping.
      ___c. One falls asleep suddenly and without warning.
      ___d. One is unable to remember one's dreams.

True/False

1. ___True ___False   William James characterized one's awareness of one's self and one's surroundings as a "stream of consciousness."

2. ___True ___False   Information can be processed unconsciously.

3. ___True ___False   Freud described consciousness by using the analogy of an iceberg, where only the tip of one's mental life is fully conscious at any one time.

4. ___True ___False   The most reliable indicator of sleep is the electroencephalogram.

5. ___True ___False   REM sleep is accompanied by a muscular relaxation called atonia.

TOPIC 4B: VOLUNTARY ALTERATIONS OF CONSCIOUSNESS

Multiple Choice

1. With regard to hypnosis, which statement is most clearly TRUE?
   ___a. There is no good way to predict who can be hypnotized.
   ___b. Under hypnosis, anyone can be made to do anything.
   ___c. Hypnosis can ease the experience of real, physical pain.
   ___d. When under hypnosis, one has no idea of what one is doing.

2. Which of these is the POOREST predictor of whether one can be hypnotized?
   ___a. the extent to which one engages in fantasy or daydreaming
   ___b a history of being an avid reader or actor
   ___c. the extent of one's passivity
   ___d. if one is male or female

3. Which of the following does NOT occur when a person is successfully meditating?
   ___a. Bodily processes slow.   ___c. Heart rate decreases significantly.
   ___b. Oxygen intake increases markedly.   ___d. Alpha waves appear on an EEG record.

4. All drugs that alter one's state of consciousness are referred to as
   ___a. psychoactive.   ___c. illicit.
   ___b. hallucinogenic.   ___d. uppers or downers.

5. What one word best differentiates drug abuse from drug use?
   ___a. legality   ___c. psychological
   ___b. maladaptive   ___d. amount

6. Worldwide, the most common of all chemical stimulants is
   ___a. heroin.   ___c. alcohol.
   ___b. nicotine.   ___d. caffeine.

7. The active chemical substance in marijuana is also found is
   ___a. chocolate.   ___c. cola drinks.
   ___b. hashish.   ___d. heroin.

8. Albeit indirectly, more deaths can be attributed to _____ than to any other psychoactive drug.
   ___a. heroin   ___c. nicotine
   ___b. cocaine   ___d. LSD

9. Everything else being equal, alcohol use and abuse is LEAST likely to occur among
   ___a. persons of low socioeconomic status. ___c. Orthodox Jews.
   ___b. American Indian adolescents.   ___d. Irish-Americans.

True/False

1. ____True ____False Hypnosis can help us remember details of traumatic experiences.

2. ____True ____False Stimulants, depressants, and hallucinogens influence cognitions, but do not influence affects or behaviors.

3. ____True ____False Alcohol, taken in the proper dosage, is a stimulant to thinking.

4. ____True ____False At the present time, there is no known useful medical application for marijuana.

Key Terms and Concepts
Topic 4A

consciousness_____

_____

subliminal perception_____

_____

blindsight_____

_____

REM sleep_____

_____

manifest content_____

_____

latent content_____

_____

activation-synthesis theory_____

_____

insomnia_____

_____

narcolepsy_____

_____

sleep apnea_____

_____

Topic 4B

hypnosis_____

_____

meditation_____

_____

psychoactive drugs_____

_____

stimulants_____

_____

depressants_____

_____

hallucinogens_____

_____

Answers to Practice Test Questions

TOPIC 4A: CONSCIOUSNESS AWAKE AND ASLEEP

Multiple Choice

1. **c**   I hope I didn't catch you on this one, which actually goes back to Chapter 1. John Watson founded *Behaviorism*, which denied the usefulness of consciousness as a scientific concept.
2. **b**   James claimed that our consciousness is selective, continuous, personal, and changing, not stable.
3. **a**   Altered states of consciousness need not be bizarre or strange, and include sleeping. They are simply changes in the way we perceive the environment and ourselves.
4. **a**   Although there has, of late, been a renewed interest in the unconscious, the notion is a very old one, predating psychology, going back to some early philosophers.
5. **c**   Freud describes a conscious, preconscious, and an unconscious level of awareness, but never said anything about a postconscious mind.
6. **d**   It may be a bit conservative, but the only statement here for which there is any evidence at all is the last one.
7. **c**   Except for measures of muscle tension-relaxation, these indicators are very unreliable.
8. **b**   This item provides a decent definition for what is called alpha activity.
9. **d**   In fact, a preponderance of delta waves is the best indicator of a stage of deep sleep.
10. **d**   Although the first three statements may be true, only the fourth is most generally true. Remember, in a multiple-choice exam, the task is to find the <u>best</u> alternative.
11. **b**   EEG records tell us nothing about muscle activity, and shows virtually no alpha or theta waves during REM sleep. They appear almost like waking waves.
12. **a**   During REM sleep, one is likely to become paralyzed, not because of muscle tension but because of a total muscle relaxation, called "atonia."
13. **c**   About the only change would be that you would REM more than usual when you were finally left to sleep.
14. **d**   As reasonable as the other alternatives may sound, there is only good evidence for the last of these four.
15. **a**   The chronic (occurring regularly over time) inability to get a good night's sleep defines the sleep disturbance called insomnia.
16. **b**   Apnea refers to a cessation of breathing. When one stops breathing while asleep, we have "sleep apnea"—a potentially dangerous condition.

True/False

1. **T**   He sure did—making the point that one's consciousness could not be held still and analyzed into bits and pieces.
2. **T**   It can be. That processing is likely to be very simple, straightforward, and not of great significance to us, but there is little doubt that some information is processed without awareness.
3. **T**   Most of our mental life, Freud argued, was unconscious. Like the tip of an iceberg, only a small portion is readily available in our conscious mind.
4. **T**   Self-report is the most unreliable indicator.
5. **T**   Indeed, while we are in REM sleep, we become immobile—not because our muscles tense, but because they have so thoroughly relaxed, a state called atonia.

TOPIC 4B: VOLUNTARY ALTERATIONS OF CONSCIOUSNESS

Multiple Choice

1. **c**   All four statements sound reasonable (as they should in a good multiple-choice item), but here, only the third is actually true.
2. **d**   Granted that some of the first three alternatives do look a bit weird, but they all do predict hypnotize-ability—being male or female does not.
3. **b**   When one is successfully meditating, bodily processes slow, heart rate decreases, alpha waves increase, and oxygen intake decreases as well.
4. **a**   Alternatives **a**, **c**, and **d** may be true of some drugs, but collectively, such drugs are referred to as psychoactive.
5. **b**   This one requires some thought. By definition, we find that drug abuse in some way interferes with normal functioning to the extent that it is maladaptive, getting in the way of one's proper adaptation to the environment and to others.
6. **d**   Here we have a trivia item. Sorry. Caffeine is the most common stimulant. Alcohol, remember, is a depressant.
7. **b**   The active ingredient in marijuana (THC) is also found in hashish.
8. **c**   Sure, heroine, cocaine, and LSD can kill, but smoking, and hence the addictive nicotine, is responsible for many more deaths.
9. **c**   One truly has to be careful about such generalizations—remember always we are talking "in general, in the long run, more often than not" here. Within these groups, we would expect alcohol consumption to be least troublesome among orthodox Jews.

True/False

1. **T**   Hypnosis can do little to help us learn and remember information we have not yet encountered, but it can help to reduce anxiety and thus enable us to remember details of anxiety-producing events that we might not be able to remember otherwise.
2. **F**   If you think about this one long enough, it almost becomes silly. Of course these drugs can and often do affect the way one feels and behaves as well as the way one thinks.
3. **F**   Sorry. No matter the dosage in which it is taken, alcohol is a depressant drug.
4. **F**   As a matter of fact, marijuana seems to be helpful in the treatment of glaucoma and as an anti-nausea agent for patients undergoing chemotherapy. The main issue now, in this country, is legalizing an otherwise illegal substance for these purposes.

A Few Flash Card Possibilities for Chapter 4
(Remember: These are only suggestions. The best flash cards are those you make yourself.)

FREUD'S LEVELS OF CONSCIOUSNESS	conscious, preconscious, and unconscious
ELECTROENCEPHALOGRAM EEG	used to measure overall electrical activity of the brain—indicator of sleep levels
ALPHA ACTIVITY	brain wave pattern indicative of quiet relaxation with eyes closed
REM SLEEP	rapid eye movement sleep; indicative of dreaming
ATONIA	paralysis of totally relaxed muscles found in REM sleep
INSOMNIA	the inability to fall (or stay) asleep
SLEEP APNEA	sleep disorder in which one totally stops breathing
STIMULANTS	psychoactive drugs that increase nervous system activity
HALLUCINOGENS	drugs that alter perceptions and mood

EXPERIENCING PSYCHOLOGY

Let's Try a Little Meditation

A reasonable meditation session usually lasts for about 20 minutes, but giving it a good try for five minutes will be long enough to provide you with an example of what the procedure is all about. It also will be long enough to realize how difficult it is to withdraw from normal waking consciousness and all of its demands for your attention. As best you can, follow these instructions as literally as possible. (It might help if someone were to read these directions to you, softly and slowly.)

- Sit in a comfortable chair, with nothing on your lap or in your hands.

- Sit with your legs uncrossed. Cup one hand loosely inside the other on your lap, or even a bit higher if that is more comfortable.

- Close your eyes gently and relax. Begin with your feet, then your ankles, then your calves, and progress to your face, letting all of your muscles relax.

- Breathe slowly through your nose. Each time you breathe, count slowly from 1 to 10, then take another breath.

- Focus on your breathing and your counting. The object is to exclude all other thoughts from your consciousness. When distracting thoughts occur, try to ignore, focusing again on your breathing and counting.

After five minutes or so, open your eyes and return to normal consciousness. How did you do? Were you really able to exclude all intruding thoughts from your awareness? What kinds of thoughts interfered with your meditation? Thoughts about the past? Thoughts about the future? If you were to try this every day, how long do you think it would take you to be able to successfully meditate—in the sense of reserving a period of time for keeping intruding thoughts to a minimum?

Chapter 5

Learning

STUDY TIP #5

"What Should I Study?"

You know my first reaction to this question, don't you? Everything. And that's not just my initial reaction. It's to be expected from all of your professors. We really do like what we're teaching. We really do think that this is just the most wonderful stuff in the world, and we want everybody to know everything.

We often hear academics talking about "empowering students to think critically" about this or that. And such is a fine goal. Indeed, we would like all of our students to be able to think critically about psychological issues, make their own judgments about psychological claims, and see how psychological concepts are personally relevant. It seems to me, however, that we should back off a little. Let's make sure that we know what we are talking about. Let's get the facts straight before we get involved in deep, abstract, philosophical discussions about psychology.

It was Ivan Pavlov we associate with classical conditioning, not B. F. Skinner. There are similarities and there are differences between classical conditioning and operant conditioning. Once you are comfortable with these ideas we can move on to discussing how Pavlovian conditioning or Skinnerian conditioning can be used in advertising or politics. But such a discussion will be rather pointless if the basic concepts are not well understood.

My point? First things first. It is advantageous to learn the terminology, the vocabulary, first. To help with that task, we have placed most important terms and their definitions in the textbook's margins. Then look for the major ideas or main points of each section. It is somewhat simplistic, but we have tried to reflect these main points in the "Before You Go On" questions throughout each Topic. The logic is clear: Before you go on, pause and consider what you have just read. Does it make sense? Can you answer the question we have asked there? If you can, fine, forge ahead. If you cannot, then don't just keep going on. Stop. Reflect. Reread and think about the section you have just finished.

Outline ~ Chapter 5: Learning

TOPIC 5A: CLASSICAL CONDITIONING

I.   What Is Learning?
    A. **Learning** is demonstrated by a relatively permanent change in behavior that occurs as the result of practice or experience.
        1. Learning cannot be observed directly.
        1. Only overt behavior can be measured.
        1. Learned changes are neither fleeting nor cyclical.
        1. Learned changes are due to experience, not maturation or adaptation.
    B. Conditioning and learning are not technically synonymous, but the most basic types of learning will be called conditioning in this text.
    B. Organisms can learn maladaptive habits as easily as positive, adaptive ones.

II. Pavlov and Classical Conditioning
    A. Ivan Pavlov was a Russian physiologist who won a Nobel Prize in 1904 for his study of the processes of digestion.
        1. Pavlov focused on the salivation reflex in dogs.
        1. Every time Pavlov presented food powder to dogs, they would reflexively salivate.
    B. Pavlov noticed that his dogs began salivating before the food was put in their mouths.
        1. The dogs would salivate at the sight of the food or at the sight of the assistant who delivered the food.
        1. This phenomenon is called classical conditioning.
    C. **Classical conditioning** is a learning process in which a neutral stimulus is paired with a stimulus that elicits an unconditioned response. After conditioning, the conditioned stimulus alone elicits a conditioned response.
        1. If food powder is presented to a dog, salivation results.
        1. The stimulus (food powder) is an **unconditioned stimulus (UCS)**, which reflexively and reliably elicits a response.
        1. Salivation is an **unconditioned response (UCR)**, which is reliably and reflexively elicited by a stimulus.
        1. A neutral stimulus (such as a tone) produces a minimal response or a response of no particular interest.
            a. An **orienting reflex** is a simple, unlearned response of attending to a new or unusual stimulus.
            a. **Habituation** is a form of learning in which an organism comes to ignore a stimulus of little or no consequence.
        5. When the dog learns not to orient toward the tone, the experiment begins.
        5. A **conditioned stimulus (CS)** in classical conditioning is when an originally neutral stimulus (such as a tone) when paired with a UCS (food powder), evokes a new response (salivation).
            a. Each pairing is called a trial.
            a. The **conditioned response (CR)** is the learned response (such as salivation in response to a tone) evoked by the CS after conditioning.
        7. The term "conditioned" indicates the learned component of classical conditioning.
        7. "Unconditioned" means that there is no learning involved.
        7. The CR and UCR are not identical.
            a. The CR is usually weaker than the UCR, regardless of the number of pairings.
            a. It is best to present the CS, followed shortly (within a second or so) by the UCS.
            a. Pavlovian conditioning is basically a matter of "ding-food-slobber.")

III. Processes and Phenomena of Classical Conditioning
  A. The stage of classical conditioning during which the CS and UCS are paired and the strength of the CR increases is called **acquisition.**
  A. **Extinction** is the process in which the strength of a CR decreases with repeated presentations of the CS alone (without the UCS).
  A. **Spontaneous recovery** occurs after extinction and following a rest interval.
    1. If the CS is then paired with the UCS, the strength of the CR increases and is called relearning.
    1. If the CS is presented without the UCS, the strength of the CR diminishes as it did during extinction.
  D. **Generalization** is a process by which a conditioned response is elicited by stimuli different from, but similar to, the CS.
  D. **Discrimination** learning is the phenomenon in classical conditioning in which an organism learns to make a response to only one CS, but not to other CSs.

IV. The Significance of Classical Conditioning for People
  A. A significant aspect of classical conditioning is its role in the development of emotional responses to stimuli in the environment.
  A. The case of "Little Albert" provides a good model for the classical conditioning of emotional responses.
    1. The project was conducted by John Watson and Rosalie Rayner at Johns Hopkins.
    2. At first, a white rat was a neutral stimulus" for Albert, eliciting no sign of fear.
    3. As the rat was handed to Albert a very loud noise was made.
    4. A sudden loud noise is an unconditioned stimulus for fear.
    5. After just one (or, perhaps, a few) pairing, Albert showed fear of the rat.
    6. Albert's mother removed Albert from the experiment before the fear could be counter-conditioned.
    7. Several have questioned the ethics of the Little Albert demonstration.

V. An Application: Treating Fear with Classical Conditioning
  A. Mary Cover Jones (1924) made one of the earliest attempts to apply classical conditioning to the elimination of a fear.
  B. Over 30 years later, a technique called systematic desensitization was introduced by Joseph Wolpe to treat phobic disorders—an intense, irrational fear of an object or event that leads a person to avoid contact with it.
  C. There are three stages of systematic desensitization.
    1. First, the therapist trains the person to relax.
    2. An anxiety hierarchy is constructed, listing in order stimuli that gradually decrease in their ability to elicit anxiety.
    3. The person relaxes, thinks about the least anxious stimulus on the list, and continues to proceed to the next highest, etc.
  D. **Counterconditioning** refers to the process of learning a new response to replace an old one.
    1. A person cannot be relaxed and anxious at the same time.
    2. This process works best for fears or anxieties associated with specific, easily identifiable stimuli.

VI. An Insight: Classical Conditioning's Role in Drug Addiction
  A. With continued use of a drug, *tolerance* may develop such that more and more drug is required to achieve the same (desired) effect.
  B. Tolerance may be a biological phenomenon, but it also may be a classically conditioned response.
    1. Aspects of the environment become stimuli that produce a classically-conditioned reaction that leads to tolerance.
    2. In a new environment the same amount of drug—without the conditioned tolerance cues—can lead to overdose.

VII. Can Any Stimulus Serve as a CS?
    A. Although Pavlov thought otherwise, research suggests that one cannot pair just any stimulus with an unconditioned stimulus and expect conditioning to result.
    B. Effective CSs provide information about the environment (e.g., when a bell rings, food is likely to appear).
    C. Some responses are simply more likely to be associated with some stimuli than with others (e.g., pleasant feelings of a vacation with memories of a sunset at the beach).

VIII. Must the Interval Between the CS and the UCS Be Brief?
    A. Pavlov thought so, and in most cases a brief interval *is* best
    B. The formation of aversions to certain tastes demonstrates that the interval between the CS and UCS may be hours long rather than seconds.
    C. A related issue illustrates that it is biologically adaptive for an organism to learn based on one encounter not to eat things that make it ill.

TOPIC 5B: OPERANT CONDITIONING AND COGNITIVE APPROACHES TO LEARNING

I. The Basics of Operant Conditioning
    A. **Operant conditioning** changes the rate or probability of responses on the basis of the consequences that result from those responses.
    B. Thorndike's **law of effect** claims that responses that lead to a "satisfying state of affairs" tend to be repeated; responses that do not lead to a satisfying state of affairs tend not to be repeated.
    C. As Skinner put it, operant conditioning show us that behaviors are controlled by their consequences.

II. Demonstrating Operant Conditioning
    A. B.F. Skinner built a special operant chamber that some have called a "Skinner box."
        1. In the box, food pellets can be dispensed through a tube into the food cup when a lever or bar is pressed.
        2. The base rate of responding refers to the number of times a rat will press the lever as it is exploring its environment before the food dispenser is activated.
    B. As predicted by Thorndike's law of effect, the rate of the lever pressing will increase when food appears after a lever press.
    C. The learning that occurred was in the rate of the response, not its nature.

III. The Course of Conditioning
    A. **Shaping** reinforces *successive approximations* of the response you want to condition.
    B. **Acquisition** is the process in operant conditioning in which the rate of a reinforced response increases.
    C. **Extinction** refers to the decrease in the rate of a response as reinforcers are withheld.
    D. The return of an extinguished response following a rest interval is called **spontaneous recovery.**
        1. If reinforcement is withheld, extinction occurs.
        2. If reinforcement is used, reacquisition occurs.

IV. Generalization and Discrimination
    A. **Generalization** is the process in which responses conditioned in the presence of a specific stimulus appear in the presence of other, similar, stimuli.
    B. **Discrimination** training occurs when responses made to appropriate stimuli are reinforced, and responses to inappropriate stimuli are ignored or extinguished.
        1. It is largely a matter of *differential reinforcement.*
        3. Learning when it is okay to do something and when it is not is an example of discrimination learning.

V. Reinforcement
    A. **Reinforcement** is a process that increases the rate, or probability, of the response it follows.
    B. A **reinforcer** is the actual stimulus used in the process of reinforcement that increases the probability or strength of a response
    C. If a stimulus presented after a response increases the strength of that response, then that stimulus is a reinforcer regardless of its nature.
    D. What will or will not be reinforcing is sensitive to individual differences and to cultural influences, and has nothing to do with the intent of the person delivering the stimulus

VI. Primary and Secondary Reinforcers
    A. A **primary reinforcer** is a stimulus (usually biologically or physiologically based) that increases the rate of a response with no previous experience or learning required.
    B. A **secondary reinforcer** may be referred to as conditioned, acquired, or learned; it increases the rate of a response because of an association with other reinforcers.
        1. Money, praise, high letter grades, and promotions are examples.
        2. Contingency contracting involves a token economy system that provides secondary reinforcers for appropriate behaviors.
        3. Bribery involves contracting to reward someone to do something that both parties view as inappropriate.

VII. Positive and Negative Reinforcers
    A. A **positive reinforcer** is a stimulus given to an organism after a response is made that increases or maintains the rate of response.
    B. A **negative reinforcer** is a stimulus that increases or maintains the rate of a response that precedes its removal.
    C. **Escape conditioning**—learning to get out of an unpleasant or painful situation once in it—is an example of negative reinforcement because the satisfying state of affairs earned by the learner is pain taken away, not a reward given.
    D. **Avoidance conditioning**—learning not to get into an unpleasant or painful situation before it occurs—is also an example of negative reinforcement.
        1. If a signal precedes a shock, an animal will learn to respond to the signal to avoid the shock (a negative reinforcer).
        2. If there is no way to avoid or escape from a painful stimulus an animal may display **learned helplessness** and stop even trying to avoid or escape from it.

VIII. Schedules of Reinforcement.
    A. The procedure of reinforcing each and every response after it occurs is called a **continuous reinforcement (CRF) schedule.**
        1. Earning a reinforcer after each response may reduce the effectiveness of that reinforcer.
        2. Responses acquired under a CRF schedule tend to extinguish very quickly.
    B. A **partial reinforcement schedule** reinforces a response less frequently than every time it occurs.
        1. With a **fixed-ratio schedule (FR)**, one establishes a ratio of reinforcers to responses (e.g., one reinforcer after every five responses).
        2. With a **fixed-interval schedule (FI)**, time is divided into set, fixed intervals, and a reinforcer is delivered when the next response occurs.
        3. With a **variable-ratio schedule (VR),** one varies the ratio of reinforcers to responses, but maintains a given ratio as an average.
        4. A **variable-interval schedule (VI)** calls for a reinforcer at the first response after a time interval whose length is randomly varied.
        5. These schedules are occasionally called *intermittent schedules of reinforcement.*
    C. The **partial reinforcement effect** refers to the phenomenon that a behavior maintained on a partial schedule of reinforcement is more resistant to extinction that one maintained on CRF.
    D. No matter how they are scheduled, reinforcers should come immediately after the desired response is made.

IX. Will the Reinforcement of *Any* Behavior Increase it Rate?
   A. With patience, nearly any behavior can be operantly conditioned to change its rate of occurrence.
   B. As the Brelands demonstrated, however, if an animal is trained to do something that is not natural to that animal, its behaviors will revert rather quickly to their normal pattern, a phenomenon called **instinctive drift**.

XI. Punishment
   A. Punishment occurs when a stimulus delivered to an organism decreases the rate, or probability, of a response that preceded it.
      1. It is delivered after a response has been made with the intention of reducing the rate of the response.
      2. Punishment is usually in some way hurtful or painful, either physically or psychologically.
      3. The distinction between a punisher and a negative reinforcer is in the timing of the stimulus, whether it is administered or removed, and its effect on behavior.
   B. Noting the effect on behavior is the only way to determine if a response is punishing.
   C. **Punishment** can be an impressive modifier of behavior.
      1. To be effective, it should be delivered immediately after the response.
      2. It needs to be administered consistently.
      3. Punishment may decrease overall behavior levels.
      4. When responses are punished, alternatives should be introduced, that is punishing a response conveys no information about what alternative response might be acceptable.
      5. Spanking or hitting a child has several negative consequences, including the fact that it provides a model of aggressive behavior.

XII. Cognitive Approaches to Learning
   A. **Cognitive approaches** to learning accent changes that occur in an organism's system of mental representations of itself and its world.
   B. Cognitive learning involves the acquisition of knowledge or understanding and need not be reflected in behavior.

XIII. Latent Learning and Cognitive Maps
   A. In experiments with rats, Tolman and Honzik demonstrated latent learning.
      1. **Latent learning** is hidden learning that is not demonstrated in performance until it is reinforced.
      2. Although rats learned their ways around a complicated maze, they made no effort to move through it efficiently until there was reason (a food reward) to do so.
      3. Tolman believed that the rats formed a **cognitive map** or mental representation of their physical environment.
   B. Humans and other animals demonstrate latent learning and the formation of cognitive maps.

XII. Social Learning and Modeling
   A. Albert Bandura's **social learning theory** refers to the idea that learning often takes place through observation and imitation of models.
      1. It is social because it is learned from others.
      2. It is cognitive because what is learned through observations or modeling are changes in cognitions and may never be expressed in behavior.
   B. There are three possible outcomes associated with learning from the behavior of others.
      1. A person can learn a new behavior.
      2. A person can inhibit a behavior if the model is seen punished for it.
      3. A person can disinhibit a behavior after watching a model, thus performing behaviors that had previously been inhibited (reduced in frequency of occurrence).
   C. The classic study of observational learning was reported in 1963 by Bandura, Ross, and Ross.
      1. This study involved children observing an adult model behave aggressively toward a plastic "Bobo" doll toy.

2. The children who had seen the aggressive behaviors of the model were more aggressive in their play than were the children in the control group who did not have the observational experience.

D. **Vicarious reinforcement** leads to acquisition of new behaviors or disinhibition of behavior.

E. **Vicarious punishment** leads to inhibition of behavior.

F. There is now little doubt that children can and do acquire aggressive/violent behaviors simply by watching television and playing video games.

G. Learning through observation and imitation is a common form of human learning.

Practice Test Questions

TOPIC 5A: CLASSICAL CONDITIONING

Multiple Choice

1. To say that learning is "demonstrated" by changes in behavior is to suggest that
   ___a. if we cannot remember something, we did not learn it in the first place.
   ___b. some changes in behavior do not last very long, or are cyclical.
   ___c. the only way we can be sure if people have learned anything is to ask them if they have.
   ___d. learning is an internal process inferred from performance.

2. As Pavlov noted, when a dog is first brought to the laboratory and stood on a table, and a bell is sounded, the first thing that we will notice is
   ___a. an orienting reflex.   ___c. habituation or acclimation.
   ___b. an unconditioned stimulus.   ___d. no response from the dog.

3. In the Pavlovian example of classical conditioning, the UCR was _____ and the CR was _____.
   ___a. a bell; salivation   ___c. a bell; food powder
   ___b. food powder; salivation   ___d. salivation; salivation

4. If we were to demonstrate spontaneous recovery in a classical conditioning procedure, it would occur following extinction and
   ___a. the introduction of a new stimulus, similar to the CS.
   ___b. a period of re-pairing the CS and the UCS.
   ___c. a rest interval.
   ___d. the UCS.

5. Which process is virtually the opposite of generalization?
   ___a. discrimination   ___c. acquisition
   ___b. reinforcement   ___d. habituation

6. We say that systematic desensitization is an application of classical conditioning. If this is so, what serves as the UCR at the beginning of treatment?
   ___a. an irrational fear
   ___b. an object or event that causes fear
   ___c. a state of calm or relaxation
   ___d. an object or event that causes calm or relaxation

7. Classical conditioning may be relevant in drug addiction in what sense?
   ___a. Some drug addicts really know that they should stop using, but don't know how.
   ___b. The environment in which drugs are taken can be conditioned to increase tolerance.
   ___c. Which drug an addict takes depends upon which produces the most reinforcement.
   ___d. No matter what a user does, some drugs are more addictive than others.

8. A stimulus will most effectively serve as a CS if
   ___a. it is repeatedly presented after the presentation of the UCS.
   ___b. it naturally produces an orienting reflex.
   ___c. its presentation reliably predicts the UCS.
   ___d. it is repeatedly paired with the appropriate CR.

9. In demonstrating taste aversions, the UCS will be
   ___a. a feeling of nausea or stomach pain.
   ___b. some food with a distinctive taste.
   ___c. any agent that naturally causes nausea or stomach pain.
   ___d. behaviors that allow the organism to avoid certain tastes.

True/False

1. ____True ____False Ivan Pavlov won a Nobel Prize for Psychology in 1902.

2. ____True ____False In a demonstration of classical conditioning, the first response a subject is likely to make is an orienting reflex.

3. ____True ____False Emotional responses that have been classically conditioned will not extinguish, no matter how many times the CS is presented alone.

4. ____True ____False Because of discrimination training, a child bitten by a German Shepard dog may become frightened of a cocker spaniel.

5. ____True ____False The strength of the UCR sets limits on the strength of the CR.

5B: OPERANT CONDITIONING AND COGNITIVE APPROACHES TO LEARNING

Multiple Choice

1. The basic thrust, or premise, of operant conditioning is that
    ___a. under the proper circumstances, any organism can learn to make any response.
    ___b. organisms only learn responses that are in their own best interest.
    ___c. behaviors are shaped or controlled by their consequences.
    ___d. people learn only if they really want to.

2. If operant conditioning is successful, what is most likely to be changed?
    ___a. the rate or probability of a response
    ___b. cognitive representations within the organism
    ___c. the stimuli that produced the learned response
    ___d. the strength or nature of a response

3. A rat in an operant chamber is given a pellet of food each time it presses a lever. After 100 pellets have been provided for lever pressing, the rat no longer gets any pellets when it presses the lever. What is most likely to occur next?
    ___a. The lever-pressing response will extinguish.
    ___b. The rat will become frustrated, anxious, and aggressive.
    ___c. The rat will continue to press the lever at the same rate.
    ___c. The rat's operant rate will spontaneously recover.

4. You want to reinforce Mickey for hanging his coat in the closet, but he never does so. He simply drops his coat on the floor as he walks trough the door. Which of these procedures would be most effective now?
    ___a. physical punishment   ___c. shaping
    ___b. discrimination learning   ___d. negative reinforcement
5. In operant conditioning, discrimination training is most a matter of
    ___a. learning right from wrong.
    ___b. discovering the differences between reinforcement and punishment.
    ___c. differential reinforcement.
    ___d. extinction followed by spontaneous recovery.

6. Primary reinforcers are
    ___a. learned.   ___c. acquired.
    ___b. conditioned.   ___d. biologically-based.

7. The major difference between positive and negative reinforcement is whether
    ___a. something is given or taken away   ___c. responses are rewarded or punished
    ___b. rates of responses go up or down   ___d. reinforcers are innate or learned

8. Which of the following provides the best example of NEGATIVE reinforcement?
    ___a. paying Billy a dollar for each "A" or "B" on his report card
    ___b. having a root canal procedure to ease the pain of a severe toothache
    ___c. spanking Amy for playing with the water in the toilet bowl
    ___d. using a token economy to modify the behaviors of a severely retard child

9. Using each of the following reinforcement schedules, different rats are trained to press levers at the same high rate. The lever pressing of rats trained on a _____reinforcement schedule will now extinguish most quickly.
    ___a. continuous   ___c. fixed-interval
    ___b. fixed ratio   ___d. variable interval

10. Which statement concerning punishment is most justified?
    ___a. Because it creates anxiety, it should never be used with children.
    ___b. Physical punishment is more effective than psychological punishment.
    ___c. Punishment is really only effective if it has been threatened repeatedly.
    ___d. Punishment decreases the rate of the responses that it follows.

11. In general, cognitive approaches to learning tend to emphasize
    ___a. the interaction of genetics and experience.
    ___b. knowing ahead of time what will serve as a reinforcer.
    ___c. changes inside the organism that may not be reflected in behavior.
    ___d. the role of learning in the acquisition of emotions.

12. If learning is "latent," it is, by definition,
    ___a. of no real value to the organism.
    ___b. not (yet) reflected in behavior.
    ___c. learned, but not remembered.
    ___d. displayed only in social situations.

13. When birds bury seeds for use in the winter months,
    ___a. they generally have no idea where to find them when the need arises.
    ___b. they hide so many seeds that they cannot fail to find at least a few to get by on.
    ___c. they form a cognitive map and actually remember where the seeds are hidden.
    ___d. the birds leave little "markers" on the ground to guide their search in winter.

14. Which of the following does your text offer as an example of social learning theory at work?
    ___a. "how-to-do-it" programs on PBS television
    ___b. Head Start preschool programs
    ___c. college programs for returning adult students
    ___d. software programs for word processing.

15. Of the following, what is it that makes Bandura's social learning theory social?
    ___a. the fact that it is a very cognitive approach to learning
    ___b. the concepts of vicarious reinforcement or punishment
    ___c. the requirement that learning be the result of practice or experience
    ___d. the fact that it can only be found in humans and not in nonhumans

True/False

1. ____True ____False   Skinner stated the Law of Effect after observing rats (and pigeons) in his operant chambers.

2. ____True ____False   Shaping is an operant conditioning technique accomplished by the method of successive approximations.

3. ____True ____False   You may be punishing responses even though you are intending to reinforce them.

4. ____True ____False   Everything else being equal, negative reinforcement is a good thing to happen to you.

5. ____True ____False   Because it requires a certain amount of intelligence, only humans are capable of forming cognitive maps.

6. ____True ____False   Children are more likely to imitate the behaviors of persons who are reinforced for their behaviors than they are to imitate the behaviors of persons who are punished for their behaviors.

Key Terms and Concepts
Topic 5A

learning _____

_____

classical conditioning _____

_____

unconditioned stimulus _____

_____

unconditioned response _____

_____

orienting reflex _____

_____

habituation _____

_____

conditioned stimulus _____

_____

conditioned response _____

_____

acquisition _____

_____

extinction _____

_____

spontaneous recovery _____

_____

stimulus generalization _____

_____

discrimination learning _____

_____

phobic disorder_____

_____

counter-conditioning_____

_____

Topic 5B

operant conditioning_____

_____

law of effect_____

_____

shaping_____

_____

reinforcer_____

_____

primary reinforcer_____

_____

secondary reinforcer_____

_____

positive reinforcer_____

_____

negative reinforcer_____

_____

escape conditioning_____

_____

avoidance conditioning_____

_____

learned helplessness_____

_____

continuous reinforcement (CRF) schedule_____

_____

partial reinforcement schedule_____

_____

fixed ratio (FI) schedule_____

_____

fixed interval (FI) schedule_____

_____

variable ratio (VR) schedule_____

_____

variable interval (VI) schedule_____

_____

partial reinforcement effect_____

_____

instinctive drift_____

_____

punishment_____

_____

latent learning_____

_____

cognitive map_____

_____

social learning theory_____

_____

vicarious reinforcement_____

_____

vicarious punishment_____

_____

Answers to Practice Test Questions

TOPIC 5A: CLASSICAL CONDITIONING

Multiple Choice

1. **d** Alternative **a** is simply not true. Alternatives **b** and **c** may be true, but are not related to the word "demonstrated," which makes **d** the correct choice.
2. **a** The very first thing that will happen is that a bell will be sounded and, reflexively, the dog will orient toward it.
3. **d** Actually, because the bell and the food powder in the first three alternatives are stimuli and not responses, the only possible answer here is the last alternative.
4. **c** Spontaneous recovery is the reappearance of a conditioned response following extinction and immediately after a rest interval.
5. **a** By definition, discrimination conditioning is usually used to offset the effects of the opposite process of generalization.
6. **a** This is a tough one. The person comes to desensitization with a (learned) irrational fear, which now acts *as if it were* a UCR to be replaced with a newly acquired CR of relaxation. All of that means that the first alternative here is the best one.
7. **b** Although some of the other alternatives may be true, the second is the only one that has to do with classical conditioning. Because of this phenomenon, taking the same amount of drug in a new (unconditioned) environment can cause an overdose.
8. **c** Pavlov did not recognize this reality, but we now know that a stimulus will serve as an effective CS only if it signals or predicts the occurrence of the UCS that follows it.
9. **c** Alternatives **a** and **d** are responses and, thus, cannot be a UCS. The food, originally neutral, is the CS, and anything that causes nausea or stomach pain acts as the UCS.

True/False

1. **F** I really like this item (and I have used it in several upper-division classes, but not in the beginning course). It is false for two reasons. Pavlov won his prize in 1904, not 1902, but that's pretty picky. There is no Nobel Prize for psychology—Pavlov's was in medicine.
2. **T** Yes, this is the first response, which needs to be habituated before actual conditioning begins.
3. **F** Some particularly strong emotional responses may take quite a while to extinguish, but eventually they will.
4. **F** Bitten by a German Shepard dog, a child may very well become frightened by a cocker spaniel, but the process involved is not discrimination, but generalization, nearly the opposite.
5. **T** This is true. Remember: no matter how many times the CS and UCS are paired, the CR is never quite as strong as the UCR was at the start.

TOPIC 5B: OPERANT CONDITIONING AND COGNITIVE APPROACHES TO LEARNING

Multiple Choice

1. **c** I doubt that many psychologists would even agree with the statements made in alternatives **a**, **b**, and **d**, which makes the third alternative the correct choice here.
2. **a** The relatively permanent change in behavior that occurs as a result of operant conditioning is a change in the rate or probability of a response.
3. **a** This is a wordy item, but the most likely thing to happen is that the rat's rate of lever pressing will decrease, which is indicative of extinction.
4. **c** If Mickey doesn't do what you want him to do, there will be nothing for you to reinforce, so in this situation, you will have to try shaping first.
5. **c** Because we reinforce some stimuli and not others, we say that discrimination training is a matter of differential reinforcement.
6. **d** Actually, the first three alternatives all say pretty much the same thing, which is a major clue that the answer is the last alternative. "Primary" as a descriptor in psychology often refers to something that is based in evolution, biology, or physiology.
7. **a** Positive reinforcers are given to organisms after an appropriate response, while negative reinforcement involves taking away something (that is usually unpleasant or painful).
8. **b** Because the root canal procedure takes away the pain of the toothache, the end result is very reinforcing (how reinforcing depends on how painful the toothache was). The reinforcement here is negative reinforcement.
9. **a** Responses learned under a continuous reinforcement schedule will extinguish more quickly than those learned under any other type of reinforcement schedule.
10. **d** Actually, the first three alternatives are each quite false. The only thing that we can say for sure is that punishment decreases response rates—by definition.
11. **c** Cognitive approaches emphasize cognitions, cleverly enough. That means that they focus on changes inside the organism that may or may not be evidenced in overt behavior.
12. **b** "Latent" means "hidden from view," or "not presently observable." Hence, the second alternative is the best choice.
13. **c** This seems strange, but, in fact, birds can (and do) create incredibly elaborate cognitive maps of their territories in which they bury their seeds for future use.
14. **a** Maybe it's just me, but I think that all those PBS television shows that are aimed at teaching us how to do all sorts of things—from tuning car engines, to installing a deck, to upholstering furniture and making quilts—follow the lead of social learning theory, in a "see how I do it, then try it yourself" sort of way.
15. **b** Vicarious reinforcement and vicarious punishment deal with the consequences of observing someone else being reinforced or punished and are, therefore, social concepts.

True/False

1. **F** Actually, it was Thorndike who stated the Law of Effect after observing his cats in a puzzle box.
2. **T** This statement is true by definition—"shaping" and "successive approximations" are nearly synonymous terms.
3. **T** It is important to remember that the intention of the person doing the reinforcing (or the punishing) is quite irrelevant in operant conditioning. What matters is the effect that one's actions have on the behavior of the "learner," which makes this statement true.
4. **T** Because negative reinforcement involves the removal of some noxious, unpleasant, painful stimulus and results in the increase of one's rate of responding, it is surely a good thing to have happen to you.
5. **F** You didn't fall for this one, did you? Remember, Tolman first demonstrated cognitive maps in rats. As it happens, it is very easy to generate human examples, but the point is that this phenomenon is not restricted to humans.
6. **T** They certainly are.

A Few Flash Card Possibilities for Chapter 5

(Remember: There are just suggestions. The best flash cards are those you make yourself.)

LEARNING	change in behavior that occurs as the result of practice or experience
CLASSICAL CONDITIONING	learning in which an originally neutral stimulus comes to elicit a new response
ACQUISITION	process in operant conditioning in which the rate of reinforced responses increases
COUNTER CONDITIONING	technique in which a new response is acquired to replace an old learned one
PHOBIA	an intense irrational fear that prompts avoidance behaviors
OPERANT CONDITIONING	a procedure that changes the rate or the probability of a response on the basis of the consequences that result from that response
LAW OF EFFECT	Thorndike's law: responses leading to a satisfying state of affairs tend to be repeated; those that do not, are not
SHAPING	reinforcing successive approximations of a response you want to condition
EXTINCTION	in operant conditioning, the decrease in the rate of a response as reinforcers are withheld
SOCIAL LEARNING THEORY	the position that learning takes place through the observation and imitation of others (models)
COGNITIVE MAP	a mental representation of the learning situation or of the physical environment

EXPERIENCING PSYCHOLOGY

Playing Pigeon: A Shaping Exercise

This activity works best in small groups—it's nearly a party game. The point is to select one "player" to be your pigeon. The others in the group are to shape the behavior of the pigeon by using positive verbal reinforcers, such as "good," or "right" as the pigeon successively approximates the desired behavior. Desired behaviors for your pigeon might include such things as:

- Sit on the floor.
- Put your thumb in your mouth.
- Scratch your right leg.
- Put your hands over your ears.
- Stand on a chair.
- Take off your left shoe.
- Pull on your hair.
- Sit down and cross your legs.
- Clap your hands.
- Spin around in a circle (twice).

Obviously, the "shapers" must know the goal behavior, but the pigeon must not. When you begin, the pigeon should start emitting behaviors, and the group should begin to shape the pigeon's behaviors toward the goal (the target behavior). Make sure that the pigeon receives no feedback other than the verbal reinforcer. See how long it takes to shape your pigeon. Anything less than 5 minutes is good.

Once your group has had some success shaping behaviors by using positive reinforcers, try to shape one of the above behaviors using punishers, that is, by saying, "bad" or "no-no!" This is more difficult, isn't it? Can you make any progress in 5 minutes?

Chapter 6

Memory

STUDY TIP #6

"How Should I Study?"

The whole idea of studying—indeed, the whole idea of going to college in the first place—is to learn and remember something that you did not know or remember before. Studying is the active process of placing information into one's memory in such a way that it can be located and retrieved later. The information that one places into memory during study is not just restricted to simple facts, but also includes knowledge of new ways of discovering information, thinking about information in new ways and evaluating information. In simple terms, it is a process in which stuff "out there" gets placed into memory in a usable way.

The first thing to realize is that studying is **an active process**. It is one in which you have to become actively involved. Sorry, but no matter how long you sit there with a book on your lap, nothing is going to happen until you start getting involved with what you are reading. Sorry, but if you are sitting in class daydreaming about last weekend's date, nothing is going to get learned, no matter how brilliant the lecture.

The essence of study is found in what psychologists call "elaborative rehearsal." To study effectively is to take to-be-learned material and elaborate on it. Think about it. Make it meaningful. Relate it to something you already know, to something you have learned elsewhere. For example, we use several stories and examples in the text in an effort to make the material meaningful. But these are our stories; they are our examples. It is much more useful to generate your own.

One of the things that makes psychology an easier course of study than some others is that it is (usually) fairly easy to relate what you are studying to some personal experience. When the text talks about various schedules of reinforcement, think about how each would affect your performance. When your instructor lectures about Piaget's theory of development stages in children, think about a younger brother, sister, niece or nephew, or perhaps, your own child or children. The more you can relate what you are learning to what you already know, the better will be your learning, and the better will be your retention.

Outline ~ Chapter 6: Memory

TOPIC 6A: HOW CAN WE BEST DESCRIBE HUMAN MEMORY?

I. Memory As Information Processing
   A. **Memory** is a set of systems involved in the acquisition, storage, and retrieval of information.
   B. Using one's memory involves three interrelated processes.
      1. **Encoding** is the active process of putting information into memory—a matter of forming cognitive representations of information.
      2. **Storage** is the process of holding encoded information in memory.
      3. **Retrieval** involves the process of locating, removing, and using information stored in memory.

II. Sensory Memory
   A. **Sensory memory** stores large amount of information for a few seconds or less.
   B. There are sensory memory systems for each sense, but two are usually considered.
      1. Visual sensory memory, or **iconic memory**, is the sensory store associated with vision.
      2. **Echoic memory** is the sensory storage system associated with the sense of hearing.
   C. Information is not encoded in sensory memory; it is stored just as it is received.

III. Short-Term Memory (STM)
   A. Information from sensory memory can be processed more fully by moving it into short-term memory.
   B. **Short-term memory (STM)** is a level, or store, in human memory with limited capacity and, without the benefit of rehearsal, a brief duration.
   C. This STM is often called working memory.
      1. Information from sensory memory or from long-term memory can be moved into STM, where we can work with it.
      2. Getting information into STM requires that one attend to it

IV. The Duration of STM
   A. **Maintenance rehearsal** is the simple repetition of information already in STM.
   B. STM can hold information for approximately 15 to 20 seconds.

V. The Capacity of STM
   A. George Miller suggested that STM had a capacity of seven, plus or minus two, chunks of information.
   B. A **chunk** is the representation in memory of a meaningful unit of information.

VI. Long-Term Memory (LTM)
   A. **Long-term memory (LTM)** refers to memory for large amounts of information that is held for long periods of time.
   B.   It is not known how long information remains stored in LTM.
   C. It is possible that memory is reconstructed from recollections of past experiences.
   D.   Simple repetition of information is seldom sufficient to process it into long-term memory.
   E. **Elaborative rehearsal** refers to thinking about, organizing, and forming images of information to make it meaningful; or relating information to something already in LTM.
      1. This term was proposed by Craik and Lockhart in 1972.
      2. It is not an either-or process; information can be elaborated to greater or lesser degrees.

VII. Are There Different Types of Long-Term Memories?
   A. **Declarative memory** includes semantic memory and episodic memory from which information can be intentionally recalled.
      1. Vocabulary, concepts, language rules, and facts are stored in **semantic memory.**

        a. **Clustering** refers to the process of recalling related items of information together on the basis of shared associations.

        b. Subjective organization refers to the process of imposing personal organization if there is a list of unrelated words to recall.

        c. Hierarchical network models propose that concepts or propositions are stored in interrelated, predictable ways.

    2. In **episodic memory**, life events and personal experiences are stored.

        a. It is time-related, and experiences are stored in chronological order.

        b. A separate category is autobiographical memory, which contains events that are particularly significant.

  B. **Nondeclarative memory** (procedural memory) involves the acquisition, retention, and retrieval of performance skills such as a tennis stroke or golf swing.

VIII. On the Accuracy of Long-term Memories

  A. Determining the accuracy of past experiences is difficult.

  B. According to Bartlett, people tend to form features of what is experienced.

    1. Through a process called **reconstructive memory,** features are retrieved and reconstructed to form a report of what was encoded and stored.

    2. Recent research and theory support Bartlett's general idea.

        a. Features are scattered widely over different parts of the brain.

        b. Therefore, no single part of the brain houses a complete memory.

  C. Sometimes, the reconstruction process results in inaccurate reports of what is in memory.

    1. Inadequate connections among the features associated with an event stored in memory can lead to inaccurate reconstruction.

    2. At encoding, inadequate separation of episodes from other similar episodes may cause a person not to remember a feature specific to a given episode.

  D. Retrieval cues may match more than one set of features representing more than one episode.

  E. A **repressed memory** is one that is so disturbing that a person has pushed it into the unconscious where it is no longer readily available for retrieval.

    1. There is controversy as to whether memories recovered during therapy are actual or false memories.

    2. There is ample research showing that memories can be implanted.

    3. This is an important issue for psychology, as well as the legal system.

  F. Eyewitness testimony is another area in which the accuracy of long-term memory is of critical importance.

    1. **Compromise memory** involves the blending of conflicting information in memory so that an "averaged" version of information will be recalled.

    2. There is much debate about whether eyewitness testimony is accurate.

IX. Where and How are Memories Formed in the Brain?

  A. Scientists assume that most human memories are stored in the cerebral cortex, but recognize that other, lower structures are involved.

    1. The hippocampus seems most necessary for memory formation.

    2. **Retrograde amnesia** refers to the loss of memory for events that occurred before the onset of amnesia.

    3. **Anterograde amnesia** occurs when one is unable to remember events occurring after the onset of amnesia.

  B. Memories are formed when changes occur in the cerebral cortex that are, in part, influenced by the action of the hippocampus.

  C. Memory formation can be influenced by changes at the synapse.

    1. With repetition or experience, the flow of impulses across synapses becomes easier.

    2. The neurotransmitter, glutamate, causes a change in the ion balance on the postsynaptic membrane, so that the neuron may be stimulated more readily.

    3. Other research claims that what matters are changes (increases in the number of receptor sites) in the postsynaptic membrane.

TOPIC 6B: FACTORS THAT AFFECT FORGETTING

I. How We Measure Retrieval
    A. Direct, Explicit Measures of Memory
        1. **Recall** asks someone to produce information to which he or she has been previously exposed.
            a. In free recall, a person can recall information in any order, but is given the fewest retrieval cues.
            b. In serial recall, a person is required to recall information in the order presented.
            c. In cued recall, retrieval cues are provided.
        2. In **recognition,** a person is asked to identify previously experienced material.
            a. First, the person must retrieve information stored in memory.
            b. Second, the person must match that memory with material to be recognized and decide whether the material was seen before.
    B. Indirect, Implicit Measures of Memory
        1. **Relearning** is the change in performance that occurs when one is required to learn material for a second time and almost always requires fewer trials than did the original learning.
        2. Procedural memory (knowing how to do things) is another example of an indirect measure of memory.

II. How We Encode Information
    A. The Power of Context
        1. The **encoding specificity principle** asserts that how we retrieve information depends on how it was encoded in the first place.
        2. **State-dependent memory** refers to the idea that retrieval depends on the extent to which a person's state of mind at retrieval matches the person's state of mind at encoding.
        3. **Flash-bulb memories** refer to memories that are unusually clear and vivid.
    B. The Usefulness of Meaningfulness
        1. **Meaningfulness** refers to the extent to which new information evokes associations with information already in LTM.
        2. Meaningfulness resides in the learner, not in the material to be learned.
    C. The Value of Mnemonic Devices
        1. Mnemonic devices are encoding techniques that can aid retrieval of information
            a. Narrative chaining occurs when unorganized material is woven into a meaningful story.
            b. **Imagery** at encoding can improve retrieval, such as the key word method of study.
            c. **The method of loci** involves taking a well-known location and visually placing material to be recalled in various places.

    D. The Role of Schemas
        1. A **schema** is an organized mental representation of the world that is adaptive and formed by experience.
            a. A person scheme helps to organize information about the characteristics of people.
            b. A role scheme includes information and expectations about how people in certain roles should behave.
            c. Event schemes house ideas about how events should occur.
        2. Retrieval is enhanced when information to be remembered is consistent with prior, existing information.

III. How We Schedule Practice
      A. Overlearning
            1. **Overlearning** is the process of practicing or rehearsing material over and above what is needed to learn it.
            2. Overlearning improves retrieval, but a diminishing returns phenomenon occurs.
      B. Scheduling, or Spacing, Practice
            1. In massed-practice conditions, there is no break between learning trials.
            2. In distributed-practice, rest intervals are interspersed among the learning trials.
            3. Short and meaningful study periods are more efficient than study periods massed together.

IV. How We Overcome Interference
      A. **Retroactive interference** occurs when interfering activities come after the learning that is to be remembered or retrieved.
      B. **Proactive interference** occurs when previously learned material interferes with the retrieval of material learned later.

Practice Test Questions

TOPIC 6A: HOW CAN WE BEST DESCRIBE HUMAN MEMORY?

Multiple Choice

1. Psychologists talk about passing information through three levels or compartments of memory called, in order,
    ___a. encoding, storage, and retrieval.   ___c. central, peripheral, and somatic.
    ___b. primary, secondary, and tertiary.   ___d. sensory, short-term, and long-term.

2. For approximately what length of time is information typically held in one's sensory memory?
    ___a. less than a second
    ___b. a few minutes
    ___c. a day or two
    ___d. At least some information is held there permanently.

3. The minimal requirement for keeping information in short-term memory with maintenance rehearsal is that we
    ___a. elaborate it in some way.   ___c. organize it.
    ___b. make it meaningful.   ___d. re-attend to it.

4. The amount of information held in STM (i.e., its capacity) can be extended (at least a little bit) if we can _____ that information.
    ___a. rehearse   ___c. chunk
    ___b. attend to   ___d. elaborate

5. The best way to encode information into long-term memory is
    ___a. rote repetition.   ___c. maintenance rehearsal.
    ___b. taking extensive notes.   ___d. by elaborating it.

6. Elaboratively rehearsing information is largely a matter of organizing it and
    ___a. making it meaningful.   ___c. retrieving it.
    ___b. re-attending to it.   ___d. repeating it.

7. Imagine a 42-year-old man who has not ice-skated since he was 12 years old. Even though it has been 30 years, he finds that can still skate quite well. His ability to ice skate has been stored in his _____ long-term memory.
    ___a. physical   ___c. episodic
    ___b. procedural   ___d. semantic

8. The answer to which question is most likely to be found in episodic memory?
    ___a. When and where did you learn to ride a bicycle?
    ___b. When and where did Wundt open his laboratory?
    ___c. What sorts of information are stored in episodic memory?
    ___d. What is the result of dividing 134 by 12?

9. If any sort of memory is to be repressed, what sort of memory is it likely to be?
    ___a. nearly anything in STM   ___c. facts stored in semantic LTM
    ___b. events stored in episodic LTM   ___d. habits stored in procedural LTM

10. When psychologists suggest that an aspect of memory is well organized (into categories or networks, for example) to which aspect of memory are they referring?
    ___a. episodic   ___c. meta-memory
    ___b. short-term   ___d. semantic

11. Referring to memory as "reconstructive"
    ___a. is a notion that goes back to the early 1930s.
    ___b. implies that all of our memories are stored just as we experienced them.
    ___c. is virtually the same as Freud's concept of repression.
    ___d. reflects the fact that specific memories are stored in specific areas of the cerebral cortex.

12. A diagnosis of anterograde amnesia implies that short-term memories cannot be made into long-term memories. This unfortunate situation is most likely to result from lesions or damage to the
    ___a. occipital lobe.   ___c. hippocampus.
    ___b. hypothalamus.   ___d. corpus callosum.

13. When memories are formed, what is the LEAST likely change to occur in the brain?
    ___a. The number of synapses increases.   ___c. The amounts of neurotransmitters change.
    ___b. Neural thresholds become lower.   ___d. New neurons are formed by experience.

True/False

1. ____True ____False   For information to be processed into memory, the very first thing that we do to or with that information is to learn it.

2. ____True ____False   The type of memory, or level of processing, with the largest capacity is our sensory memory.

3. ____True ____False   Of the three levels or types of memory, perceptual attention influences short-term memory the most.

4. ____True ____False   The most efficient strategy for encoding information in semantic long-term memory is to use elaborative rehearsal.

5. ____True ____False   Information in semantic long-term memory is probably stored in chronological order, that is, is stored in the order in which it was received.

TOPIC 6B: FACTORS THAT AFFECT FORGETTING

Multiple Choice

1. When psychologists talk about "retrieval failure," what assumption do they make?
   ___a. We are dealing with short-term memory.
   ___b. Information is available, even if it is not accessible.
   ___c. There must be some sort of brain damage involved.
   ___d. The material was never stored in the first place.

2. Information is most difficult to retrieve when retrieval is requested by asking for
   ___a. recognition.　　　　　　　　　___c. recall.
   ___b. relearning.　　　　　　　　　___d. some implicit measure.

3. Research that involves _____ is dealing with implicit measures of learning.
   ___a. recognition　　　　　　　　___c. serial recall
   ___b. schema　　　　　　　　　　___d. relearning

4. Implicit measures of memory are most appropriate for information stored in
   ___a. semantic memory.　　　　　　___c. reconstructed memory.
   ___b. procedural memory.　　　　　___d. episodic memory.

5. Most people cannot remember all of the features on a one-dollar bill. Which of the following phrases best describes the basic problem in such instances?
   ___a. lack of availability　　　　　___c. improper encoding
   ___b. poorly worded questions　　　___d. proactive interference

6. What does the "encoding specificity hypothesis" tell us?
   ___a. Retrieval is enhanced to the extent that retrieval cues match encoding cues.
   ___b. We tend to remember pleasant things more readily than we remember unpleasant ones.
   ___c. Retrieval is enhanced to the extent that we use explicit measures rather than implicit ones.
   ___d. The effects of retroactive interference are greater than the effects of proactive interference.

7. Studies of "state dependent" memory provide support for
   ___a. recognition being superior to recall.　　___c. the encoding specificity hypothesis.
   ___b. retrograde amnesia.　　　　　　　　　___d. the value of mnemonic techniques.

8. Mnemonic techniques enhance or improve retrieval because they
   ___a. involve the continued repetition of information.
   ___b. make material more meaningful.
   ___c. involve the right side of the brain as well as the left.
   ___d. lengthen the storage of LTM.

9. Making up a story that contains all of the words on a list to be learned is a mnemonic device called
   ___a. the peg word method.　　　　　___c. mental imagery.
   ___b. the method of loci.　　　　　　___d. narrative chaining.

10. Organized, but general, representations of knowledge stored in one's LTM are
    ___a. mnemonic devices.　　　　　　___c. episodes.
    ___b. schemas.　　　　　　　　　　___d. retrieval strategies.

11. After a list of words is presented to Bob 8 times, we have evidence that he has learned the list. If we want Bob to engage in 200% overlearning of this list, how many ADDITIONAL presentations would be required?
    ___a. 0　　　　　　　　　　　　　___c. 16
    ___b. 8　　　　　　　　　　　　　___d. 20

12. Which is true most often?

    ___a. Retroactive interference is less disruptive than is proactive interference.

    ___b. Overlearning increases the capacity and the duration of STM.

    ___c. Overwhelming anxiety explains most retrieval failures on classroom exams.

    ___d. Distributed practice is superior to massed practice.

13. If, during the course of a semester, you have nine classroom exams, for which exam will PROACTIVE interference be the greatest?

    ___a. the first

    ___b. the fifth (the one in the middle)

    ___c. the ninth

    ___d. Proactive interference effects would be the same for all nine exams.

14. You are in an experiment to demonstrate the retroactive interference that may occur between two learning tasks, A and B. You are assigned to the Experimental Group. The first thing that you will be asked to do is

    ___a. take a test on your retrieval of A.

    ___b. learn Task A.

    ___c. learn Task B.

    ___d. rest while the Control Group learns Task A.

True/False

1. ____True ____False   At least on classroom exams, retrieval measured by recall is superior to retrieval measured by recognition.

2. ____True ____False   We may think of explicit memory retrieval as an unconscious process.

3. ____True ____False   Flashbulb memories are stored in procedural long-term memory.

4. ____True ____False   Mnemonic devices have an impact on retrieval, but not on encoding.

5. ____True ____False   Retrieval is a skill that can be enhanced with practice.

Key Terms and Concepts
Topic 6A

memory_____

_____

encoding_____

_____

storage_____

_____

retrieval_____

_____

sensory memory_____

_____

short-term memory (STM)_____

_____

maintenance rehearsal_____

_____

long-term memory_____

_____

elaborative rehearsal_____

_____

declarative memory_____

_____

nondeclarative memory_____

_____

semantic memory_____

_____

category clustering_____

_____

episodic memory_____

_____

reconstructive memory_____

_____

repressed memory_____

_____

compromise memory_____

_____

retrograde amnesia_____

_____

anterograde amnesia_____

_____

Topic 6B

recall_____

_____

recognition_____

_____

relearning_____

_____

encoding specificity hypothesis_____

_____

state-dependent memory_____

_____

flashbulb memories_____

_____

meaningfulness_____

_____

mnemonic devices_____

_____

schema_____

_____

overlearning_____

_____

retroactive interference_____

_____

proactive interference_____

_____

Answers to Practice Test Questions

TOPIC 6A: HOW CAN WE DESCRIBE HUMAN MEMORY?

Multiple Choice

1. **d** The key to this item is that we're talking about "levels" or "compartments," otherwise, alternative **a** would look pretty good. The best alternative here is the last one.
2. **a** Of all of our different varieties of memory, the duration of sensory memory is, by far, the shortest. Some folks say less than one second, some say about a second, but even an alternative that says "a few minutes" is way too long.
3. **d** You have to be careful on this one. The word "minimal" is very important here. Any one of these alternatives will do the job, but the minimum necessary is simply paying attention to it again.
4. **c** The best term (although arguments could be made for some of the other alternatives) is the technical term "chunk," largely because the others are more related to duration than to capacity.
5. **d** The best way is to "work with it," using elaborative rehearsal.
6. **a** We say that elaborative rehearsal gets information into LTM, so "retrieving it" won't do. Alternatives **b** and **d** say the same thing and are related to STM, so the answer is that it involves making the material (more) meaningful.
7. **b** These abilities are most likely in procedural memory.
8. **a** Mostly because it is personal and autobiographical, the answer to the question about learning to ride a bicycle is probably in episodic memory. Note that actually remembering how to do so would be in procedural memory.
9. **b** Long-term memories of traumatic, anxiety-producing experiences—of the sort usually found in one's episodic memory—are the sorts that are typically repressed.
10. **d** There is little doubt that all of our memory processes are organized in some fashion, but issues of organization are mostly related to semantic memory.
11. **a** That our recall of experience is reconstructed from bits and pieces of stored information is a point of view that goes back to Barlett in 1932. The other three alternatives are just simple false.
12. **c** Because the hippocampus is involved in "moving" experiences from STM to LTM, and because a difficulty in doing so is what anterograde amnesia is, the quality answer is the third one.
13. **d** It's difficult to say, of course, exactly what changes take place in the brain when memories are formed, but we know for sure that new neurons are not formed or created. Remember from Chapter 2 that we are born with more neurons than we'll ever have again.

True/False

1. **F** No, actually, before we learn it we must attend to and perceive it, but before that we must sense that information.
2. **F** Whereas LTM seems to be virtually without limit in terms of capacity, sensory memory is going to be limited by our sensory ability. Sensory memory capacity is large, but not as large as that of LTM.
3. **T** Indeed, because paying attention is so central to STM, we find its capacity limited.
4. **T** This statement is simple in that it does not bother to tell us just what elaborative rehearsal is, but in its simplicity, it is true.
5. **F** Information in semantic memory is no doubt well organized, and one of the ways in which it may be organized is chronologically. Having said that, I still am going to claim that the answer here is false because there are so many other, better, more common ways of organizing material in semantic memory—and because chronological organization better fits episodic memory.

TOPIC 6B: FACTORS THAT AFFECT FORGETTING

Multiple Choice

1. **b** When we talk about retrieval failure, we are probably going to assume that the information that cannot be remembered is in memory, but cannot be gotten out for some reason, which is essentially what the second alternative is saying.
2. **c** In virtually every case (although do note that there are exceptions) recall is more difficult than any other measure.
3. **d** When we ask someone to relearn previously learned—and perhaps forgotten—material, we are really testing to see if any of that material is still there—implicitly.
4. **b** In truth, material in procedural memory seems to actively resist explicit measures of retrieval.
5. **c** The simple thing to say is that we cannot remember these features because we have never really tried to learn them, which is to say that they have never been properly encoded.
6. **a** I think that **a** is a fairly good, concise statement of the encoding specificity hypothesis. Note that although alternatives **b** and **d** are essentially true statements, they are not related to the question.
7. **c** State-dependent memory studies have to do with the person's "state of mind" at encoding and at retrieval, and verify what we predict with the encoding specificity hypothesis.
8. **b** More than anything else they may do, mnemonic devices enhance the meaningfulness of what we are encoding.
9. **d** This item provides a good description of what is involved in narrative chaining.
10. **b** This item provides a good definition of schemas.
11. **c** If Bob engages in no more trials, overlearning = 0%; 8 trials = 100%; 16 trials = 200%, and 20 trials = 250% overlearning.
12. **d** Answer **a** is virtually never true. Answer **b** incorrectly talks about STM instead of LTM. Answer **c** sounds good, perhaps, but it is untrue, while answer **d** is nearly always true.
13. **c** The very last test will always provide the most proactive interference—interference from materials learned earlier.
14. **b** You may want to go back and review the design for both the retroactive and proactive interference experiments. The correct choice here is that as an experimental subject, you will begin by learning Task A.

True/False

1. **F** No, in fact, quite the opposite is true.
2. **F** No. Explicit measures are necessarily conscious processes, such as recognition and recall.
3. **F** This is terribly unlikely—so much so that I'd call it false. What we call flashbulb memories are more likely to be stored in episodic memory.
4. **F** If you think about this one for a minute, you will see how silly it is. Yes, mnemonic devices impact on retrieval, but they do so by having their real impact at the time of encoding, putting information into memory in a more meaningful way.
5. **F** In fact, practicing the retrieval of learned information is exactly what you are doing right now. I hope it helps. It should.

EXPERIENCING PSYCHOLOGY

Tapping Into Flashbulb Memories

We have defined *flashbulb memories* as experiences stored in long-term memory that are particularly clear and vivid, and easy to retrieve. Most likely, these memories are stored in episodic memory, and although their recollection may be easy and vivid, they may not all be accurate.

By and large, one's personal collection of flashbulb memories varies from one generation to another.

To explore flashbulb memories in more detail, you might try a few things. First, ask someone in his or her twenties, someone in his or her forties, and someone in his or her sixties for two or three flashbulb memories that most easily come to mind.

Did you notice how easy it is to have people understand the basic notion of flashbulb memories? To what extent was there any overlap in the sorts of events that constitute flashbulb memories for people of different ages? Can you assess the extent to which the flashbulb memories you noted were accurate representations of the events recalled? Did you note any distortions? Did you note any consistent ways in which these memories were recalled? Were there any differences in the *kinds of events* that people recalled? Even though they may have recalled different events, were there any similarities in the details of there recollections, that is did they tend to mention what they were doing at the time, or who was with them, or how they felt when the event occurred?

Chapter 7

"Higher" Cognitive Processes

STUDY TIP #7

Tend To Your Own Stress Levels

Let's take a break from tips about studying *per se* to talk about something very common among college students: **stress**. Stress is a reaction to stressors. It is an unpleasant, arousing, and disruptive reaction to frustrations, conflicts, and life events. To be alive in the world and paying attention is to experience stress. We may try to structure our lives in ways to reduce our experienced stress, but, in general, stress is unavoidable. Relevant to our current discussions, stress interferes with one's study. To study efficiently requires focused attention, concentration, and all the mental energy you can muster. If you are distracted and distressed by stress, anxiety, anger, and confusion, quality study time will be one of the first victims.

The very best way to deal with stress in your life is to deal with (if not eliminate) the stressor that caused it. In the meantime, however, there are several steps that you can take that will help you feel better and work more effectively. It is important, for example, to get enough rest. Being sleep-deprived is in itself stressful. It is important to do whatever you can to stay physically healthy. Engaging in physical exercise can be helpful. Learning techniques of relaxation can be very effective.

And here's a point that is particularly important for college students who are experiencing stress: Social support has enormous advantages. Do not suffer stress alone. If you do not have an adequate circle of friends on campus with whom to share your troubles, seek help elsewhere. Check with your campus counseling center or the office of student services. See your psychology instructor. He or she may not be in a position to help, but I'll bet that your instructor knows of places you can go to get help dealing with excessive levels of stress in your life. If you are too "stressed out" to use them, none of my "Study Tips" will be of much use.

Outline ~ Chapter 7: "Higher" Cognitive Processes

TOPIC 7A: Thinking, Problem-Solving, and Language

I.   Some Thoughts about Thinking
- A. **Thinking** is a general term used to encompass such cognitive processes as reasoning and problem-solving that use or extend upon existing cognitions.
   1. The so-called "lower" cognitive processes include perception, learning, and memory.
   2. The "higher" cognitive processes, then, work with existing, already-formed cognitions.
- B. **Concepts** are mental representations of classes, or categories, of events or objects of experience.
   1. In a sense, concepts are "ideas," or the units of thinking.
   2. They seldom represent just one, specific instance, but rather represent one's stored awareness of a set of events or objects.
   3. Most concepts in our experience are "fuzzy," without specific definition.
   4. The best example of a concept is called a **prototype**.
- C. **Reasoning** is a higher cognitive process in which one comes to a conclusion based on either a set of general principles or on the basis of an assortment of accumulated facts and observations.
   1. Such a manipulation of cognitions qualifies as a "higher" cognitive process.
   2. **Inductive reasoning** leads one to come to a conclusion that follows from separate, specific facts, and observations.
   3. **Deductive reasoning** leads one to come to a conclusion about a specific event based on the application of a few general principles (stored concepts).

II. Problem-Solving
- A. A **problem** exists when there is a discrepancy between one's present state and one's perceived goal state and there is no readily apparent way to get from one to the other.
- A. A problem has three major components.
   1. An initial state—the situation as it is, or is perceived to exist, at the moment
   1. A goal state, or end product
   1. Possible routes or strategies for getting from the initial state to the goal state
- C. Well-defined problems are those in which both the initial state and the goal state are clearly defined.
- C. With an ill-defined problem one has no clear idea of what one is starting with or what an ideal solution would be.

III. Problem Representation
- A. One should try to understand the nature of a problem, and try to make it meaningful by relating it to information available in memory.
- A. Useful problem representation often involves the sorting out of what is important and what isn't.

IV. Problem-Solving Strategies
- A. A **strategy** is a systematic plan for generating possible solutions that can be tested to see if they are correct.
- A. An **algorithm** is a strategy that guarantees that eventually one will arrive at a solution if the strategy is correctly applied.
   1. Algorithms systematically explore and evaluate all possible solutions until the correct one is found.
   1. This is sometimes referred to as a generate-test strategy.
- C. A **heuristic** is an informal, rule-of-thumb strategy of generating and testing problem solutions.
   1. Heuristics are more economical for solving problems than are algorithms, but there is no guarantee of success.

1. With a means-end analysis the final goal is kept in mind, but sub-goals are used to reach the final goal.

V. Barriers to Effective Problem-Solving
   A. Mental set and functional fixedness can interfere with problem solving.
      1. A **mental set** is a tendency to perceive or respond to something in a given, or set, way.
         a. An inappropriate mental set can interfere with problem-solving
         b. An appropriate mental set can speed problem-solving
      1. **Functional fixedness** is an inability to discover an appropriate new use for an object because of experience using the object in some other function.
   B. Biased heuristics can interfere with effective problem solving and decision-making.
      1. The **availability heuristic** is the assumption that whatever comes to mind must be more common, or probable, than things difficult to recall.
      1. The **representativeness heuristic** is the assumption that any judgments made about the most prototypic member of a category will hold for all members of the category.
      1. The **positive test strategy** claims that if something works, don't drop it to try something else.
   C. To solve problems successfully, one must break out of the constraints of improper mental sets, functional fixedness, and some heuristic strategies.

VI. Creative Problem-Solving and Creative Thinking
   A. **Creativity** is the potential to produce novel ideas that are task-appropriate and of high quality.
      1. Creativity is often a matter of learning <u>not</u> to do something or doing something in a different way.
      2. Just being different or unique is not to be creative.
      3. Creativity is seldom found to be correlated with "general intelligence."
         a. One must have knowledge of the area in which he or she is working.
         b. What is perceived as a creative outcome often takes considerable time, effort, and practice.
   B. Creative problem solving often involves **divergent thinking**; that is, the creation of many ideas or possible solutions from one idea.
   C. With **convergent thinking**, one takes many ideas or bits of information and tries to reduce them to just one possible solution
   D. Creative problem solving can be divided into four interrelated stages (Wallas, 1926).
      1. Preparation
      1. Incubation
      1. Illumination
      1. Verification
   E. Good problem solvers show more awareness of what they are doing during the course of problem solving than do poor problem solvers.

VII. Let's Talk: What is Language?
   A. **Language** is a large collection of arbitrary symbols that have a shared significance for a language-using community and that follow certain rules of combination (Morris, 1946).
   A. Communication is the act of transferring information from one point to another.
   A. One property of all true languages is **arbitrary symbolic reference**, which means that there need be no resemblance between a word and its referent.
   A. **Semanticity** refers to the meaning that words take on in a language.
   A. **Productivity** refers to the property of language that with a limited number of language symbols, we can express an infinite number of ideas.
   A. Another property of language is **displacement**, the ability to communicate about the "not here and not now."

VIII. Describing the Structure in Language
  A. *Psycholinguistics* is a discipline consisting of scientists trained in psychology and linguistics who analyze language.
  A. Individual speech sounds of a language are called **phonemes**.
     1. How phonemes are combined to form words and phrases is governed by phonological rules.
     1. There are approximately 45 phonemes in English.
  C. The study of meaning in language is called **semantics**.
     1. A **morpheme** is the smallest unit of meaning in a spoken language.
     1. A *free morpheme* has a meaning and can stand alone.
     1. Prefixes and suffixes are examples of *bound morphemes*.
     1. The use of morphemes is governed by morphological rules.
  D. The rules that govern how sentences are formed in a language are referred to as the **syntax** of a language.
     1. The formal expression of the syntax of a language is its grammar.
     1. People have a competence for rules that govern language use.

IX. Language Use as a Social Process
  A. **Pragmatics** is the study of how social contexts affect the meaning of linguistic events.
  A. The rules of conservation are part of the pragmatics of speech.
  C. Pragmatics involves decisions based on the perception of the social situation at the moment.

TOPIC 7B: INTELLIGENCE

I. Just What *Is* Intelligence?
  A. Wechsler (1975) defined **intelligence** as, "The capacity of an individual to understand the world about him (or her) and his (or her) resourcefulness to cope with its challenges."
  A. Boring's (1923) operational definition states, "Intelligence is what the intelligence tests measure."

II. Classic Models of Intelligence
  A. Spearman (1904) proposed that intelligence consisted of a general intelligence or **g-factor**, and a collection of specific cognitive skills, or **s-factors**.
  A. L.L. Thurstone (1938) believed that intelligence consisted of seven **primary mental abilities**.
  A. J.P. Guilford (1967) claimed that intelligence could be analyzed as three intersecting dimensions involving operations, contents, and products, with 120 combinations.
  A. Vernon (1960, 1979) viewed intelligence as having a general factor and a structured set of specific factors.

III. More Contemporary Models of Intelligence
  A. Howard Gardner suggests that people can display intelligence in any one of eight ways or in a combination of them.
     1. These include intelligence displayed in the following areas: mathematical/logical, verbal/linguistic, spatial, musical, body/kinesthetic, naturalistic, interpersonal, and intrapersonal.
     1. Gardner is considering a ninth type of intelligence, "existential."
     1. Which are valued the most depend on the demands of one's culture.
  B. Robert Sternberg also sees intelligence as multifaceted.
     1. Intelligence is a matter of how one goes about solving problems that arise in their lives.
     2. Sternberg's (often interacting) components of intelligence are called *analytic*, *practical*, and *creative*.
  C. John Mayer and Peter Salovey introduced into psychology's vocabulary the term **emotional intelligence**, characterized by the ability to perceive, generate, and regulate emotions in order to promote better emotional reactions and thoughts.

IV. Intelligence Across Cultures
   A. Western ideas about intelligence are not always shared by non-Western cultures.
   A. Differences reflect what is valued in a culture.
      1. The Chinese, for example, think of intelligence in terms of a general cognitive factor, interpersonal and intrapersonal intelligence, intellectual self-assertion, and intellectual self-effacement.
      2. Native Americans are more likely than European Americans to think of intellectual giftedness in terms of those individuals who contribute most the the welfare of the group.

V. The Characteristics of Psychological Tests
   A. A **psychological test** is an objective, standardized measure of a sample of behavior.
   A. **Reliability** refers to a test's ability to produce the same or highly similar results across similar testing situations.
   A. Measures of **validity** refer to a test measuring what it claims to be measuring.
      1. The four forms of validity are face, predictive, concurrent, and construct.
      1. The more dimensions along which a test is valid, the better.
   D. Results of a test taken by a large group of people whose scores are used to make comparisons are called **norms.**

VI. The Stanford-Binet Intelligence Scale
   A. This test appeared in 1905 in France.
      1. Lewis Terman at Stanford supervised a translation and revision of the test in 1916, calling it the Stanford-Binet.
      1. The fifth edition was published in 2003.
   B. The test follows a three-level, hierarchical model of cognitive ability.
   B. The current test yields an overall g score, or general intellectual ability.
   B. Under g there are three second-level factors.
      1. Crystallized abilities represent those skills needed for acquiring and using information about verbal and quantitative concepts.
      1. Fluid-analytic abilities are those needed to solve problems that involve figural or nonverbal types of information.
      1. The third factor at this level is short-term memory.
   E. Crystallized abilities are further divided into verbal and quantitative reasoning.
   E. Fluid-analytic abilities are further divided into abstract/visual reasoning.
   E. There is a total of 15 subtests, all of which yield individual scores.
   E. **IQ** is an abbreviation for the term intelligence quotient.
      1. IQ formerly was calculated by taking a person's mental age, dividing it by his or her chronological age, and multiplying by 100.
      1. The deviation IQ uses established group norms and compares intelligence scores across age groups.
      1. Since IQ is considered a common vocabulary term, it is still used to refer to general intelligence.

VII. The Wechsler Tests of Intelligence
   A. David Wechsler published his first intelligence test in 1939.
      1. Its latest edition is the WAIS-III, published in 1997, and is used for persons between 16 and 74 years of age.
      1. There is a Wechsler Intelligence Scale for Children (WISC-III) used with those 6 to 16 years of age.
      1. The Wechsler Preschool and Primary Scale of Intelligence (WPPSI-R) was designed for 4-to 6-year olds.
   B. The WAIS-III has seven verbal subtests and seven subtests that constitute a performance scale.
   B. Each of the Weschler tests yields an overall score, verbal score, and performance score.

VIII. Group Tests of Intelligence
   A. These tests are generally paper-and-pencil tests that can be administered to many people at one time.
      1. The Army Alpha Test was published in 1917 and made rough discriminations among examinees on the basis of intelligence.
      1. The Army Beta Test was designed for illiterates.
      1. The Army now uses the Armed Forces Qualification Test for inductees.
   B. When psychological tests of cognitive ability are used to predict future behaviors, we call them **aptitude tests**.
      1. The American College Testing Program (ACT) and the Scholastic Aptitude Test (SAT) are administered to predict academic success.
      2. The SAT-I was published in 1994 to more thoroughly assess skills.
      2. The SAT-II includes a written essay section, a language proficiency test for native speakers of Japanese and Chinese, and tests for non-native English speakers.

IX. Group Differences in Measured Intelligence
   A. IQ scores reflect a particular measure of intelligence and do not equal one's intelligence.
   A. Even though, *on average*, the IQ of one group is higher than that of another, many individuals from the second group may be more intelligent than individuals in the first.
   A. Just knowing that, on average, two groups have different IQ scores tells us nothing about why that difference exists—even if the difference is a reliable one.

X. Gender Differences in IQ
   A. There are few studies that report any gender differences in IQ between men and women on any test of general intelligence.
      1. There may be no differences because the tests are constructed to minimize or eliminate any such differences.
      1. There are hints of small gender differences on a few specific intellectual skills.
         a. Males score higher than females on tests of spatial relations.
         a. Scores on mathematics skills are well correlated with the number and type of math classes taken while a student.
         a. In a recent study, significantly more boys than girls scored higher on tests of math and science.
         a. Girls scored better than boys did on tests of perceptual speed, reading comprehension, and writing skills.

XI. Age Differences in IQ
   A. When using a cross-sectional testing method, results indicate that overall IQ peaks in the early 20s, remains stable for about 20 years, and then declines sharply.
   A. When a longitudinal method is used, IQ scores rise until the late 30s or early 40s, stabilizing for about 20 years, then falling after age 60.
   A. Specific intellectual skills do not decline at the same rate, and some do not decline at all.
   A. **Fluid intelligence** refers to abilities related to speed, adaptation, flexibility, and abstract reasoning; these skills show the greatest decline with age.
   A. **Crystallized intelligence** refers to abilities depending on acquired knowledge, accumulated experiences, and general information; these skills remain constant or increase throughout one's lifetime.

XII. Racial and Ethnic Differences in IQ
   A. On average, Caucasians score 15 points higher on general intelligence than do African Americans.
   A. Japanese children between 6 and 16 score higher on IQ tests than do Caucasian American children of the same age.
   A. Researchers have tried to determine if tests are biased, or if environmental factors, genetic factors, or cultural differences in motivation influence scores.
   A. Steele and Aronson believe that a *stereotype threat* will cause members of a group to perform more poorly on tasks that relate to prevailing negative stereotypes.
   A. The argument over the causes for race differences may one day be a moot issue.

1. The very definition of "intelligence" is changing.
2. The differences between the IQ scores of African Americans and Caucasian Americans is getting smaller.

XIII. Extremes of Intelligence
    A. The most frequently occurring score is the average score, 100.
    B. 95% of all IQ scores fall between 70 and 130.

XIV. The Mentally Gifted
    A. According to The United States Office of Education, individuals can be described as gifted who excel in any of the following six areas.
        1. Psychomotor ability
        2. Visual and performing arts
        3. Leadership ability
        4. Creative or productive thinking
        5. Specific academic aptitude
        6. Intellectually gifted
    B. Lewis Terman began a study of the mentally gifted in the 1920s.
        1. His research group focused on children who had IQ scores above 135.
        2. This longitudinal study concluded that, in general, gifted children experience advantages in many areas.

XV. Mental Retardation
    A. According to the AAMD, **mental retardation** refers to sub-average general intellectual functioning, which originated during the developmental period, and is associated with impairment in adaptive behavior.
        1. IQ scores from 70 to 85 are considered to be borderline.
        2. IQ scores from 50-69 are in the mildly retarded range.
        3. IQ scores from 35-49 are in the moderately retarded range.
        4. IQ scores from 20-34 reflect severe mental retardation
        5. IQ scores less than 19 indicate profound mental impairment.
    B. Estimates indicate that at any one time approximately 3 percent of the population falls within the IQ range for retardation.
    C. **Down syndrome** occurs when a fetus develops with 47 chromosomes instead of the usual 23 pairs.
        1. Down syndrome is more likely to occur as the age of either parent increases.
        2. A person with this syndrome may fall into any level of retardation.
    D. **Fragile X syndrome** is a variety of mental retardation with a genetic basis that was discovered in the late 1960s.
    E. About one-half to three-quarters of cases of mental retardation do not have known biological or genetic causes.
    F. **Phenylketonuria**, or **PKU**, is a genetic disorder that can be detected with a blood test at birth, and treated with a prescribed diet during childhood.

Practice Test Questions

TOPIC 7A: THINKING, PROBLEM-SOLVING, AND LANGUAGE

Multiple Choice

1. Some cognitive processes can be called "higher" because they
   ___a. begin higher in the spinal cord than do other cognitive processes.
   ___b. require and use (manipulate) more basic cognitive process.
   ___c. involve language and the "lower" cognitive processes do not.
   ___d. use algorithm instead of heuristics.

2. A prototypic concept is one that
   ___a. is also referred to as a "fuzzy" concept.
   ___b. has been experienced before other members of the same category.
   ___c. tends to have more members than most others because we experience them more often/
   ___d. best represents members of the category or class of concepts.

3. When we say that we are faced with a problem, what are we MOST LIKELY to be missing?
   ___a. an awareness that a problem exists
   ___b. a goal or an objective to be reached
   ___c. a sense of how to get from where we are to where we want to be
   ___d. an appreciation of the current situation and the resources that are available

4. More than anything else, what makes a problem "well-defined" as opposed to "ill-defined"?
   ___a. the ability to know with certainty when an adequate solution has been found
   ___b. the extent to which we realize that we are faced with a problem that needs to be solved
   ___c. the adequacy of problem representation
   ___d. the choice of an adequate problem-solving strategy

5. Which provides the best example of a well-defined problem?
   ___a. How can Israeli-Palestinian differences be peacefully resolved?
   ___b. Which country in North America has the longest coastline?
   ___c. What would be required to establish a psychology laboratory in a new college?
   ___d. What is the best way to organize a surprise party for a co-worker?

6. When we say that problem solving begins with problem representation, we are suggesting that one needs to
   ___a. put the problem in numerical, or mathematical form.
   ___b. examine all possible problem-solving strategies before deciding on one.
   ___c. decide if the problem even has a solution.
   ___d. make the problem meaningful.

7. Problem representation typically is easiest when
   ___a. the problem deals with familiar information.
   ___b. the problem is well-defined.
   ___c. there is only one way in which the problem can be solved.
   ___d. the problem is ill-defined.

8. Which strategy is relatively inefficient, but guarantees a solution if a solution is possible?
   ___a. working backward   ___c. using an algorithm
   ___b. hill-climbing   ___d. means-ends analysis

9. As more and more solutions and routes to problem solutions become available, the more sensible it is to use
    ___a. a comprehensive search of all possibilities.
    ___b. a heuristic strategy.
    ___c. fewer and fewer hypotheses.
    ___d. an algorithmic approach.

10. Functional fixedness is essentially a type of
    ___a. problem representation.   ___c. creativity.
    ___b. heuristic strategy.   ___d. mental set.

11. The ultimate test of a creative solution to a problem is whether
    ___a. anyone else has ever thought of it before.
    ___b. it is artistic, balanced, or beautiful.
    ___c. it actually works to solve the problem at hand.
    ___d. it is convergent or divergent.

12. If the solution to a problem is going to occur to you, it will probably occur in the sub-process identified by Wallas (1926) as
    ___a. preparation.   ___c. illumination.
    ___b. incubation.   ___d. verification.

13. Which is LEAST descriptive of language? Language is
    ___a. rule-governed.   ___c. creative, or generative.
    ___b. correct or incorrect.   ___d. both cognitive and social.

14. When we say that language allows us to communicate about things that are not present, neither here nor now, we are saying that language demonstrates
    ___a. displacement.   ___c. a cognitive process.
    ___b. behavior that follows rules.   ___d. arbitrariness.

15. The social context in which language is produced and understood is the most central, or important, concern of
    ___a. syntax.   ___c. phonemics.
    ___b. pragmatics.   ___d. semantics.

16. The rules that govern the ways in which morphemes and words can be combined to form sentences are
    ___a. morphemic rules.   ___c. syntax.
    ___b. pragmatics.   ___d. semantics

True/False

1. ____True ____False   Languages, including English, generally contain more words than morphemes.

2. ____True ____False   The concept of a language acquisition device, or LAD, is useful in accounting for the biological or instinctive nature of the language acquisition process.

3. ____True ____False   Problems can be (and often are) solved without the use of memory.

4. ____True ____False   Computers cannot use algorithms to solve problems effectively; only humans can.

5. ____True ____False   A mental set can be helpful in a problem-solving situation.

6. ____True ____False   Divergent thinking involves generating as many potential solutions as possible, while convergent thinking involves reducing the number of possibilities in problem solving.

7. ____True ____False   Taking data and inputs and observations from many different areas and putting them together to reach one conclusion (or a small number of conclusions), represents deductive reasoning.

TOPIC 7B: INTELLIGENCE

Multiple Choice

1. Which of these is the most appropriate operational definition of intelligence? Intelligence is
    ___a. the sum of those cognitive abilities that allow us to adapt to the environment.
    ___b. that which is measured by the revised edition of the Wechsler Adult Intelligence Scale.
    ___c. the accumulation of information over one's lifetime.
    ___d. the ultimate problem-solving skill.

2. Spearman and Thurstone devised their theories of intelligence by
    ___a. introspecting about their own intellectual skills.
    ___b. making up their own tests of intelligence, or IQ.
    ___c. interviewing many people of differing intellectual abilities.
    ___d. examining the correlations among tests for different abilities.

3. A view of human intelligence proposed by Howard Gardner argues that
    ___a. intelligence will soon be measured by physiological means.
    ___b. humans are no more intelligent than any other organisms.
    ___c. there are at least eight very different ways in which to demonstrate intelligence.
    ___d. intellectual capacity is inherited and therefore related to one's race or ethnic origins.

4. Sternberg's Triarchic Model of Intelligence focuses on
    ___a. a careful description of over 100 intelligent behaviors.
    ___b. making sure that there is a test for each aspect of intelligence.
    ___c. the functions, or use of, intellectual skills in practice.
    ___d. the relationships between general and specific abilities.

5. If a psychological test is reliable, it will
    ___a. measure whatever it measures with consistency.
    ___b. measure what it claims to be measuring and nothing else.
    ___c. yield scores that can be interpreted easily.
    ___d. have a very large and representative norm group.

6. When Binet and Simon wrote their first test of intelligence, their major concern was to
    ___a. study the long-term consequences of being judged to be mentally gifted as a child.
    ___b. determine how much of one's intelligence is inherited and how much reflects the environment.
    ___c. identify those children who needed to be placed in remedial or special education classes.
    ___d. discover if intelligence was one unitary "g" factor, or several specific "s" factors combined.

7. Using the classic approach to IQ as an intelligent quotient, if 10-year-old Sally demonstrates the intellectual functioning typical of an average 8-year-old, her IQ is
    ___a. 70.   ___c. 100.
    ___b. 80.   ___d 125.

8. When David Wechsler first published his tests, what did he bring to IQ testing?

    ___a. individually administered testing

    ___b. tests that were more valid for children than for adults

    ___c. a way to assess general intelligence, or "g"

    ___d. a separate score for nonverbal performance items

9. In the context of intelligence testing, what is a "standard score?"

    ___a. the actual number of items for which the subject is given credit

    ___b. the average score earned on the test by all of those who have taken it

    ___c. a score that indicates a person's placement relative to similar persons in the norm group

    ___d. the number of items correct minus the number of items incorrect

10. What do IQ tests predict best?

    ___a. success on the job (in terms of happiness and money earned)

    ___b. the presence or absence of psychological disorders

    ___c. academic achievement

    ___d. socioeconomic level

11. In psychology today, the concept of IQ

    ___a. has been discredited to the point that psychologists hardly ever use the term.

    ___b. is taken to be synonymous with intelligence, but only for children and adolescents.

    ___c. is considered to be but one indicator, or measure, of intelligence.

    ___d. is taken to be one's mental age multiplied by one's chronological age and divided by 100.

12. If we discover that the difference between the IQ scores for Group A and Group B is significant—greater than we could expect by chance—where Group A's scores are higher than those of Group B, we would then have evidence that

    ___a. Group B has been educationally deprived.

    ___b. Group A is genetically smarter than Group B.

    ___c. Group A has a higher socioeconomic level than Group B.

    ___d. Group A is more intelligent that Group B as indicated by IQ scores.

13. For which intellectual skill do males tend to score higher than do females?

    ___a. verbal reasoning   ___c. arithmetic computation

    ___b. spatial relations   ___d. general information

14. The long-term study of the mentally gifted begun by Terman tells us that which observation about the mentally gifted is FALSE?

    ___a. They are physically healthier than average.

    ___b. They have brighter-than-average children.

    ___c. They experience more divorces than average.

    ___d. They earn more money than average.

15. Down syndrome

    ___a. can be treated by changes in diet—if the disorder is caught at birth.

    ___b. children are invariably either severely or profoundly mentally retarded.

    ___c. develops as a result of a chromosomal abnormality.

    ___d. is usually caused by alcohol or drug use by the mother during pregnancy.

True/False

1. ____True ____False   Failing to find evidence for any general (g) factor of intelligence, Thurstone proposed that what we call intelligence is made up of seven primary mental abilities.

2. ____True ____False   The current version of the Stanford Binet test yields just one score—a measure of general intelligence, "g."

3. ____True ____False   There are no differences between the average IQ scores for men and the average IQ scores for women.

4. ____True ____False   Racial differences in IQ scores that cannot be accounted for on the basis of environmental factors, must then be due to genetic factors.

5. ____True ____False   We stand a better chance of preventing mental retardation than we do of adequately treating it.

Key Terms and Concepts
Topic 7A

thinking_____

_____

concepts_____

_____

prototype_____

_____

reasoning_____

_____

inductive reasoning_____

_____

deductive reasoning_____

_____

problem_____

_____

algorithm_____

_____

heuristic_____

_____

mental set_____

_____

functional fixedness_____

_____

availability heuristic_____

_____

representativenes heuristic_____

_____

positive test strategy_____

_____

creativity_____

_____

divergent thinking_____

_____

convergent thinking_____

_____

language_____

_____

arbitrary symbolic reference_____

_____

semanticity_____

_____

productivity_____

_____

displacement_____

_____

phonemes_____

_____

semantics_____

_____

morphemes_____

_____

syntax_____

_____

pragmatics_____

_____

Topic 7B

intelligence_____

_____

g-factor_____

_____

primary mental abilities_____

_____

emotional intelligence_____

_____

psychological test_____

_____

reliability_____

_____

validity_____

_____

norms_____

_____

intelligence quotient (IQ)_____

_____

aptitude tests_____

_____

fluid intelligence_____

_____

crystallized intelligence_____

_____

mental retardation_____

_____

Down syndrome_____

_____

Answers to Practice Test Questions

Multiple Choice

1. **b** The so-called higher cognitive process (thinking, reasoning, problem-solving, language use, for example) require and manipulate the "lower" cognitive processes of perception, learning, and memory.
2. **d** This one is "by definition." A prototype is the best example of a concept or category.
3. **c** If we knew how to get from where we were to where we wanted to go, we wouldn't even have a problem, so the best alternative is the third one.
4. **a** With a well-defined problem, the goal state is very clear so we know when we are there, and we know it with some degree of certainty. We can say, "There, that problem is solved."
5. **b** Given the answer provided right above to #8, the only acceptable answer is **b**.
6. **d** Once we realize that we've got a problem, the first and most difficult step is to put that problem into terms that are meaningful to us.
7. **a** If a problem already exists in a form with which we are familiar, representation will be relatively easy.
8. **c** It may be very inefficient and very time-consuming, but one thing about an algorithmic strategy is that we are guaranteed that eventually we will find a solution if one is available.
9. **b** Heuristics (in general) allow us to cut back on the number of choices we may pursue in problem solving. The more possibilities there are, the more important to devise a heuristic strategy.
10. **d** By definition, functional fixedness is a variety of mental set.
11. **c** No matter how unique, no matter if divergent or convergent, no matter how artistic or beautiful, the ultimate test of a creative solution is whether it actually works to solve the problem at hand.
12. **c** Solutions to problems—creative or not—tend to occur in the illumination stage of problem solving. (Can't you just see the little cartoon character with the light bulb—hence, illumination—above his head, saying, "AHA!!"?)
13. **b** Language is rule-governed. It is creative or generative, and it is both cognitive and social. I'm not sure I know what it means to say that language is either correct or incorrect.
14. **a** Although language is an arbitrary, cognitive process that follows rules, communicating about the not here and the not now reflects displacement.
15. **b** Pragmatics focuses on the social contextual issues involved in language use (at least to a greater degree than the other choices listed here).
16. **c**   The terms "syntax" and "grammar" are often used interchangeably. This is what we're talking about here—making grammatically correct utterances.

True/False
NOTE: THESE TRUE/FALSE ITEMS ARE NOT IN THE ORDER IN WHICH THEY ARE COVERED IN THE TEXT. This is on purpose. You need to know the material; you seldom need to know it in the order in which it is presented.

1. **F** Quite the contrary, because morphemes include such non-words as prefixes (e.g., un- or dis-), suffixes (e.g., -ment or –ing) and plurality (e.g., -s or –es). Languages have many more morphemes than words.
2. **T** No one knows just what a LAD is, or exactly how it works, but it is the "structure" used to describe the biological aspects of language acquisition, so this item is true,
3. **F** I certainly hope that you didn't fall for this one. Think about it. How can one even understand the nature of a problem without reference to memory? This one is so easy; so obviously false, that some students can't believe it and make it more difficult than it is.
4. **F** In fact, computers can solve problems with what amounts to a heuristic strategy, but they are best at using algorithmic strategies, checking out all possibilities—quickly.
5. **T** Sure it can. If it is an appropriate mental set or expectation, a mental set can be very useful in a problem-solving situation.
6. **T** Not only is this statement true, it also provides a pretty good definition of both divergent and convergent thinking.
7. **F** Easily confused, this definition is for the other variety of reasoning: inductive.

Multiple Choice

1. **b**   Each of these defines intelligence, and reasonably so, but only the second alternative is an operational definition, specifying the operations used to measure intelligence.
2. **d**   Although they came to different conclusions when they did so, they both used the same method of examining the correlations among test scores.
3. **c**   The fact that Gardner talks about eight (or eight-and-a-half) ways of displaying intelligence (as opposed to nine or ten) is not terribly relevant. What is relevant is the basic notion that there are ways of being intelligent other than in the arena of academic excellence.
4. **c**   What makes Sternberg's approach quite different from the others is that he claims we should look at intelligent behaviors in action, in use, rather than as structures or test scores.
5. **a**   In the context of testing, reliability means what it means elsewhere: dependability or consistency.
6. **c**   Their basic job was to identify children in the French school system who needed a different (special) style of education because of some general intellectual deficit.
7. **b**   What we're looking for here is MA divided by CA, times 100, or 8 divided by 10, times 100 = 80.
8. **d**   One of Wechsler's complaints about IQ tests of his day was that they were so heavily verbal and vocabulary-oriented. He included many performance items on his tests, and allowed for the computation of a performance IQ.
9. **c**   By definition, we calculate standard scores by comparing earned scores with those achieved by members of the appropriate norm group.
10. **c**   Although IQ scores may be positively correlated with the factors named in the other alternatives, what IQ scores predict best is achievement in school, or academics.
11. **c**   Obviously, we can find psychologists who will argue with this point of view, but I think that the most conservative response here is that psychologists see IQ test scores as just one indicator of the underlying trait that we call intelligence.
12. **d**   All we know with any certainty is that Group A, on the average, is more intelligent than Group B, as indicated by IQ scores.
13. **b**   Spatial relations tests are about the only ones on which males seem to have a consistent advantage.
14. **c**   Once you realize that I am looking for a false statement (which is always a bit backwards and troublesome), it is clear that alternative **c** should be your choice.
15. **c**   Down Syndrome (and there are those who refer to this as "Down's Syndrome"—either way is okay) appears when a zygote manages to pick up an extra chromosome, making 47 instead of the usual 46 in 23 pairs.

True/False

1. **T**   This is a good, straightforward statement of Thurstone's position on intelligence.
2. **F**   No, what makes this revision different from previous ones (among other things, of course) is that it can provide a number of more specific scores than just one general, overall score.
3. **T**   Seems deceptively simple, doesn't it? And it's true.
4. **F**   Just because we cannot specify an environmental determinant does not mean or imply that one must go all the way in the other direction and assume that there must be a genetic determinant.
5. **T**   We do.

EXPERIENCING PSYCHOLOGY

By Their Label Shall Ye Know Them

Here are four simple drawings:

As best you can, reproduce each of them, using four 3x5-inch index cards. The task here is to ask several people to try to remember them and reproduce them from memory on blank 3x5 cards. For half of the people in your experiment, hand them a card and, in order, name the objects as:
- A bee hive
- The number seven
- An hourglass
- A pine tree.

For the other half of your participants, do exactly the same thing, except identify the objects as:
- A hat
- The number four
- A picnic table
- A trowel.

Once you have presented all the cards, wait about two minutes, then provide your participants with four blank cards and ask them to reproduce the four drawings as best they can. To what extent did your verbal label of the image influence the drawings that were reproduced from memory?

Chapter 8

Human Development

STUDY TIP #8

A Word About Motivation and Goals

Effective study habits are developed, not for their own sake, but to make learning more efficient. You don't go to college to study; rather, you go to learn. A good college student is one who knows how to maximize opportunities to learn. A successful college student is also one who is motivated to learn.

We can learn some things "by accident," without really intending to do so. We may not set out to learn the numbers on the uniforms of the players on our favorite team, but after watching several games, we discover that we can identify the players without a scorecard. Our most efficient learning, however, occurs when we intend to learn, when we make a conscious effort to acquire new information.

Anyone who has a firm goal in mind, who knows what he or she is striving for, and why, can be said to be well motivated. Difficulties in learning in college can arise when students have no clear-cut goals, do not really know why they are there, and are not motivated to do well. "Doing well in college" is a very general goal. To be most effective, goals and motives should be as concrete and specific as possible. "Doing well" must therefore be broken down into manageable pieces. First think about this year, then this term. Take each course in turn. What grade do you hope to earn? Then break down each course, perhaps in terms of assignments or exams. What is your goal for your next exam? To prepare for that exam how many pages of text will you study over the weekend? How many practice problems will you try? Make sure your goals are realistic. It might be noble to strive for an A+ on every quiz, exam, and assignment, but is such a goal realistic? You might have to be ready to accept some compromises. Any student (or any other type of organism) that consistently falls short of goals (even self-established goals) eventually will become frustrated, lose interest, and suffer reduced motivation.

Your goals should not be too stringent, nor should they be too long-range. It's fine to dream of becoming a doctor, but you might be better off concentrating on next week's midterm exam. Short-term goals are usually more effective motivators than are long-term goals.

Outline ~ Chapter 8: Human Development

TOPIC 8A: DEVELOPMENT DURING CHILDHOOD

I. Prenatal Development
- A. The period of development from conception to birth is the **prenatal period**.
- B. The process of prenatal development begins with fertilization, when a single sperm produced by the father unites with the egg provided by the mother.
- C. During the **germinal stage** of prenatal development, the **zygote**, the one-cell product of the union of sperm and ovum, begins to move down the fallopian tube toward the uterus.
    1. It is undergoing rapid cell growth at this time, and forms into a hollow ball called the *blastocyst*.
    2. This stage lasts from the time of fertilization until the blastocyst implants itself into the wall of the uterus, around two weeks.
        a. The outer layer of cells is programmed to develop into the placenta, the amniotic sac, and umbilical cord.
        b. The inner layer of cells is programmed to become the fetus.
- D. The **embryo stage** lasts about six weeks.
    1. All of the organ systems of the body are laid in place.
    2. During this vulnerable period, the central nervous system is at risk, and the unborn is most sensitive to external or environmental influences.
- E. The **fetal stage** includes months 3 through 9.
    1. The organs of the body continue to increase in complexity and size and begin to function.
    2. During the seventh month, most fetuses have reached the point of viability, meaning that they could survive without interference or medical intervention if born.
    3. After nearly 270 days, the fetus is ready to enter the world as a newborn.

II. Environmental Influences on Prenatal Development
- A. Maternal malnutrition often leads to increases in miscarriages, stillbirths, and premature births.
- B. Newborns with low birth weight (4 pounds or less) who do survive have a greater risk of cognitive deficits—even as they approach adolescence.
- C. Using vitamin and mineral supplements is generally a good idea, but these can be overdone as well.
- D. A balanced, sensible diet works best for mother and fetus.

III. Smoking, Drinking, and Drugs
- A. Smoking by pregnant women has harmful effects on their unborn children.
    1. Smoking during pregnancy is associated with low birth weight and premature birth.
    2. Children whose mothers smoked a pack of cigarettes a day during pregnancy have a 75 percent increase in risk for mental retardation, even when other risk factors were controlled.
    3. Smoking during and after pregnancy is associated with an increased risk of sudden infant death syndrome.
- B. **Fetal alcohol syndrome (FAS)** refers to a cluster of symptoms (for example, low birth weight, poor muscle tone, and intellectual retardation) associated with a child born to a mother who was a heavy drinker of alcohol during pregnancy.
    1. Heavy drinking is defined as drinking three or more alcoholic drinks per day or binge drinking during vulnerable periods of organ development.
    2. Lower doses of alcohol consumption during critical periods of pregnancy can produce a condition known as fetal alcohol effects.
    3. The highest rate of fetal alcohol syndrome is among the Native American population of the Southwest.
    4. Children whose mothers drank even small amounts of alcohol during pregnancy are at increased risk for behavior problems later in life.
    5. Experts agree that the best advice for a pregnant mother is total abstinence.

C. Mothers who use or abuse psychoactive drugs during pregnancy cause considerable complications for their unborn child.
  1. Even common drugs such as caffeine and aspirin have been associated with low birth weights.
  2. It is wise to avoid harmful substances, get good prenatal care, eat a healthy diet and follow the advice of a physician.

IV. What About Dad?
  A. Researchers are looking at the role of the father in determining the quality of life of the prenatal child.
  B. The main issue revolves around factors affecting the quality of the father's sperm at the moment of conception.
    1. Sperm from fathers beyond the age of 35 or 40 may be partly the source of the genetic problems of Down syndrome.
    2. The father's possible role in the transmission of STDs also is clear.

V. Sensory and Perceptual Development
  A. To some degree, all human senses are functioning at birth.
    1. The **neonate**—the newborn—can focus well on objects held one to two feet away, but everything nearer or farther appears out of focus until the child is about four months old.
    2. Neonates can hear nearly as well as adults.
    3. Newborns can respond to differences in taste and smell.
    4. Neonates can detect touch and temperature stimulation, and can feel pain.
  B. A wide range of perceptual abilities develops during the first year.
    1. Infants prefer patterned over unpatterned stimuli, and moving over stationary stimuli.
    2. There is also a preference for patterns that look like human faces over patterns that do not.
    3. Young infants can discriminate among facial expressions of emotions and within a few hours after birth can recognize a picture of their own mother..

VI. Cognitive Development – Piaget's Approach
  A. **Cognitive development** refers to the age-related changes in learning, memory, perception, attention, thinking, and problem solving.
  B. Developmental psychologists look at cognitive development from two perspectives.
    1. The **structural-functional approach,** developed by Jean Piaget, says that structures (schemas) change with development, while functions remain fixed. Cognitive development is seen as a series of qualitative changes in intelligence.
    2. The **information processing approach** focuses on quantitative changes in basic information processing systems like memory, attention, and learning.
  C. A **schema** is an organized mental representation of the world that is adaptive and formed by experience.
  D. Piaget proposed that there are two basic functions or mechanisms that help a child adapt to the environment.
    1. **Organization** refers to one of the functions in Piaget's theory and involves a predisposition to integrate individual schemas into organized units.
    2. **Adaptation** involves a child adapting cognitive abilities to the demands of the environment, and comprises two complementary processes.
      a. **Assimilation** occurs when a child incorporates new information into an existing scheme.
      b. **Accommodation** allows the infant to modify its schemas to account for new experiences.

VII. Piaget's Stages of Development
  A. In the **sensorimotor stage** (birth to two years), children discover by sensing (sensori-) and doing (motor).
    1. Children learn about causality in this stage.

2. Children learn about **object permanence**, an appreciation that an object no longer in view can still exist and reappear later.
3. Imitation also develops during this stage.

B. In the **preoperational stage** (two to six years), a child's thinking is self-centered or egocentric.

C. In the **concrete operations stage** (seven to eleven years) children begin to develop many concepts and show that they can manipulate those concepts.
1. Rule-governed behavior begins in this stage.
2. **Conservation** involves the awareness that changing the form or the appearance of something does not change what it really is.

D. In the **formal operations stage** (twelve years and up), the logical manipulation of abstract, symbolic concepts appears.

VIII. Reactions to Piaget

A. Considerable research has supported many of Piaget's insights about children.

B. There are two major criticisms of Piaget's theory.
1. The borderlines between his proposed stages are much less clear-cut than his theory suggests.
2. Piaget underestimated the cognitive talents of preschool children.

C. Further criticisms suggest that object permanence appears earlier than age 2, and that Piaget's theory gives little attention to the impact of language development and the gradual increase in the capacity of a child's memory.

D. Piaget's theory was so detailed and thought provoking that it will challenge researchers for years to come.

IX. Cognitive Development – The Information-Processing Approach

A. The Development of Learning
1. Classical conditioning and operant conditioning can be demonstrated with neonates.
2. Imitation can be observed in infants as young as one week old.

B. The Development of Memory
1. Memory can be demonstrated in very young infants.
2. Children as young as three can understand the temporal nature of events and form scripts of those events in memory.
3. The most impressive gains take place between three and 12 years of age, both in short-term memory and long-term memory.
4. Elaboration is a sophisticated memory strategy that is "discovered" late in childhood and is rarely used before adolescence.

X. Moral Development

A. Piaget believed that children are unable to make moral judgments until they are at least three or four years old.

B. Lawrence Kohlberg proposed three levels of moral development.
1. **Preconventional morality** in which the prime interest of the child is simply with the punishment that comes from breaking a rule.
2. **Conventional morality** is based on an accepted social convention, where approval matters as much or more than anything else.
3. **Postconventional morality** is the highest level of moral reasoning in Kohlberg's theory in which moral reasoning reflects complex, internalized standards.

C. The basic thrust of Kohlberg's theory has merit and cross-cultural applications.

D. Problems with the theory exist because few people operate at the higher stages, particularly in cultures that emphasize communal or group membership.

E. *Collectivism* and *individualism* illustrate that what is true for one culture may not be for another, and neither is better or more moral.

F. There may be a "disconnect" between what people may *believe* is the right and moral thing to do, and what they actual do in their behaviors.

G. Carol Gilligan believes that the moral reasoning of females is different from that of males.
1. Women, Gilligan argues, are more likely to focus on caring, personal responsibility and relationships, while males focus on rules, justice, and individual rights.

2. Gilligan does not suggest that one approach to moral reasoning is any better or worse than the other.

XI. Erikson's Psychosocial Theory of Development
    A. Erik Erikson proposed an eight-stage theory of life-span development that has a cross-cultural basis.
    B. The first four stages are relevant for children:
        1. *Trust vs. mistrust*, during the first year of life, when the child either develops a basic sense of safety or insecurity and anxiety.
        2. *Autonomy vs. self-doubt*, from ages one and one-half to three years, when a child learns independence or experiences inadequacy.
        3. *Initiative vs. guilt*, from three to six years of age, when confidence is developed, or feelings of a lack of self-worth result.
        4. *Competence vs. inferiority*, from six years to puberty, adequacy in basic social and intellectual skills occurs, or a lack of self-confidence and feelings of inferiority may develop.

XII. Developing Gender Identity
    A. **Gender** refers to one's maleness or femaleness; socially ascribed characteristics of males and females, as opposed to their biological characteristics.
    B. Cognitive psychologists believe that once children can discriminate between the sexes, they develop schemas for gender-related information.
        1. Encouraged by parents, children at an early age (1-year-old) have defined preferences for choices of toys.
        2. By the age of 3 or 4 children tend to gravitate toward same-sex play groups.
    C. **Gender identity** is the sense or self-awareness of one's own maleness or femaleness.
        1. Most children develop gender identity by the age of 2 or 3.
        2. Once gender identity is established, it is very resistant to change.
        3. By late childhood and early adolescence, peer pressure intensifies gender differences.

XIII. Developing Social Attachments
    A. **Attachment** is a strong emotional relationship between a child and his or her mother or primary caregiver.
    B. Strong attachments are most likely to be formed if the parent is optimally sensitive and responsive to the needs of the child.
        1. Attachment formation is a two-way process.
        2. It is more than simply a matter of spending time with a child
        3. Secure attachments need not be with the mother only; they may involve the father or some other significant caregiver.
        4. Attachment patterns may have life-long ramifications.
    C. There are many benefits that result from secure attachment.
    D. High-quality daycare facilities can foster both cognitive and social development.
        1. The quality of attachment in a daycare situation depends entirely on the quality of care provided.
        2. Both quality maternal care and daycare can work together to form secure attachments in infants and children.

TOPIC 8B: DEVELOPMENT IN ADOLESCENCE AND ADULTHOOD

I. Adolescent Development
    A. **Adolescence** is the period between childhood and adulthood, often begun at puberty and ending with full physical growth, generally between the ages of 12 and 20.
    B. Adolescence can be described from a biological, psychological, or social perspective.
        1. In biological terms, adolescence begins with **puberty**, the stage of physical development at which one becomes capable of sexual reproduction.

2. A psychological perspective emphasizes the development of cognitions, feelings, and behaviors that characterize adolescence.
3. A social perspective defines adolescence in terms of being "in between," not yet an adult, but no longer a child.
C. G. Stanley Hall and Anna Freud believed that adolescence was a time of turmoil and stress.
D. Many studies indicate that adolescents typically make adjustments in psychologically healthy ways.

II. The Challenge of Puberty
A. The growth spurt is signified by a marked increase in height and weight, and usually occurs at an earlier age in girls than boys.
B. Puberty occurs when one becomes physically capable of sexual reproduction.
1. In females, this is indicated by the first menstrual period, called **menarche**.
2. Boys seldom know when their puberty begins.
C. Boys and girls who reach puberty before or after most of their peers are referred to as early or late bloomers.
1. The consequences of reaching puberty early are more positive for males than for females.
2. Being a late bloomer has negative implications for both males and females, although few consequences are lasting.

III. The Challenge of Identity Formation
A. One of the major tasks of adolescence is the resolution of an **identity crisis,** where there is a struggle to define a sense of self, what to do in life, and what one's attitudes, beliefs, and values should be.
1. The search for identity is the fifth stage of psychosocial development in Erikson's hierarchy.
2. According to Erikson, there may be role confusion at this time.
B. Most of the conflicts between adolescents and their parents occur early in adolescence and generally are resolved by the end of adolescence.
C. Marcia has identified four ways that identity issues can be resolved during adolescence: identity achievement, foreclosure, identity diffusion, and moratorium.
D. In eight cross-cultural studies, Waterman found evidence of Marcia's groupings.

IV. The Challenges of Drug Use
A. Many adolescents experiment with drugs.
B. Smoking (79) and drinking alcohol (81%) lead the list of drug-related activities teens have tried at least once by the ninth grade.
C. Drug use among teenagers is on the decline.
D. Drug abuse is destructive, but there is a distinction between use and abuse.

V. The Challenges of Sexuality
A. Adolescents are a sexually active group.
1. According to a recent CDC report, 49.9 percent of high school teens had engaged in sexual behavior.
2. Males tend to view their first sexual experience more favorably than do females.
B. Teen pregnancy has become a significant social problem.
1. Teen pregnancy rates in the U.S. are nearly twice as high as other industrialized countries, and nine times higher than the rates in the Netherlands and Japan.
2. A higher percentage of males than females reported a use of alcohol or drugs prior to their last sexual intercourse.
3. In the year 2000, there were nearly one-half million births to women between the ages of 15 and 19.
C. Many adolescents are ignorant of the consequences of their own sexual behaviors.
D. Teen mothers are more likely to drop out of school, be on welfare, have inadequate access to health care, and suffer economic hardships.

VI. Development During Early Adulthood
  A. The transition from adolescence to adulthood is marked by choices and commitments.
  B. Levinson has called it the "era of greatest energy and abundance and of greatest contradiction and stress."

VII. Marriage and Family
  A. Erikson claims that early adulthood revolves around the choice of intimacy or isolation.
      1. Eighty-five percent of Americans marry at least once.
      2. Mate selection is a complex process that involves availability, eligibility, and attractiveness (physical and psychological).
  B. David Buss believes that a person is likely to marry someone who is similar in almost every variable.
  C. Approximately 50 percent of all first marriages end in divorce.
  D. One of the best predictors of a successful marriage is the extent to which partners were able to maintain close relationships before marriage.

VIII. The Transition to Parenthood
  A. **Generativity** reflects a concern for family and for one's impact on future generations.
  B. As parents, men and women take on the responsibilities of new social roles of mother and father.
  C. There is overwhelming evidence that marital satisfaction tends to drop during the child rearing years of a marriage.
  D. Marital satisfaction increases again once the children leave the nest.
      1. The U-shaped curve representing marital satisfaction before, during, and after the child rearing years is one of the most reliable in the social sciences.
      2. Other research confirms that indicators of marital satisfaction tend to go down in the months immediately following the birth of a first child.
  E. The most common explanation as to why dissatisfaction increases after the birth of a child is due to role conflict and role strain.

IX. Career Choice
  A. One's choice and satisfaction of occupation affect self-esteem and identity.
  B. Dual-career families are quite common
  C. Women make up about half of the professional workforce in the United States..
  D. Career selection is driven by family influence and the potential for earning money.
  E. Choosing a career involves exploration, crystallization, choice, career clarification, induction, reformation, and integration.
  F. If a poor choice is made, one can work through the process again.

X. Development During Middle Adulthood
  A. One must adjust to the physiological changes of middle age.
  B. Middle-aged persons face a major set of challenges in learning to deal with family members.
      1. Dealing with teens and elderly parents places some middle-aged adults in what has been called the sandwich generation.
      2. Family members provide 80 percent of all day-to-day health care for the elderly.
  C. Another task of this age is determining how to leave a mark on future generations.
  D. Relating to one's spouse and developing leisure-time activities can be a challenge for those who have previously been devoted to children and career.

XI. Development During Late Adulthood
  A. The transition to late adulthood generally occurs in the early to mid-sixties.
  B. By 2050, the number of people 65 and older will be nearly 78.9 million with an average life span of 82.1 years, the majority being women.

XII. What It Means to Be Old
    A. **Ageism** is the name given to discrimination and prejudice against a group on the basis of age.
    B. Adults over 65 can be divided into young-old and old-old groups.
        1. The distinction is based on the psychological, social and health characteristics rather than actual age.
        2. This distinction reinforces the notion that aging is not some sort of disease.
    C. Adult children are more capable of caring for their parents in their old age.
        1. Fewer that 15% of Americans over the age of 65 live in nursing homes.
        2. Nursing home residence increases to about 25% by age 85.
    D. Not all people retire successfully.
        1. Availability of economic resources matters.
        2. Social relationships help retirement succeed.
        3. One's personal health, education, and self-esteem also mater.
    E. With increased age often come increased physical problems.
        1. But, only 28% of the elderly report their health as fair or poor.
        2. Chronic illnesses (such as arthritis and osteoporosis) are more common in the elderly.
        3. The average 85-year old takes 8-10 prescription medications.
    F. Close family relationships and involvement in effective exercise programs predict successful aging.

XIII. Death and Dying
    A. Dealing with death is the last major crisis all must face.
    B. Although Kübler-Ross posited five stages in dealing with death, the descriptions may be idealized.
    C. Each person must face death in his or her own way.
        1. There is no "best" way to go about dying.
        2. The elderly are less morbid about dying than are adolescents.
        3. They may fear the process but do not fear the fact of their own death.

Practice Test Questions

TOPIC 8A: DEVELOPMENT DURING CHILDHOOD

Multiple Choice

1. Which of these developmental periods lasts the longest?
   ___a. embryonic period   ___c. prenatal period
   ___b. germinal period   ___d. fetal period

2. At which stage, or at what time, is the developing human at greatest risk of a physical defect?
   ___a. as a zygote   ___c. as a growing fetus
   ___b. during the embryonic stage ___d. during the birth process

3. Which of these typically has the most adverse effect on the developing human organism?
   ___a. the mother's inability to gain weight during pregnancy
   ___b. inadequate calcium intake during pregnancy
   ___c. having to take antibiotics, such as penicillin, during pregnancy
   ___d. alcohol use or abuse during pregnancy

4. Which of these senses is least well developed in the neonate?
   ___a. vision   ___c. hearing
   ___b. smell   ___d. taste

5. On what basis were Piaget's stages of development determined?
   ___a. the actual, chronological age of the child
   ___b. whether the child uses accommodation or assimilation
   ___c. the extent to which the child is egocentric or social
   ___d. how schemas are formed or modified with experience

6. Of the several criticisms of Piaget's theory of development, which is LEAST reasonable?
   ___a. It lacks attention to cognitive processing.
   ___b. The divisions between stages are not as clear as Piaget asserted.
   ___c. Piaget underestimated to abilities of preschool children.
   ___d. It lacks a significant concern for cross-cultural differences.

7. The memory strategy of elaboration is generally first put in use
   ___a. within days after birth.
   ___b. by the time the frontal lobe has developed (about age 2).
   ___c. only after children have begun school (even kindergarten).
   ___d. early in adolescence.

8. Melanie is 9 years old. She can easily get to school and back, a distance of six city blocks. On the other hand, she has great difficulty telling you how she manages the trip to school and back each day. Melanie is in Piaget's _____ stage of cognitive development.
   ___a. sensorimotor   ___c. concrete operations
   ___b. preoperational   ___d. formal operations

9. Kohlberg's theory of development focuses mainly on the development of
   ___a. cognitive representations, called schemas.
   ___b. strategies that children use to learn.
   ___c. morality and a sense of right and wrong.
   ___d. how children and adolescents interact with each other.

10. Of these, which is the largest difference between Piaget's theory and Erikson's theory of development? Erikson's theory
____a. relies less on the notion of stages.
____b. was based on experiments, not observations.
____c. is more relevant for boys than for girls.
____d. describes development through the lifespan.

11. Which observation about the development of gender identity is most supported by cross-cultural evidence?
____a. Girls relate better with their mothers, while girls relate better with their fathers.
____b. Children show no particular preferences for toys; they prefer to play with whatever their parents what them to.
____c. Right from birth, there are significant differences in temperament or "difficulty" between boys and girls.
____d. By the age of three or four years and throughout their early school years, children prefer same-sex playmates.

12. If secure attachment is going to occur, it will occur for most children (nearly two-thirds) when they are
____a. born.   ____c. five years old.
____b. one year old.   ____d. about to become teenagers.

True/False

1. ____True ____False   Fetal alcohol syndrome includes the likelihood of intellectual retardation.

2. ____True ____False   because of its beneficial effects on cardiovascular functioning, pregnant women are now being advised to drink at least 1, but no more than 3 glasses of red wine each day.

3. ____True ____False   In humans, the sense of smell does not begin to develop until at least two to three months after birth.

4. ____True ____False   In developing his theories of cognitive development, Piaget seems to have underestimated the cognitive skills of very young, preschool children.

5. ____True ____False   Carol Gilligan has argued that with regard to moral development, there are no sex differences in morality, but that males and females approach moral dilemmas differently.

6. ____True ____False   Whether a child will become securely attached depends on the behaviors of the child as well as the behaviors of the care-giver.

TOPIC 8B: DEVELOPMENT IN ADOLESCENCE AND ADULTHOOD

Multiple Choice

1. Which of these observations about adolescence is most valid?
    ___a. It is a developmental stage through which many individuals will not pass successfully.
    ___b. It is a developmental stage defined in terms of stress, turmoil, and abnormality.
    ___c. It is a developmental stage through which most pass in psychologically adaptive ways.
    ___d. It is a developmental period—the only one—defined in biological terms.

2. Which "biological" phenomenon is LEAST associated with the onset of adolescence?
    ___a. penile erections and nocturnal emissions in boys
    ___b. a growth spurt in both boys and girls
    ___c. menarche in girls
    ___d. the appearance of secondary sex characteristics

3. Which observation concerning menarche is TRUE?
    ___a. It is found more commonly in boys than in girls.
    ___b. It occurs, on average, at a younger age than it did 100 years ago.
    ___c. It generally occurs two to three years before puberty begins.
    ___d. It is produced, or triggered, by an increased level of androgens.

4. At the time of their puberty, or in their early adolescence, who seems to benefit the MOST?
    ___a. early-blooming males   ___c. late-blooming males
    ___b. early-blooming females   ___d. late-blooming females

5. Which of Piaget's stages of development is best associated with adolescence?
    ___a. identity formation   ___c. identity achieved
    ___b. postconventional reasoning   ___d. formal operations

6. Which observation concerning adolescent drug use is TRUE?
    ___a. Adolescents experiment with and use drugs more than adults do.
    ___b. Adolescents are more likely to use illegal drugs than legal drugs.
    ___c. The use of drugs by adolescents declined a bit in the 1980s, but is again on the rise.
    ___d. Adolescents who have never used drugs experience fewer adjustment problems than do those who have experimented with drugs.

7. Which of the following explanations for teen pregnancy is least acceptable or least reasonable?
    ___a. Teenagers are ignorant about matters of human sexuality.
    ___b. Many teenagers simply want to start their own families.
    ___c. Teenagers have negative attitudes about contraceptive use.
    ___d. Pregnancy simply occurs "by accident," without intention.

8. What two concepts, taken together, best characterize the beginning of adulthood?
    ___a. independence and interdependence   ___c. growth and development
    ___b. death and dying   ___d. assimilation and accommodation

9. For Erikson, early adulthood is best characterized in terms of
    ___a. competence vs. inferiority.   ___c. intimacy vs. isolation.
    ___b. ego-identity vs. despair.   ___d. generativity vs. stagnation.

10. The evidence suggests that—in general, of course—a woman is most likely to choose to marry someone who
    ___a. she believes to be most like herself.
    ___b. she believes will earn the most money in his lifetime.
    ___c. is physically most attractive.
    ___d. is most unlike, or opposite from, her father.

11. Of all the concerns that one might have about the characteristics of a mate, the one trait that varies most widely from culture to culture seems to be

___a. chastity. ___c. earning potential.

___b. intelligence or wisdom. ___d. kindness.

12. Which of the following best characterizes the elderly in the United States?

___a. Most of them (more than 50%) require supervision of the sort found in nursing homes.

___b. Most of them (more than 50%) are preoccupied with thoughts of their own deaths.

___c. Most (more than 75%) are vigorous and healthy.

___d. Most (nearly 65%) list their health as a serious problem.

13. According to Kubler-Ross, the final stage in facing one's own death is the stage of

___a. anger. ___c. acceptance.

___b. denial. ___d. joy.

True/False

1. ____True ____False Most adolescents are seriously troubled, rebellious, and uncooperative.

2. ____True ____False Boys profit from early maturity more than girls do, and they suffer more from late maturity.

3. ____True ____False Any sort of experimentation with drugs by adolescents will have long-term negative consequences.

4. ____True ____False Most young adults are unhappy or dissatisfied with their first career choice.

5. ____True ____False Most Americans (male and female) experience a real mid-life crisis, accompanied by the realization that "time is running out," and that they may not get to do all that they wanted to do.

Key Terms and Concepts
Topic 8A

prenatal period_____

_____

zygote_____

_____

germinal stage_____

_____

embryonic stage_____

_____

fetal stage_____

_____

fetal alcohol syndrome_____

_____

neonate_____

_____

cognitive development_____

_____

structural-functional approach_____

_____

information-processing approach_____

_____

schemas_____

_____

adaptation_____

_____

assimilation_____

_____

accommodation_____

_____

sensorimotor stage_____

_____

object permanence_____

_____

preoperational stage_____

_____

concrete operations stage_____

_____

conservation_____

_____

formal operations stage_____

_____

preconventional morality_____

_____

conventional morality_____

_____

postconventional morality_____

_____

gender_____

_____

gender identity_____

_____

attachment_____

_____

Topic 8B

adolescence_____

_____

puberty_____

_____

menarche_____

_____

identity crisis_____

_____

generativity_____

_____

Answers to Practice Test Questions

TOPIC 8A: DEVELOPMENT DURING CHILDHOOD

Multiple Choice

1. **c**   Be careful here. The germinal period and periods of the embryo and the fetus all taken together make up the prenatal period. Within that period, the fetal period is the longest.
2. **b**   It is when the organism is in the form of an embryo that it is most sensitive to the formation of physical defects.
3. **d**   Alcohol abuse is certainly the most devastating factor leading to birth defects of these listed, but even moderate alcohol consumption is generally discouraged.
4. **a**   The newborn, or neonate, has sensory capacities that are much greater than was once thought, but they are all not equally developed. Of these, vision is the last to become fully functioning.
5. **d**   The different stages of Piaget's theory are defined in terms of how the child goes about forming or modifying schemas on the basis of his or her interaction with the environment.
6. **a**   Actually, such a "criticism" would be absurd. Piaget's is, after all, a theory of cognitive development.
7. **d**   memory strategies in general do not appear until the school years. Using elaboration techniques is a strategy that does not really get put into use until very late in childhood or, more commonly, at the beginning of adolescence.
8. **c**   Melanie is probably in Piaget's stage of concrete operations, which would be typical for a nine-year-old. (Did it bother you that this item is "out of order"? This is something for which you need to be alert.)
9. **c**   Kohlberg's is referred to as a theory of moral development.
10. **d**   Erikson's stages of development are equally relevant for boys and girls and were based on observation. What makes his stages different is that they extend through adolescence and adulthood, whereas Piaget's do not.
11. **d**   There is virtually no evidence to be found—in any culture—for the first three observations, whereas the fourth choice has considerable support, even across many cultures.
12. **b**   About 65 percent of children in the United States (and around the world) will form attachments during their first year.

True/False

1. **T**   There are many signs and symptoms associated with fetal alcohol syndrome (retarded physical growth, poor coordination, poor muscle tone, etc.). By definition, one sign is mental retardation.
2. **F**   Hardly! Pregnant women are being advised to abstain from any and all alcoholic beverages.
3. **F**   Not only does it begin to develop long before birth, but at birth, the neonate's sense of smell is rather well developed.
4. **T**   Yes, this is one of the most common criticisms of Piaget's theory.
5. **T**   Most of Kohlberg's theory of moral development was based on the study of males. Gilligan suggests that females may have a different style of morality than do males.
6. **T**   There is simply no doubting that attachment formation is a two-way process.

TOPIC 8B: DEVELOPMENT IN ADOLESCENCE AND ADULTHOOD

Multiple Choice

1. **c**   Although some (including G. Stanley Hall and Anna Freud) would claim that alternative **b** is correct, current thinking would make alternative **c** your best choice. Alternatives **a** and **d** are almost silly.
2. **a**   Penile erections and nocturnal emissions typically occur for some time before puberty in boys, which is indicated by the presence of live sperm cells.
3. **b**   Menarche occurs in girls, not boys; defines the beginning of puberty; is triggered by estrogens, not androgens, and—for reasons not fully understood—seems to be occurring at a younger age than ever before in history.

4. **a**   At least at the time of their adolescence, early-maturing boys seem to experience an "advantage" over the other named groups.
5. **d**   The first three alternatives are not even associated with Piaget.
6. **c**   Alternatives **a** and **b** are clearly false. Alternative **d** is also false, but newer and controversial. Alternative **c** is the one that is most clearly true.
7. **b**   Alternatives **a**, **c**, and **d** are all reasonable and commonly cited explanations for the high rate of teenage pregnancy.
8. **a**   Although at first they may appear contradictory, independence and interdependence characterize early adulthood.
9. **c**   Here again, this item hinges on your knowledge of Erikson's stages. Early adulthood is associated with conflicts between intimacy and isolation.
10. **a**   Aren't some of these alternatives funny? What I am getting at here is the observation that mate selection is most often based on similarities, not that "opposites attract."
11. **a**   And the range of concern is very wide from one culture to another.
12. **c**   There is no doubt that the only alternative here that is even close to being true is the third one.
13. **c**   Not everyone "buys" Kubler-Ross's scheme, of course, but her stages are, in order: denial, anger, bargaining, depression, and acceptance.

True/False

1. **F**   To some of us (and to parents of adolescents in particular) this may appear to be true, but it isn't. It reflects more of an incorrect stereotype than reality.
2. **T**   This is about as nice a summary statement about early and late maturation as I can muster.
3. **F**   Again, some of us may want to think of this statement as true, but the evidence suggests that it is, in fact, false. What matters here, of course, is largely a matter of degree.
4. **T**   This true statement is lifted nearly verbatim from the text.
5. **F**   We often hear this used as an "excuse" for some pretty silly behaviors by middle-aged adults, but there is little hard evidence for a general period or stage of development that we can characterize as a mid-life crisis.

EXPERIENCING PSYCHOLOGY

An Ageism Survey

Ageism is a discriminatory practice or negative stereotype formed solely on the basis of age. Although ageism can occur with regard to persons of any age, it is most often directed at the elderly. Here is a simple, 10-item, true/false quiz about the elderly. Use it to see if you can detect any signs of ageism in the responses.

Indicate whether each of the following statements is "true" or "false." Consider "younger" to refer to persons under 65 years of age and "older" to refer to those over 65 years of age.

- Older people are more likely than younger people to attend church.

- Older people are more cautious and less likely to make risky decisions than are younger people.

- As people age, they tend to become more like each other.

- Older people have more difficulty than do younger people in adapting to a changing environment.

- A decrease in life satisfaction is usually experienced by older persons.

- The majority of persons over 65 live in nursing home or assisted-living institutions.

- Mental disorders occur more frequently among older people than among younger people.

- Depression is more common in older people than in younger people.

- Decreasing intelligence as measured by IQ tests, and other measures of cognitive functioning, is one of the inevitable changes that occurs with increasing age.

- Aging of the brain leads the way for the deterioration of other bodily systems and functions.

Scoring this "quiz" is very easy as each item is worded so that it is false.

Chapter 9

Personality

STUDY TIP #9

The Key To Effective Listening In Class

"But I never missed a class!" is a claim that instructors often hear from students who have not done well on an exam, and who have not yet learned the difference between attending a class and taking an active part in that class. This difference has a significant impact on how well students learn. The real key is preparation.

It is always easier to listen to and understand information with which you are familiar than it is to try to listen to and understand totally unfamiliar information. To be sure, few lectures or class activities are designed to be about something you knew very well before you took the class. The material will have to be somewhat new; that's what you're paying for. But if you prepare carefully, lectures and class discussions will not seem totally alien. Once a semester is under way, preparing for class will be relatively easy. You will have had time to develop some sense of what will be happening in class.

At the very least you should review recent lecture notes and preview the text for each class meeting. Perhaps the most important thing to do is to familiarize yourself with the vocabulary terms that might come up in class. If you're familiar with the vocabulary **before** you go to class, your listening for ideas, unifying themes, and over-arching concepts will be easier because you won't have to struggle with the definitions of new terms. You will then have more time to concentrate, select, organize, and summarize your thoughts in coherent notes.

Good listening is a matter of attitude. To be an effective listener, you must be in the proper frame of mind. As you take your seat, you have to rid your mind of thoughts of the activities of the day. You cannot do a good job of listening to a lecture if you're thinking about last night's date or this afternoon's lunch. You'll have difficulty attending to what is going on in class if you're still focused on a disagreement with a loved one. You can't contribute to a class discussion if all you're prepared to talk about is last weekend's game. Get your mind warmed up: What's the professor going to be talking about today? What contributions will you be expected to make? How will today's class fit in with what you already know? When you find yourself totally surprised at what is being said in class you have not prepared adequately.

Outline ~ Chapter 9: Personality

TOPIC 9A: THEORIES OF PERSONALITY

I. Introducing Personality Theories
    A. A **theory** is an organized collection of testable ideas used to explain a particular subject matter.
    B. **Personality** includes the affects, behaviors, and cognitions that characterize a person with some consistency in a variety of situations.
    C. There are three potential goals for personality theories:
        1. theoretical: to account for a person's characteristic patterns of thought, emotion, and behavior—and the mechanisms behind those patterns
        2. empirical: to gather and analyze observations on how personalities, environmental situations, and behaviors are inter-related
        3. institutional: to bring together many of psychology's sub-fields so as to better understand the whole person

II. The Psychoanalytic Approach
    A. The **psychoanalytic approach** is associated with Sigmund Freud and his followers.
    B. Two basic premises characterize the approach.
        1. Freud believed that innate drives could explain human behavior.
        2. He accepted the power of unconscious forces to mold and shape behavior.
    C. Freud believed that there were three levels of consciousness: the conscious, preconscious, and unconscious.
    D. Freud believed that innate biological drives, or instincts, rule personality.
        1. **Life instincts (eros),** or impulses for survival, motivate sex, hunger, and thirst.
        2. **Death instincts (thanatos)** are impulses of destruction.
            a. When these are directed inward, they give rise to feelings of depression or suicide.
            b. When they are directed outward, they result in aggression.
        3. Freud believed that life is an attempt to resolve the conflicts between these two natural instincts.
    E. Freud proposed that personality consisted of three separate, though interacting structures: the id, ego, and superego.
        1. The **id** is the instinctive aspect of the personality that seeks immediate gratification and resides in the unconscious mind.
            a. The driving force of the id is **libido**, or sexual/sensual energy.
            b. The id operates on the **pleasure principle**, the basic function of which is to find satisfaction for pleasurable impulses.
        2. The **ego** develops through one's experience with reality, and is the rational, reasoning part of one's personality.
        3. The **superego** reflects the internalization of society's rules and one's sense of morality or conscience.
            a. The superego operates on the **idealistic principle**, which demands that one do what is right and proper, no matter what the circumstances.
            b. The superego has no contact with reality.
        4. The **reality principle** is the force that governs the ego, arbitrating between the demands of the id and the conscience of the superego.
    F. If the ego cannot find acceptable ways to satisfy the drives of the id, or if it cannot deal with the demands of the superego, conflict and anxiety result.
        1. Freud proposed that **defense mechanisms** are unconsciously applied techniques that protect the self (ego) against strong feelings of anxiety.
            a. **Repression**, or motivated forgetting, is a matter of forgetting some anxiety-provoking event or desire.
            b. **Sublimation** involves the repression of unacceptable sexual or aggressive impulses and channeling them into socially acceptable behaviors.

        c.   **Denial** occurs when a person refuses to acknowledge the realities of an anxiety-provoking situation.

        d.   **Rationalization** occurs when one makes up excuses for one's behaviors rather than facing the real reasons for them.

        e.   **Fantasy** provides an escape from anxiety through imagination or daydreaming.

        f.   **Projection** is a matter of seeing in others one's own unacceptable, anxiety-provoking thoughts, motives, or traits.

        g.   **Regression** occurs when one returns to earlier, more primitive levels of behavior that were once effective.

        h.   **Displacement** refers to directing one's motives or behaviors at a substitute person or object rather than expressing them directly.

    2.   Using defense mechanisms is a normal reaction, but they can become maladaptive.

G. **Neo-Freudians** were analysts who were bothered by the strong emphasis on biological instincts and lack of concern for social influences.

    1.   Alfred Adler (1870-1937) proposed that goals and incentives motivate people.

        a.   He believed that one's goal in life is the achievement of success or superiority.

        b.   An inferiority complex can cause one to feel less able than others to solve life's problems and get along in the world.

    2.   Carl Jung (1875-1961) believed that the major goal in life was to unify all aspects of personality, conscious and unconscious , introverted and extroverted.

        a.   Jung believed there was a personal unconscious and a collective unconscious.

        b.   He thought that the collective unconscious included archetypes, universal forms, and patterns of thought that transcend history.

    3.   Karen Horney (1885-1952) focused on basic anxiety as a prime motivator.

        a.   She claimed that there were three distinct ways in which people interact with each other: moving away, toward, and against each other.

        b.   She disagreed with Freud's position regarding the biological basis of differences between men and women.

H. The psychoanalytic approach is complex and comprehensive, and has supporters and critics.

III. The Behavioral-Learning Approach

    A.   American psychology was oriented toward the lab and theories of learning.

        1.   John B. Watson (1878-1958) emphasized the role of the environment and learning in shaping one's behaviors.

        2.   B.F. Skinner's (1904-1990) variety of behaviorism focused on observable stimuli and observable responses and for relationships among them.

        3.   John Dollard (1900-1980) and Neal Miller (b. 1909) posited that a system of habits developed in response to cues in the environment, and that behavior was motivated by primary and learned drives.

        4.   Albert Bandura (b. 1925) considered internal cognitive processes of the learner, observation, and social influence to be important to personality.

    B.   Critics suggest that these approaches dehumanize personality and that they are too deterministic.

    C.   Supporters value the approaches for their emphasis on experimentation and for the forms of behavior therapy that have evolved.

IV. The Cognitive Approach

    A.   In this approach, it is thought that many of the cognitive processes humans use intersect with patterns of though and perception.

        1.   According to George Kelly (1955) each person has a set of personal constructs that directs thoughts and perceptions.

        2.   Walter Mischel (1973) proposed a cognitive model that included "person variables."

           a.   Cognitive and behavioral construction competencies

           b.   Encoding strategies and personal constructs

          c.   Subjective stimulus values

          d.   Self-regulatory systems and plans

      3.   Cantor and Kihlstrom (1987) proposed the notion of **social intelligence**, which are all the skills, abilities, and knowledge that a person brings to all social situations, and uses to solve life tasks.

      4.   Cantor and Langston (1989) identified defensive pessimism and optimism as life task-strategy packages.

  B.   The cognitive approach to personality fits in well with what is known about human cognition, and its future seems bright.

V.   The Humanistic-Phenomenological Approach

  A.   This optimistic approach claims that people have the ability to shape their destiny, and that biological, instinctive, or environmental influences can be overcome or minimized.

      1.   Carl Rogers (1902-1986) thought that the most powerful of human drives was to become fully functioning.

      2.   Abraham Maslow (1908-1970) focused on the positive, and thought that the major goal in life was to self-actualize.

  B.   This approach has strengths, but is criticized for being a vision for the nature of personality rather than a scientific theory.

VI. The Trait Approach

  A.   Guilford defined a **trait** as "any distinguishable, relatively enduring way in which one individual differs from others."

  B.   Traits fall on a continuum and are descriptive of personality dimensions.

  C.   Gordon Allport (1897-1967) proposed two types of personality traits: common traits and personal traits.

      1.   Common traits are dimensions of personality shared by most.

      2.   Allport claimed that there were three subtypes of personal traits.

          a.   A cardinal trait is one that is so overwhelming that it influences virtually everything a person does.

          b.   A central trait is a disposition that characterized someone in five to ten words.

          c.   Secondary traits are found in specific circumstances.

  D.   Raymond Cattell (1905-1998) offered an empirical approach with the correlational procedure called factor analysis to identify groups of highly related variables.

      1.   Cattell relied on psychological tests, questionnaires, and surveys.

      2.   He argued that there are two types of personality traits.

          a.   Surface traits are clusters of behaviors that go together and are easily observed.

          b.   Source traits are not directly observable but determine which surface traits become expressed in behavior.

  E.   The Big Five Model describes the traits that have the most research support and include the following:

      1.   Extroversion/Introversion

      2.   Agreeableness or Friendliness

      3.   Conscientiousness

      4.   Neuroticism/Emotionality

      5.   Openness to Experience and Culture/Intelligence

  F.   There continues to be debate concerning the number of traits that are important in personality and predicting behavior.

  G.   The value of personality traits varies from culture to culture.

TOPIC 9B: ISSUES RELATED TO PERSONALITY

I.   Is There a Personality?
     A. Walter Mischel (1968) challenged the consistency of personality, and proposed that traits were consistent only when viewed in similar or consistent situations.
     B. *Interactionism*, or the transactional approach, says that how a person behaves is a function of an interaction of stable personality characteristics and one's perception of the situation.

II. The Origins of Personality
     A. The most popular biological approach is temperament theory, which suggests that one's temperamental qualities are inborn and influence behavior.
         1. This theory proposes that individuals are born with a characteristic way of responding to the environment and to others.
         2. The ways of responding are rooted in the way a person's brain, nervous system, and endocrine system operate.
         3. There is consistency with temperament over time.
         4. Temperamental characteristics interact with the environment to affect behavior.
     B. The Learning Theory of personality development suggests that personality is acquired by the traditional mechanisms of learning.
         1. Reinforcement strengthens behavior.
         2. Behaviors maintained on a partial schedule of reinforcement are more resistant to extinction than those maintained on a continuous schedule.
         3. Children learn from watching models.
         4. Children learn attitudes, self-concept, and internal standards for behavior through these mechanisms.
     C. The Psychoanalytic Theory of personality development has the following propositions.
         1. Conscious and unconscious forces guide behavior.
         2. The basic structure of personality develops over time.
         3. Personality develops across a series of stages.
         4. One's personality develops according to how well one moves through the stages.
     D. Freud believed that at each stage of development, a crisis had to be resolved, or **fixation,** an over-investment of psychic energy would occur.
         1. Fixation in the Oral Stage (birth to 1 year) would result in overeating, nail biting, smoking, or talkativeness.
         2. In the Anal Stage (age 1 to 3 years) satisfaction is gained through control of bladder and bowel habits.
             a. Toilet training accompanied by high levels of stress and anxiety can lead to anal fixation.
             b. Adults who are overly neat and orderly or extremely disorganized and messy can demonstrate the anal stage.
         3. The Phallic Stage (age 3 to 5 years) signals the awareness of one's sexuality.
             a. Resolution of the Oedipus/Electra complex is the central crisis of this stage.
             b. The superego begins to develop here.
         4. During the Latency Period (age 6 until puberty) there is no crisis to be resolved and sexual development is on hold.
         5. During the Genital Stage (after puberty) there is a renewal of sexual impulses.

III. Gender and Personality
     A. Gender differences tend to be insignificant and inconsistent, except in regard to overt, physical aggression.
     B. The differences in aggression are found at all ages and in all cultures.

IV. Personality Measurement or Assessment
     A. The three goals of personality assessment are diagnosis, theory building, and behavioral prediction.
     B. **Behavioral observation** involves drawing conclusions about one's personality based on observations of behaviors.

C. The data of the **interview**, a conversational interchange, provides one of the oldest, most widely used, but not necessarily most accurate method of personality assessment.
D. The **Minnesota Multiphasic Personality Inventory (MMPI)** is a popular paper-and-pencil personality test designed to aid in the diagnosis of people with mental disorders.
    1. The MMPI-2 is a revision published in 1989 that was designed to update and improve the original test.
    2. It consists of 567 true-false questions and is considered a criterion-referenced test.
    3. A trained psychologist must interpret the pattern of responses.
E. The California Personality Inventory (CPI) assesses 18 personality traits.
F. Cattell's 16 PF Questionnaire was designed in conjunction with his trait theory approach.
G. The Taylor Manifest Anxiety Scale has gained wide acceptance as a measure of anxiety.
H. The Endler Multidimensional Anxiety Scale claims to distinguish between anxiety and depression.
I. A **projective technique** asks a person to respond to ambiguous stimuli in the hopes that the person will reveal aspects of his or her personality.
    1. The **Rorschach inkblot test** is a projective technique in which a person is asked to say what he or she sees in a series of inkblots.
    2. The **Thematic Apperception Test (TAT)** consists of a series of pictures about which a person is asked to tell a story.
J. The scoring and interpretation of projective tests are usually subjective and impressionistic.

Practice Test Questions

TOPIC 9A: THEORIES OF PERSONALITY

Multiple Choice

1. Ideas, thoughts, or memories of which we are not immediately aware, but which we can think about with reasonably little effort, are said by Freudians to be stored in our _____ level of awareness.
    ___a. immediate
    ___b. unconscious
    ___c. preconscious
    ___d. subconscious

2. Freud might "explain" war and man's inhumanity toward man in terms of
    ___a. thanatos.
    ___b. libido.
    ___c. wish-fulfillment.
    ___d. eros.

3. The aspect or structure of one's personality that is most responsible for feelings of guilt or blame is the
    ___a. id.
    ___b. superego.
    ___c. libido.
    ___d. ego.

4. Otis did not take the time to study for his test in psychology and, as a result, failed it badly. Otis blames the instructor for asking so many "picky" questions and blames the author of his text for writing such a "poor and useless" book. It sounds like Otis is engaging in
    ___a. repression.
    ___b. fantasy.
    ___c. projection.
    ___d. rationalization.

5. The so-called Neo-Freudians left Freud and devised their own theories of personality because they objected to—more than anything else—Freud's heavy emphasis on
    ___a. instincts and biological concepts.
    ___b. the importance of early childhood.
    ___c. parent-child social interactions.
    ___d. the idea of levels of consciousness.

6. The concept of "inferiority complex" is best associated with
    ___a. Freud.
    ___b. Jung.
    ___c. Adler.
    ___d. Horney.

7. More so than any other theorists discussed, psychologists such as Watson, Dollard, Miller, and Skinner tended to talk about personality in terms of
    ___a. conscious choices made by individuals faced with difficult decisions to make.
    ___b. explaining a person's behaviors by referring to environmental factors.
    ___c. personality traits that remained relatively stable once they were formed.
    ___d. cognitive representations of the world that guide one's behaviors.

8. Which of these is the most valid criticism of the behavioral approach to personality?
    ___a. It emphasizes the environment so much, there is little left for the inner, individual person.
    ___b. It relies too heavily on concepts borrowed from biology and physiology.
    ___c. Focusing on only one level of consciousness, it leaves out much of the rich fabric of unconscious processes.
    ___d. Most of the terminology of this approach is very loosely defined.

9. To say that a personality theory is phenomenological is to say that it emphasizes
    ___a. instinctive, biological mechanisms.
    ___b. how people see themselves and their environments.
    ___c. unconscious, unknown and unknowable influences.
    ___d. learning and conditioning.

10. Personality traits have been defined most commonly
    ___a. in terms of how one's personality is tied to survival.
    ___b. to describe how someone scores on a personality test.
    ___c. to explain individual differences among people.
    ___d. by statistical procedures such as factor analysis.

11. In the context of personality theories, what makes the Big Five so remarkable?
    ___a. The five major theorists involved have agreed on what personality is.
    ___b. We now can determine when the environment is most important and when personality is most important.
    ___c. There seems to be a consensus on how best to describe personality.
    ___d. There are actually five levels of consciousness, not just the three that Freud described.

True/False

1. ____True ____False   Freud based his approach to personality on his experiences as a therapist.

2. ____True ____False   B. F. Skinner never had a theory of personality, claiming that learning theory would do just fine.

3. ____True ____False   Unlike Freud, Carl Rogers never engaged in psychotherapy.

4. ____True ____False   Most trait theories, including the so-called "Big Five" theory, do not include intelligence as a personality trait.

TOPIC 9B: ISSUES RELATED TO PERSONALITY

Multiple Choice

1. Which concept can best describe how the so-called "person-situation" debate has been resolved?
    ___a. a no-win situation   ___c. evolutionary
    ___b. useless or pointless   ___d. interactionism

2. If we hear someone talking about "dispositional traits" and "situational traits" to what is she or he referring?
    ___a. nature/nurture   ___c. growth/development
    ___b. internal forces/external forces   ___d. male issues/female issues

3. According to Freud, the first time one becomes aware of and finds pleasure in one's own genitals is when one enters the _____ stage of development, at about the age of three years.
    ___a. sexual   ___c. phallic
    ___b. latency   ___d. genital

4. For which of these assertions is there the most evidence?
    ___a. Males are more physically aggressive than are females.
    ___b. Males are more analytical in their thinking than are females.
    ___c. Females are more creative in their problem solving than are males.
    ___d. Females are generally more sociable than are males.

5. As opposed to intellectual assessment, personality assessment
    ___a. seldom uses psychological tests.
    ___b. attempts to measure you at your best.
    ___c. is used to predict behavior.
    ___d. measures normal, or typical, behaviors.

6. To say that a test, such as the MMPI-2, is "criterion referenced" implies that
      ___a. questions do not have right or wrong answers.
      ___b. people from different known groups respond to items differently.
      ___c. the test is designed to predict who might become mentally ill in the future.
      ___d. test scores have been factor analyzed.

7. The test in which one is assumed to project his or her personality into descriptions of ambiguous inkblots is the
      ___a. Thematic Apperception Test.
      ___b. Minnesota Multiphasic Personality Inventory.
      ___c. Rotter Incomplete Sentences Test.
      ___d. Rorschach Test.

True/False

1. ____True ____False   All of your personality traits change over time.

2. ____True ____False   Both the Rorschach and the TAT are projective tests.

Key Terms and Concepts
Topic 9A

theory_____

_____

personality_____

_____

psychoanalytic approach_____

_____

life instincts (eros)_____

_____

libido_____

_____

death instincts (thanatos)_____

_____

id_____

_____

pleasure principle_____

_____

ego_____

_____

reality principle_____

_____

superego_____

_____

idealistic principle_____

_____

defense mechanisms_____

_____

repression_____

_____

sublimation_____

_____

denial_____

_____

rationalization_____

_____

fantasy_____

_____

projection_____

_____

displacement_____

_____

neo-Freudians_____

_____

inferiority complex_____

_____

social intelligence_____

_____

trait_____

_____

Topic 9B

temperament theory_____

_____

behavioral observation_____

_____

interview_____

_____

Minnesota Multiphasic Personality Inventory (MMPI-2)_____

_____

projective technique_____

_____

Thematic Apperception Test_____

_____

Answers to Practice Test Questions

TOPIC 9A: THEORIES OF PERSONALITY

Multiple Choice

1. **c**   The key here is "reasonably little effort." This indicates that the information is stored at the preconscious level.
2. **a**   In fact, Freud had quite a bit to say about war and its destructive power. He suggested that humans must have some sort of drive for destruction, which he called thanatos, to match their drive for life and survival, which he called eros.
3. **b**   It is our superego that informs us of moral issues and keeps us in touch with "right and wrong." When forces of the id overwhelm the superego, the result is often guilt.
4. **d**   Otis is rationalizing. He is making up excuses for his behaviors instead of facing—the anxiety-producing—reasons for them.
5. **a**   There were many grounds on which people broke away from Freud. Of these, the first statement here summarizes a problem that many had.
6. **c**   As you know by now, I usually don't like questions about names, but I think that for each of the theorists discussed in this chapter, you ought to have at least one or two well-formed associations, such as Adler and inferiority complexes. This might be a good place to remind you of the value of flash cards for studying.
7. **b**   The psychologists listed here would say that forces outside the organism—forces in the environment, not the person—should be used to explain behavior.
8. **a**   Although a reasonable criticism of all behavioral approaches, this one is most often leveled at Skinner's.
9. **b**   Phenomenology has to do with perception. Here the issue is the perception of one's self and the perception of others. Here again we have the point that what matters most is what is perceived, not what is.
10. **d**   Personality traits are dimensions of description and have been determined most often by factor analyzing test scores of many persons to see which characteristics might be interrelated.
11. **c**   The Big Five are personality traits (or clusters of traits). What makes them remarkable is the extent of consensus about their universality.

True/False

1. **T**   Actually, Freud was a physician and therapist first and a personality theorist later. He based his theories on many things, including observations of his patients and himself.
2. **T**   In fact, we may argue that Skinner never really had much of a learning theory either, but to the extent that learning theories were developed, they would suffice for Skinner.
3. **F**   Roger's form of therapy was quite different from Freud's, of course, but Rogers developed a very popular form of psychotherapy.
4. **F**   Virtually all personality theories, including the listing of the "Big Five," include intelligence (or something very much like it) as an important aspect of one's personality.

TOPIC 9B: ISSUES RELATED TO PERSONALITY

Multiple Choice

1. **d**   We've seen this term before in other contexts. Here we are talking about the interaction of situational and dispositional influences on behavior.
2. **b**   Referring to one's disposition is to make reference to internal, personality characteristics, whereas situational traits refer to forces of the environment.
3. **c**   It's a little word, but the key word here is "first."
4. **a**   If I had not put the "physically" in this alternative, even it would be in doubt. There is virtually no evidence for the last three alternatives.
5. **d**   On an intelligence test, I want you to do as well as you can, but on an assessment of personality, I want you to act normally and give me your characteristic responses, not what you think might make you look better.
6. **b**   What makes the MMPI-2, for example, criterion-referenced is that each item tends to be answered differently by people from different known groups.
7. **d**   Which is why it is referred to as the Rorschach Inkblot Test.

True/False

1. **F**   A very tough call on this one, because in fact, many personality characteristics do remain remarkably stable over time.
2. **T**   They are projective tests in the sense that they are so ambiguous that the person must project aspects of his or her personality into test responses.

EXPERIENCING PSYCHOLOGY

Assessing One Aspect of Personality

Humanistic approaches to personality emphasize the analysis of the factors that enter into a person's perceptions and evaluations of his or her life experiences. Carl Rogers refers to these perceptions as the *self-concept*. Mark Snyder (*The Many Me's of the Self Monitor*, Belmont, CA: Brooks/Cole, 1980) has prepared a Self-Monitoring Scale that indicates the extent to which one is aware of one's own wants, needs, and traits; that is, is aware of one's own "self."

These statements concern personal reactions to a number of different situations. No two statements are exactly alike, so consider each statement carefully before responding. If a statement is true, or mostly true, as applied to you, circle the **T**. If the statement is false, or usually not true, as applied to you, circle the **F**.

T　**F**　1. I find it hard to imitate the behavior of other people.

T　**F**　2. I guess I put on a show to impress or entertain certain people.

T　**F**　3. I would probably make a good actor.

T　**F**　4. I sometimes appear to others to be experiencing deeper emotions than I really am.

T　**F**　5. In a group of people, I am rarely the center of attention.

T　**F**　6. In different situations and with different individuals, I often act like very different people.

T　**F**　7. I can only argue for ideas I already believe.

T　**F**　8. In order to get along and be liked, I tend to be what other people expect me to be more than anything else.

T　**F**　9. I may deceive people by being friendly when I really dislike them.

T　**F**　10. I am not always the person I appear to be.

SCORING: Give yourself one point for each of the questions 1, 5, and 7 that you answered **F**, and give yourself one point for each of the remaining items that you answered with a **T**. If your total points are seven or more, you are probably a high-monitoring person; three or below and you are probably low on self-monitoring.

Three points to ponder: (1) To what extent does the situation determine the extent to which one acts openly and honestly in the presence of others? (2) Can you think of any behaviors or characteristics that should be correlated with one's degree of self-monitoring? (3) How would you proceed to test the reliability and the validity of this scale, and how would you create norms for it?

Chapter 10

Motivation and Emotion

STUDY TIP #10

On Taking Useful Notes In Class

Attending class and listening carefully are important because lectures are presented to you only once. This is also why you'll need some written record of the information presented orally in class. Good lecture notes, written in your own style, are valuable tools for learning. There is a large body of research devoted to note taking. Here, I'll just touch on two principles that will help you learn psychology—or any other discipline.

1. *Select and organize what you hear.* It is probably already apparent to you that there is no way that you can write down everything that is said in class. This can be an advantage. Note taking should be an active process of selecting and organizing information. Although it is generally better to take too many notes than it is to take too few, it is important to be an active listener who participates in class, not a passive, mechanical writer. The notes you take will be yours, so put them in a form that you can use. Except for technical terms and new vocabulary, use your own words. Copying information is not learning it. Develop shortcuts. Feel free to abbreviate, but only if you will able to understand your symbols and notes when you go back to study them. From time to time, taking no notes at all may be best. Thinking about what is being said, or participating in a class discussion may be more meaningful.

2. *Edit and review your notes.* Classroom notes are always a "work in progress." Immediately after class, while material is still fresh, review your notes, fill in gaps, underline for emphasis, note unclear sections that need further work, and use your margins to jot down information you did not have time to record during class. Several times a week, as part of your study, continue the editing process. Use your textbook or other notes, outside readings, or consult with your instructor for correct spellings, missing details, clarification, and the like. After each quiz or exam in the course, go back and critically evaluate your own notes. To what extent did they help? How can they be improved? Did you write too much? Too little? Was the format you used the best possible for you?

Outline ~ Chapter 10: Motivation and Emotion

TOPIC 10A: MOTIVATION

I.   Instincts
    A. **Motivation** is the process that arouses, directs, and maintains behavior.
    B. In the past, behaviors often were explained in terms of an **instinct**—an unlearned, complex pattern of behavior that occurs in the presence of certain stimuli.
    C. William McDougall believed that humans were motivated by 18 instincts.
        1. As more behaviors needed explaining, the list of instincts grew.
        2. Truth is, instincts may "name," but they don't explain.
        3. Still, the approach reminds us that we may engage in some behaviors for reasons that are basically biological, physiological, and inherited.

II. Needs and Drives
    A. In Clark Hull's system, a **need** is a lack or shortage of some biological essential required for survival and resulting from deprivation.
        1. Needs give rise to drives.
        2. A **drive** is a state of tension, arousal, or activation resulting from an unlearned need that arouses and directs an organism's behavior.
            a. Primary drives are based on unlearned, physiological needs.
            b. A **secondary drive** is a state of tension resulting from a learned or acquired need that motivates an organism's behavior.
    B. Maslow's hierarchy of needs is a stage theory with the following levels:
        1. Physiological
        2. Safety and security
        3. Love and belongingness
        4. Esteem
        5. Self-actualization.

III. Incentives
    A. **Incentives** are stimuli an organism may be motivated to approach or avoid.
    B. Whereas drives are said to "push" behaviors, incentives "pull" behaviors from without
    C. Many of the principles are similar to those of operant conditioning.

IV. Balance or Equilibrium
    A. There are several theories that involve the concepts of balance or equilibrium.
    B. Walter Cannon's theory of **homeostasis** claimed that internal physiological conditions seek a balanced "set point."
    C. **Arousal** theories suggest that for every task there is an optimal and balanced level of activation required to complete the task well.
    D. Leon Festinger's theory of **cognitive dissonance** argues that we are motivated to maintain a state of balance or equilibrium among cognitions.

V. Temperature Regulation
    A. We are driven to regulate our body temperature.
    B. When body temperature changes from normal, the first reaction is physiological.
        1. The attempt is to return to set point by a process mediated by the hypothalamus.
        2. The **hypothalamus** is a small structure near the limbic system in the center of the brain, associated with temperature regulation, feeding, drinking, and sex.
    C. If automatic processes are insufficient, we are driven to engage in behavior to change body temperature.

VI. The Thirst Drive and Drinking Behaviors
    A. There are several cues to thirst.
        1. Intracellular fluid loss is monitored by the hypothalamus.
        2. A complex chain of events involving the kidneys monitors extracellular loss.
    B. Sensory qualities can give rise to external cues to thirst.

VII. The Hunger Drive and Eating Behaviors
    A. There are several internal cues to "feeling hungry."
        1. The hypothalamus has both an eat (the lateral hypothalamus) and no-eat (ventromedial hypothalamus) center.
        2. We may be sensitive to levels of blood sugar or glucose.
        3. The liver may be sensitive to levels of fat supply.
        4. There may be an overall drive to maintain a set point body weight.
        5. Genetic factors clearly are involved in weight gain and obesity.
        6. An ob gene controls the amount of a hormone named leptin in the bloodstream which tells the brain how much fat is stored in the body
    B. Eating behaviors are influenced by non-physiological, external processes, such as time-of-the-day, the appearance of food, and social pressures from others.
    C. Obesity has become of epidemic proportions in the United States.
        1. Technically, obesity is defined in terms of a body mass index of 30 or greater.
        2. Nearly one-third of American adults are obese.
        3. Obesity seems to have a clear genetic basis.
        4. There seems to be no quick and easy treatment for obesity.
            a. The body protects better against weight loss than weight gain.
            b. Fully 95 percent of those on a weight-loss program will be back at their original weight within five years.
            c. The only useful plan seems to be a gradual shift in lifestyle: eat a bit less; exercise a bit more.
    D. Eating disorders afflict approximately 8 million Americans, 90 percent of whom are women..
        1. **Anorexia nervosa** is characterized by an inability (or refusal) to maintain one's body weight through self-starvation and/or increased activity.
        2. **Bulimia** is characterized by episodes of binge eating followed by purging.
            a. Females most often experience eating disorders.
            b. There are no known causes of eating disorders, but social/cultural pressures and physiological predispositions are both suspected as being important.
            c. Prognosis for anorexia is poor with high degrees of relapse, but the outlook for bulimia is better.

VIII. Sexual Motivation and Human Sexual Behaviors
    A. Sex can be an important motivator for humans and non-humans alike.
        1. On a physiological level, the sex drive is unique.
            a. The survival of the individual does not depend upon its completion.
            b. It depletes rather than replenishes bodily energy.
            c. It requires maturation before it is apparent.
            d. Whereas in "lower species" internal physiological states are of prime importance, they are less so for higher species such as humans.
        2. For humans in particular, hormones are neither necessary nor sufficient to account for sexual behaviors.
    B. Men and women differ in but a few, but in important ways with regard to sexuality.
        1. Men demonstrate more interest in sex, fantasize about it more and have a decidedly more greater interest in engaging in sex than do women.
        2. Whereas women seek commitment in sexual relationships, men tend to seek sex first, relationships later.
        3. Men are significantly more likely to be the sexual aggressor and initiate sexual contact.
    C. **Homosexuality** is a sexual orientation involving sexual attraction and arousal to members of the same sex.
        1. **Heterosexuality** is a sexual orientation involving sexual attraction to and arousal by members of the opposite sex.
        2. The terms **gay**, which is most often used to refer to males with a same-sex orientation, and **lesbian**, the term for women with a same-sex orientation, are preferred terms of reference.
        3. Homosexuality and heterosexuality are not mutually exclusive categories.

4. In terms of sexual responsiveness, there is little difference between persons of homosexual and heterosexual orientations.
5. Homosexual orientation is related to an interaction among genetic, hormonal and environmental factors.
6. There are no differences in sex hormone levels in adult homosexuals and adult heterosexuals.
7. There are small but significant differences in the structure of the hypothalamus between gay and heterosexual men.

IX. Psychologically Based Motives
    A. The **need to achieve (nAch)** is the acquired need to meet or exceed some standard of excellence in one's behavior.
        1. The **Thematic Apperception Test**, a projective personality test requiring a subject to tell a series of short stories about a set of ambiguous pictures, measures the nAch.
        2. People with high nAch seek tasks in which success is not guaranteed but in which there is a reasonable chance of success.
        3. The need to achieve probably is learned, usually in childhood.
    B. The **need for power** involves the need to be in control, to be in charge of the situation and others.
        1. The need for power in itself is neither good nor bad.
        2. There are no reliable differences between men and women in measured needs for power.
    C. The **need for affiliation** is a need to be with others, to work with others toward some end, and to form friendships and associations.
    D. The **need for intimacy** is a need to form and maintain close, affectionate relationships with others.
        1. Intimacy involves self-disclosure.
        2. Women are more likely than men to show high intimacy needs.
    E. Loneliness is a psychological state arising when our actual social relationships are discrepant from the relationships we would like to have.

TOPIC 10B: EMOTION

I. Defining and Classifying Emotions
    A. There are four components of an emotional reaction.
        1. One experiences a subjective feeling of affect.
        2. One has a cognitive reaction, i.e., "knows what happened."
        3. There is an internal physiological reaction.
        4. Finally, there is an overt behavioral reaction.
    B. Emotions are motivators in that they arouse behaviors.
    C. Classifying the "subjective feeling" component of emotion has been very difficult.
        1. Wilhelm Wundt proposed three, intersecting dimensions.
        2. Carroll Izard proposed nine primary emotions.
        3. Robert Plutchik argued for eight basic emotions, each related to survival and adaptation.
        4. Richard Lazarus defined basic emotion in terms of being motivated to approach or avoid.
    D. The only issue on which there is any consensus is that emotions represent a valenced state, meaning that they could be classified as positive or negative.

II. Physiological Aspects of Emotion
    A. Emotionality involves the autonomic nervous system (ANS).
        1. The parasympathetic division of the ANS is actively involved in maintaining a relaxed, calm, unemotional state.
        2. When one is emotional, his or her **sympathetic division of the ANS** takes over, producing several reactions.
            a. The pupils of the eye dilate.

       b. Heart rate and blood pressure are elevated.
       c. Blood is diverted away from the digestive tract toward the limbs and brain.
       d. Respiration increases.
       e. Moisture is brought to the surface of the skin in the form of perspiration.
       f. Blood sugar levels increase.
       g. Blood will clot more readily than usual.

B. The two brain structures most involved in emotionality are the limbic system and the hypothalamus.

C. The role of the cerebral cortex in emotionality seems to be largely inhibitory and cognitive.

III. Outward Expressions of Emotion

    A. Charles Darwin was one of the first to understand that facial expressions provide indicators of an organism's emotional state.

    B. Whereas non-human animals have many instinctive patterns of behavior to communicate emotional state, humans have language.

    C. Much research by Paul Ekman has demonstrated a reliable relationship between emotional states and facial expressions across cultures.

    D. Emotions can have several behavioral manifestations.

       1. **Aggression** is a behavior intended to inflict harm on another organism or a symbol of that organism.

       2. The **frustration-aggression hypothesis** argues that aggression is always a consequence of frustration.
           a. We now know that this hypothesis is too simplistic.
           b. When frustration is accompanied by anger, aggression is more likely.

       3. What factors lead to the arousal of anger?
           a. How we judge the intent of a person who frustrates us
           b. The perception that we have been treated unjustly
           c. A need to restore justice and equity
           d. Feelings of powerlessness

       4. Aggressive drivers tend to be young, poorly educated males with a history of violence and drug or alcohol problems.

Practice Test Questions

TOPIC 10A: MOTIVATION

Multiple Choice

1. Which of these is LEAST involved in motivational states?
   ___a the arousal of behavior   ___c. the directing of behavior
   ___b. the memory of behavior   ___d. the maintenance of behavior

2. Of these, which psychological process is LEAST affected by one's motivations?
   ___a. memory   ___c. perception
   ___b. learning   ___d. sensation

3. What is the major problem with using the concept of instinct to explain human behavior?
   ___a. There are too many human instincts to keep track of.
   ___b. There are too few human behaviors that have a biological basis.
   ___c. Referring to instincts may describe behaviors, but it doesn't explain them.
   ___d. Too many human instincts have opposites, such as needs to socialize and needs to be alone.

4. In Hull's theory (as an example) what gives rise to a drive?
   ___a. a need   ___c. a behavior
   ___b. a motive   ___d. a goal or incentive

5. Approaches to motivation that focus on stimuli outside the organism are approaches that focus on
   ___a. incentives.   ___c. arousal.
   ___b. drives.   ___d. homeostasis.

6. Which of these terms is most like Cannon's concept of homeostasis?
   ___a. drive   ___c. fulfillment
   ___b. sensation-seeking   ___d. balance

7. Which brain structure is MOST involved in temperature regulation?
   ___a. the hypothalamus   ___c. the brain stem
   ___b. the limbic system   ___d. the corpus callosum

8. Most of the water in our bodies is contained
   ___a. in our bloodstream.
   ___b. within the cells of our bodies.
   ___c. in sweat glands.
   ___d. in spaces between the cells in our bodies.

9. Which is likely to be LEAST involved in motivating us to eat or not eat?
   ___a. the physical appearance of food   ___c. how empty our stomachs are
   ___b. our hypothalamus   ___d. reactions of our liver

10. Which of these statements is TRUE about bulimia, but FALSE about anorexia nervosa?
    ___a. It is an eating disorder found mostly in young women.
    ___b. It involves a preoccupation with one's weight and body size.
    ___c. With proper treatment, the prognosis for a full recovery is good.
    ___d. In virtually all cases, at least some hospitalization will be required.

11. In what way is the sex drive in humans most different from the sex drive in rats?
    ___a. It does not appear until after puberty.
    ___b. Its satisfaction does not determine the survival of the individual.
    ___c. It is strongly affected by learning and experience.
    ___d. Its physiological basis is largely hormonal.

12. With regard to homosexuality, which observation is most TRUE?

     ___a. Sexual preference is a matter of choice freely made.

     ___b. Gay males have excess levels of female hormones in their systems.

     ___c. Homosexuality is a dimension, a matter of degree, not either/or.

     ___d. Most homosexuals (male and female) have not tried heterosexual sex.

13. At the moment, which of these can be taken as the most reasonable hypothesis for the development of a homosexual orientation?

     ___a. genetic differences in X and Y chromosomes

     ___b. the lack of a father-figure in single-parent homes

     ___c. unsatisfying or frustrating sexual encounters in early adolescence

     ___d. hormonal imbalances that occur during prenatal development

14. If given a choice, a person with a high need to achieve (aAch) would probably chose a job in which he or she

     ___a. could succeed with very little effort.

     ___b. would be in a position to control the fate of others.

     ___c. would be working with as many people as possible.

     ___d. could do well, but only with effort and hard work.

True/False

1. ____True ____False   The concepts of balance, equilibrium, and set-point refer only to physiological conditions or physiological processes.

2. ____True ____False   Arousal theory tells us that one's performance on a task will continue to improve as one's level of arousal continues to increase.

3. ____True ____False   Although our hypothalamus may inform us that we are hungry or thirsty, learning and experience inform us about what to eat or drink.

4. ____True ____False   The prognosis for anorexia nervosa is significantly better than the prognosis for bulimia.

5. ____True ____False   Whereas men are motivated by a need to achieve, women are motivated by a fear of failure.

TOPIC 10B: EMOTION

Multiple Choice

1. Of the following, which question reflects a current debate concerning the nature of emotions?
   ___a. Do facial expressions express emotions?
   ___b. Are cognitions required for an emotional experience?
   ___c. Does becoming emotional involve the ANS?
   ___d. Do emotions serve any useful adaptive functions?

2. Which change is LEAST likely during an emotional reaction?
   ___a. Heart rate decreases.   ___c. Blood flow is diverted to the limbs.
   ___b. Digestion stops.   ___d. Pupils dilate.

3. According to the characterization presented in the text, which of these is NOT included in our conceptualization of an emotional reaction?
   ___a. a subjective feeling, or affect
   ___b. a cognitive awareness of what is happening
   ___c. a judgment of whether the emotion is adaptive
   ___d. an overt behavioral reaction

4. How many basic emotions are there?
   ___a. 4   ___c. 9
   ___b. 8   ___d. It depends.

5. Which aspect of the brain is most directly involved in emotion?
   ___a. the thalamus   ___c. the brain stem
   ___b. the limbic system   ___d. the basal ganglia

6. In emotional states, the major role of the cerebral cortex seems to be to
   ___a. trigger reactions in lower centers, like the limbic system.
   ___b. increase heart rate and blood pressure.
   ___c. cognitively interpret the situation at hand.
   ___d. cause the organism to engage in fight or flight.

7. Which expression of emotion is uniquely human?
   ___a. verbal description   ___c. body language
   ___b. facial expression   ___d. posture and gestures

True/False

1. ___True ___False Emotions that we classify as "negative" seldom have any survival value.

2. ___True ___False Most psychologists agree that there are four basic, or primary, emotions.

3. ___True ___False The only emotions that appear to be universal are joy and fear.

Key Terms and Concepts
Topic 10A

motivation_____

_____

instincts_____

_____

need_____

_____

drive_____

_____

secondary drive_____

_____

incentive_____

_____

homeostasis_____

_____

arousal_____

_____

cognitive dissonance_____

_____

obesity_____

_____

anorexia nervosa_____

_____

bulimia nervosa_____

_____

homosexuality_____

_____

heterosexuality_____

_____

gay_____

_____

lesbian_____

_____

need to achieve (nAch)_____

_____

Thematic Apperception Test (TAT)_____

_____

need for power_____

_____

need for affiliation_____

_____

need for intimacy_____

_____

loneliness_____

_____

Topic 10B

emotion_____

_____

valenced state_____

_____

sympathetic division (of the ANS)_____

_____

aggression_____

_____

frustration-aggression hypothesis_____

_____

Answers to Practice Test Questions

TOPIC 10A: MOTIVATION

Multiple Choice

1. **b**   We say that motivation arouses, directs, and maintains behavior. Now memory is surely involved in motivation—it's involved in nearly everything—but it is less central than the other three.
2. **d**   Actually, the more complex, or "higher" a psychological process, the more likely that motivation will be a significant factor. The best choice here is the nearly physiological process of sensation.
3. **c**   There is value to the notion of instinct, of course, but with regard to human behavior, instinct tends more to name and describe than to explain anything.
4. **a**   Don't get rattled just because I dropped a name in here. In virtually anyone's system—including Hull's—needs give rise to drives.
5. **a**   Drives, arousal, and homeostasis all refer to conditions or states within the organism, whereas incentives are thought of as being "out there" in the environment.
6. **d**   By definition, homeostasis is a condition of balance or equilibrium.
7. **a**   This one is fairly obvious. The hypothalamus would be the best guess if you weren't sure—it seems to be involved in almost all physiological drives.
8. **b**   Most of the water in our bodies is stored within the cells.
9. **c**   Clearly it has an impact, but curiously, of these choices, the sense of fullness of the stomach is the least important.
10. **c**   Alternatives **a** and **b** are both true. Alternative **d** is true of anorexia, but not bulimia.
11. **c**   Alternatives **a**, **b**, and **d** are true of the sex drive for both humans and rats. The sex drive and sexual behaviors in rats do not seem to be much affected by learning or experience.
12. **c**   Only the third alternative is true, and beyond that, the others are very false.
13. **d**   The total picture is far from clear. We're quite sure that none of the observations made in the first three alternatives are even relevant, and we are becoming quite convinced that the fourth alternative makes the best statement that we can make right now..
14. **d**   The best alternative here is the last one.

True/False

1. **F**   At one point in history, we might have been able to say that this statement was true, but now we see that these concepts can be applied well beyond physiological functioning.
2. **F**   Well, at first, maybe, but what makes this statement false is that if arousal continues to rise, eventually it will become so high as to be debilitating.
3. **T**   If the truth of this statement is not obvious, you only need think about it for a moment longer.
4. **F**   No, in fact, quite the opposite is true.
5. **F**   With regard to achievement and failure, there is little evidence that there are any sensible gender differences at all.

TOPIC 10B: EMOTION

Multiple Choice

1. **b**   I don't think that any of the others are debatable at all, but there is now quite a discussion centering on the role—or even the necessity—of cognition for emotional experiences.
2. **a**   Heart rate increases, it doesn't decrease—in fact, think of this item in terms of "what would you like to have happen if you were faced with a bear in the woods?"
3. **c**   It is not possible to have an emotional reaction without the processes named in alternatives **a**, **b**, and **d**. If there is ever a judgment made about the adaptive value of an emotion, it would be made later.
4. **d**   This one is sort of silly, isn't it? Different theorists have different ideas, and for now the safest thing that we can say is that it depends—mostly on which theorist you'd like to believe.

5. **b**   As we've seen, all of the parts of the brain tend to work together and all of its aspects are involved in all reactions, but having said that, it is the limbic system that is most involved in emotionality.

6. **c**   The main role of the cerebral cortex is to bring a cognitive, thoughtful analysis to the situation that is being experienced.

7. **a**   This has less to do with emotion than it does with the difference between humans and nonhumans. Only humans can talk (verbalize) about how we feel.

True/False

1. **F**   Actually, some of the "negative" emotions—fear, for example—may have more survival value than some of the "positive" emotions.

2. **F**   Here's this one again. Previously, it was item #4 in multiple-choice form. Psychologists have come to no general agreement on the number of primary emotions—and are wondering if there even is such a thing as a primary, basic, emotion.

3. **F**   The text addresses the universality of facial expressions of emotion and suggests that anger, fear, disgust, sadness, and happiness are all expressed in the same way across cultures. This does not mean that there are not even more emotional expressions in common, as yet not confirmed.

EXPERIENCING PSYCHOLOGY

Joy to the World

This is a little exercise that demonstrates just how complex emotions can be—particularly for those who would like to organize or categorize "basic" human emotions.

JOY or **HAPPINESS** is commonly considered to be a basic emotion. There are a great many words in our language that are somehow related to the basic concept of joy or happiness. Here is a list of some of them:

BLISS	AMUSEMENT	CHEERFULNESS	GAIETY
GLEE	JOLLINESS	JOVIALITY	DELIGHT
GLADNESS	ENTHRALLMENT	ENJOYMENT	HAPPINESS
JUBILATION	ELATION	SATISFACTION	ECSTASY
EUPHORIA	ENTHUSIASM	ZEST	EXCITEMENT
THRILL	PLEASURE	CONTENTMENT	TRIUMPH
PRIDE	EXHILARATION	EAGERNESS	OPTIMISM
HOPE	JOY	RAPTURE	MIRTH
LEVITY	RELIEF	GIDDYNESS	

Write each of these (and any others you can think of) on a sheet of paper. Read each of the following statements to others and ask them to indicate which of these words best describes the situation being described. For which item(s) on the list was there the most agreement? Did you notice any sex differences in which terms were chosen?

1. *Colleen didn't think that she would be accepted at the college she most wanted to attend, but she just received notification that she had been accepted.*
2. *Tom's uncle told him that he was sending him a check. Tom was expecting a check for about $100. He has just opened the envelope from his uncle and found a check for $3000.*
3. *One of Juanita's professors has just read her paper to the class as an example of a thoughtful and well-written paper.*
4. *An instructor who usually dresses very conservatively has just walked into class wearing an oversized T-shirt with a picture of Mickey Mouse on the front.*
5. *A male student that Mary admires very much has just asked her if she will meet with him and help him with his math assignment.*
6. *Sam's mother had a brain tumor surgically removed two days ago. Sam has just received word from his father that the tumor was not malignant.*
7. *Jan's best friend has just told her that she and Jack, whom Jan admires and likes a lot, are planning to get married at the end of the term.*
8. *Julio worked hard campaigning for Alice Hawkins for student body president. He has learned that she has been elected with 71 percent of the votes.*
9. *It is Father's Day. The picnic is over, and Ralph is thinking about what great kids he and Evelyn have and how beautiful his six grandchildren are.*
10. *Gail went to visit her friend Margaret. When she arrived, seventeen of her friends were there to give her a surprise birthday party.*
11. *The party that Judy had worked so hard to plan was a great success. The guests have all gone home, and Judy is exhausted. She is thinking about the party as she settles herself into bed.*
12. *Joe's favorite team just won the Super Bowl.*

Chapter 11

Psychology, Stress, and Physical Health

STUDY TIP #11

<u>The Essentials of Textbook Study</u>

No matter what the course, there will be more information stored in your textbook than could ever be presented in class. Therefore, learning how to get information from your text is one of the most important skills you can acquire while in college. Here are a few general ideas.

1. *Prepare for textbook study.* Develop expectations about all that you read. Read the chapter preview; skim the summary; glance at the headings, subtitles and illustrations. Even before you begin reading, you should have a series of questions in mind. "What is this all about?" "How can I make sense of this?" "How will this show up on an exam?"

2. *Read textbooks differently.* Reading a chapter in a textbook is not studying. Studying is a process in which you must get actively and personally involved. It requires a great deal more concentration than does reading for pleasure. It involves you asking and seeking answers to questions. There are times when you should actually stop reading! Stop, pause, and <u>think</u> about what you've just read. Does it make sense? If not, do not go on making matters worse.

3. *Make textbook study an active process.* You must be mentally active and alert while studying so that you can search, question, and think. Underlining or highlighting in textbooks has become a common practice. It is often misused. The purpose of highlighting is to emphasize passages in the text so that essential points can be reviewed economically. When 80 percent of a page is underlined for emphasis, however, it is the remaining 20 percent that usually appears more striking.

4. *Use the textbook's margins.* You can increase the value of your textbook as a study aid by using its margins for your personal notations. Make your text a storehouse of references. Cross-reference textbook material with information in your notes. If it's your book, use it—don't be afraid to write in it.

Outline ~ Chapter 11: Psychology, Stress, and Physical Health

TOPIC 11A: STRESS, STRESSORS, AND HOW TO COPE

I.   Stressors: The Causes of Stress
    A.   **Stress** is defined as a complex set of reactions to real or perceived threats to one's well being that motivates adaptation.
    B.   The sources or stimuli for stress are called **stressors.**

II. Frustration-Induced Stress
    A.   Frustration-induced stress results from the blocking or thwarting of goal-directed behavior.
        1.   *Environmental* or *social frustration* refers to blocking of goal-directed behavior by something or somebody in the environment.
        2.   Personal frustration results from internal or personal reasons.
    B.   Fault and blame are not relevant here.

III. Conflict-Induced Stress
    A.   A **conflict** is a stressor in which some goals can be satisfied only at the expense of others.
    B.   There are four major types of motivational conflicts.
        1.   *Approach-approach* conflicts result when a person is caught between two or more alternatives, each of which is positive or potentially reinforcing.
        2.   With *avoidance-avoidance* conflicts, a person is faced with several alternatives, each of which is negative or punishing in some way.
        3.   In *approach-avoidance* conflicts, there is only one goal a person would like to reach, but at the same time, would like to avoid.
        4.   *Multiple approach-avoidance* conflicts result when a person is faced with a number of alternatives, each of which is in some way both positive and negative.

IV. Life-Induced Stress
    A.   In 1967, Holmes and Rahe published the first version of their *Social Readjustment Rating Scale (SRRS).*
        1.   The scale provides a list of life events that might be potentially stressful.
        2.   There is a positive correlation between scores on the SRRS and incidence of physical illness and disease.
    B.   While stress may predispose a person to physical illness, the scale does not demonstrate cause and effect outcomes.

V.   Socioeconomic Status or SES
    A.   **Socioeconomic status (SES)** is a measure that reflects income, educational level, and occupation.
    B.   SES is related to stress in at least two ways.
        1.   Persons of higher socioeconomic status are less likely than persons of low SES to encounter negative life events such as unemployment, poor housing, and less access to quality health care.
        2.   Persons of low SES have fewer resources to deal with stressful life events when they do occur.
    C.   Richard Lazarus believes that stress is a result of life's little hassles.
        1.   Lazarus and his colleagues designed the Hassles Scale.
        2.   This scale is a better predictor of symptoms such as anxiety and depression than the SRRS.
    D.   *The Comprehensive Scale of Stress Assessment* can be used with teens.
    E.   Stressors can be pleasant and desired, even though they may bring other hassles.

VI. Reacting to the Stressors in Our Lives
    A.   Stress is a reaction to stressors.
    B.   It motivates people to do something about the perceived threats to one's well-being.

VII. Individual Differences in Responding to Stressors
    A. There are individual differences in how people respond to stressors.
    B. People who seem generally resistant to the negative aspects of stress have been labeled as having *hardy personalities*.
    C. Hardiness is related to the following three factors.
        1. Challenge
        2. Control
        3. Commitment
    D. Some researchers argue that there are sex differences in reacting to stress.
        1. Males are likely to show a "flight-or-flight" reaction.
        2. Females tend to exhibit "tend-and-befriend" reactions.
    D. Some responses to stress are more effective or adaptive than others.

VIII. Stress as a Physiological Reaction: Seyle's GAS
    A. The **general adaptation syndrome** or GAS refers to the physiological reactions one makes to stressors.
        1. The first response to the perception of a stressor is *alarm*, which activates the sympathetic division of the ANS.
        2. The second stage is *resistance*, where the drain on body resources continues.
        3. The third stage is *exhaustion*, when bodily resources become nearly depleted.
    B. Repeated exposure to stressors has cumulative effects.

IX. Effective Strategies for Coping with Stressors
    A. There are several strategies to consider, including:
        1. Identify the stressor.
        2. Remove or negate the stressor.
        3. Reappraise the situation.
        4. Inoculate against future stressors.
        5. Take your time with important decisions.
        6. Learn techniques of relaxation.
        7. Engage in physical exercise.
        8. Seek social support.
    B. Whereas the five of the above may be thought of as *problem-focused* strategies, others deal more with the unpleasantness of experiencing stress, and are called *emotion-focused* strategies.

X. Ineffective Strategies for Coping with Stressors
    A. Procrastination is a form of fixation—simply not doing something to remove the stressor.
    B. Aggression is a maladaptive reaction to stressors.
        1. The **frustration-aggression hypothesis** claimed that aggression was always caused by frustration.
        2. It is now realized that there are other sources of aggression.
    C. Anxiety is a general feeling of tension, apprehension, and dread that involves predictable physiological changes.
    D. The anxiety that results from stress can become so discomforting and maladaptive to lead a psychologist to say that a person is suffering from a psychological disorder.

TOPIC 11B: HEALTH PSYCHOLOGY

I. Psychological Factors that Influence Physical Health
    A. Health psychology is the field of applied psychology that studies psychological factors affecting physical health and illness.
        1. It may be that simply changing some "unhealthy behaviors" would be more effective and less expensive than treating illness or disease.
        2. Noting that biological factors (such as genetic predispositions) and psychological factors (such as a person's reactivity to stressors) and social factors (such as the

influence of family, social support, or one's cultural expectations) all may interact to produce certain illnesses or diseases is called the **biopsychosocial model.**

B. There is a positive correlation between some personality variables and some aspects of physical health.

C. The **Type A behavior pattern (TABP)** originally was defined as describing a person who was competitive, achievement-oriented, impatient, easily aroused, often hostile and angry, who worked at many tasks at the same time.
   1. For nearly 20 years, many studies found a positive relationship between coronary heart disease (CHD) and behaviors typical of the Type A personality.
   2. Subsequent data failed to show a clear relationship between TABP and CHD.
   3. There may be a set of behaviors within the Type A behaviors that does predict CHD.
   4. It now seems that the active ingredients of TABP related to CHD are anger and hostility.

D. A person with a **Type B behavior pattern** is described as relaxed and easygoing.

E. More research is needed on adequately diagnosing TABP and its relationship to CHD.

II. Why People Die: The Unhealthy Lifestyle
   A. People die for an infinite number of reasons, but many deaths are premature and preventable.
      1. Nearly 2.5 million Americans die each year.
      2. Although death surely cannot be prevented, many deaths are premature and related to lifestyle choices.
   B. Smoking, poor nutrition, obesity, and stress are behavioral risk factors that contribute to death.
   C. Psychologists use behavioral techniques to promote healthy and safe behaviors.

III. Helping People to Stop Smoking
   A. Cigarette smoking is responsible for over 440,000 deaths each year in the U. S.
   B. Most people who quit permanently do so without any special program of intervention.
   C. Using a nicotine patch in conjunction with therapy can be effective.
   D. Combining psychotherapeutic interventions with antidepressant medications seems promising.
   E. There has been some success with designing programs aimed at getting people to refrain from smoking in the first place.
   F. Increasing the taxes on cigarettes provides a negative incentive.

IV. Sexually Transmitted Diseases (STDs)
   A. **Sexually transmitted diseases (STDs)** are contagious diseases usually passed on through sexual contact.
   B. STDs affect millions of people each year, with 15,000,000 *new cases* reported each year in the United Steses.
      1. **Chlamydia** is caused by a bacterial infection and is one of the most common STDs in North American.
      2. **Gonorrhea** is a bacterial infection that affects millions of people.
      3. **Syphilis** has four stages, and can lead to death without treatment.
      4. **Genital herpes** is caused by a virus and is a common STD.
      5. The **human immunodeficiency virus**, or **HIV**, causes acquired immune deficiency syndrome, or **AIDS.**
         a. The United Nations HIV/AIDS office estimates that 42 million people are living with HIV/AIDS worldwide, and that over 5 million *new cases* were diagnosed in 2002 alone..
         b. There currently is no vaccine to prevent AIDS.
         c. There is no cure, but some drug combinations can increase the life span and quality of life for those with the infection.
         d. The only reasonable way to avoid AIDS is through the careful monitoring of one's behaviors.

V. Interventions to Decrease to Incidence of AIDS
   A. Successful interventions are multifaceted and involve:

1. Education.
2. Changing attitudes.
3. Increasing motivation to engage in safer sexual practices.
4. Providing people with negotiating skills.
5. Targeting people most at risk.
6. Marketing strategies.

B. Knowledge of AIDS—in and of itself—is seldom useful in getting people to actually change their behaviors.
1. Most teenagers simply do not believe that they will contract the HIV.
2. As a result, most do not use condoms.

C. AIDS has unprecedented psychological complications.
1. Stress, depression, anger, anxiety, and denial are common.
2. Males with AIDS are 7.5 times more likely to commit suicide than men in the general population.
3. Others (even family members) often shun the AIDS patient.

Practice Test Questions

TOPIC 11A: STRESS, STRESSORS, AND HOW TO COPE

Multiple Choice

1. In what way can we say that stress is like a motivator?
   ___a. It has a physiological component.   ___c. It arouses and directs behavior.
   ___b. It feels bad.   ___d. It occurs without awareness.

2. A real or perceived threat to one's sense of well-being defines
   ___a. stress.   ___c. a psychological disorder.
   ___b. anxiety.   ___d. a stressor.

3. The concept of frustration is based on which fundamental assumption?
   ___a. People are basically good and mean well.
   ___b. Motivation and emotion both involve a visceral reaction.
   ___c. Behavior is motivated, or goal-directed.
   ___d. Stress results from negative, unfortunate experiences.

4. Which of these provides the best example of frustration?
   ___a. You get a flat tire on the way to an important meeting.
   ___b. You can't decide what courses to take next semester.
   ___c. Your best friend is going to get married.
   ___d. You win the lottery and now everyone wants to be your friend.

5. As adults, which conflict situation do we tend to experience the LEAST?
   ___a. approach-approach   ___c. approach-avoidance
   ___b. avoidance-avoidance   ___d. multiple approach-avoidance

6. Scott is going to get a new car and cannot decide if he wants the white one or the red one. Scott is in
   a(n) _____ conflict.
   ___a. approach-approach   ___c. approach-avoidance
   ___b. avoidance-avoidance   ___d. multiple approach-avoidance

7. Josh used to be able to play 36 holes of golf in a day without much effort, Now, given his age and
   general physical condition, he finds it too tiring to play that much, and this—in turn—he finds
   stressful. We would best describe Josh's stress as induced by
   ___a. environmental frustration.   ___c. an approach-approach conflict.
   ___b. personal frustration.   ___d. a frustration-aggression hypothesis.

8. The most adaptive reaction to the stressors in one's life is
   ___a learning.   ___c. aggression.
   ___b. frustration.   ___d. fixation.

9. Of these mechanisms for coping with stress and stressors, which is the most ineffective or inefficient?
   ___a. engaging in cognitive reappraisal   ___c. fixating
   ___b. gathering social support   ___d. taking relaxation training

10. What, essentially, is conflicted when we are in a conflict?
    ___a. perceptions   ___c. motives
    ___b. emotions   ___d. cognitions

11. Which of the following seems to be describing something other than an avoidance-avoidance conflict?
    ___a. out of the frying pan, into the fire   ___c. damned if you do and damned if you don't
    ___b. all dressed up and no place to go   ___d. stuck between a rock and a hard place

12. When adults rate the most stress-inducing life event they can imagine, which event gets scored as the most stressful?

    ___a. the death of a spouse   ___c. a divorce

    ___b. an exam just before the holidays   ___d. an illness while pregnant

13. The very first stage of Selye's General Adaptation Syndrome is

    ___a. awareness.   ___c. denial.

    ___b. alarm.   ___d. homeostasis.

14. Persons with "hardy personalities" demonstrate each of the following EXCEPT a tendency to

    ___a. see difficulties as challenges and opportunities.

    ___b. try to get more and do more than most others.

    ___c. believe that one is in control of one's fate.

    ___d. be actively involved in what is going on in one's life.

15. Which of the following strategies is classified as "problem-focused" rather than "emotion-focused"?

    ___a. engaging in cognitive reappraisal   ___c. seeking social support

    ___b. learning techniques of relaxation   ___d. engaging in physical exercise

True/False

1. ____True ____False   Stress is so unpleasant, so negative a reaction, that we can say that the only way to be truly happy in life is to avoid stress altogether.

2. ____True ____False   The "frustration-aggression hypothesis" claims that all aggression results from frustration.

3. ____True ____False   When goal-directed behaviors are blocked or thwarted, the result is frustration.

4. ____True ____False   Avoidance-avoidance conflicts cannot be resolved, which is why they are so stressful.

5. ____True ____False   Something that is a stressor for one person, may not be for another person.

6. ____True ____False   Because making difficult decisions can be stress-inducing, psychologists recommend that tough decisions be made quickly to get them over with, so that one may deal with the resulting stress and then "move on."

7. ____True ____False   Learning techniques of relaxation, as in biofeedback, is an example of a so-called "problem-focused strategy" for dealing with stress and stressors.

TOPIC 11B: HEALTH PSYCHOLOGY

Multiple Choice

1. Whereas clinical psychology is concerned with psychological disorders, the field of health psychology is concerned with
   ___a. persons who do not have and have never had such disorders.
   ___b. personality disorders.
   ___c. physical health and well-being.
   ___d. psychological disorders that have physical symptoms.

2. Which of the following is NOT an assumption of health psychology?
   ___a. Behavioral interventions in health care are cost effective.
   ___b. If psychological disorders were better treated, there would be fewer physical health problems.
   ___c. It is likely to be easier and safer to change behaviors than to treat some diseases.
   ___d. Behaviors may increase or decrease the risk of certain diseases.

3. The most positive correlation between personality variables and physical health are for associations that predict
   ___a. stomach problems, such as ulcers.   ___c. coronary heart disease.
   ___b. skin rashes and skin disorders.   ___d. many (but not all) varieties of cancer.

4. Which characteristic or description is NOT included in the Type A behavior pattern?
   ___a. high cholesterol levels   ___c. achievement orientation
   ___b. lack of patience   ___d. general hostility

5. Which of these characteristics is a prime candidate as an "active ingredient" in the Type A behavior pattern?
   ___a. hostility and anger   ___c. being hurried
   ___b. commitment to hard work   ___d. egocentrism

6. What one behavior change would have the greatest impact on physical health in the United States?
   ___a. stopping smoking   ___c. drinking less caffeine
   ___b. eating less saturated fat   ___d. using condoms

7. Psychologists estimate that _____ of the 10 leading causes of death in the United States are in large measure behaviorally determined.
   ___a. 1   ___c. 5
   ___b. 3   ___d. 7

8. With regard to cigarette smoking, which statement is FALSE?
   ___a. There would be about 100,000 fewer deaths in the United States if no one smoked.
   ___b. There is no evidence that secondhand smoke is related to lung cancer.
   ___c. About 80 percent of those who quit smoking start up again within one year.
   ___d. We are better at getting people not to smoke in the first place than we are at getting smokers to stop.

9. Of these, a person is LEAST likely to be diagnosed as having
   ___a. chlamydia.   ___c. syphilis.
   ___b. gonorrhea.   ___d. AIDS.

10. AIDS is caused by
   ___a. having any sort of sex with someone who is HIV-infected.
   ___b. a strain of bacteria.
   ___c. improperly handled blood or semen.
   ___d. a virus.

11. Of these, the "subgroup" that has changed its behaviors most in response to the AIDS epidemic is
   ___a. homosexual males.   ___c. homosexual females.
   ___b. sexually active teenagers.   ___d. sexually active senior citizens.

True/False

1. ____True ____False   Health psychologists received their Ph.D. in I/O, or industrial/organizational psychology.

2. ____True ____False   Following a heart attack, women with Type A personalities have a survival advantage over women with Type B personalities.

3. ____True ____False   Once AIDS develops, death is certain.

Key Terms and Concepts
Topic 11A

stress_____

_____

stressors_____

_____

frustration_____

_____

approach-approach conflict_____

_____

avoidance-avoidance conflict_____

_____

approach-avoidance conflict_____

_____

multiple approach-avoidance conflict_____

_____

socioeconomic status (SES)_____

_____

general adaptation syndrome (GAS)_____

_____

emotion-focused strategies_____

_____

problem-focused strategies_____

_____

biofeedback_____

_____

frustration-aggression hypothesis_____

_____

Topic 11B

health psychology_____

_____

biopsychosocial model_____

_____

Type A behavior pattern (TABP)_____

_____

sexually transmitted diseases (STDs)_____

_____

acquired immune deficiency disease (AIDS)_____

_____

Answers to Practice Test Questions

TOPIC 11A: STRESS, STRESSORS, AND HOW TO COPE

Multiple Choice

1. **c**   Although alternatives **a** and **b** may be true (alternative **d** is meaningless), it is the third statement that best describes the relationship between stress and motivation.
2. **d**   This is a good definition of a stressor—not stress, please note. Stress is a reaction or a response.
3. **c**   By definition, frustration is the blocking or thwarting of goal-directed behavior, and is based on the assumption that, in fact, behaviors are goal-directed.
4. **a**   The first example is one of frustration—environmental frustration at that.
5. **c**   I suppose that we could argue about this one, because I do not have quality data to support my assertion that as adults we tend to "keep our options open" and are seldom faced with a situation in which there is just one option available, and thus less frequently get "trapped" in simple approach-avoidance conflicts.
6. **a**   I think that most of us will agree that we're not going to feel too sorry for Scott, momentarily stuck in an approach-approach conflict.
7. **b**   This is a long one (and a little self-disclosing), isn't it? What I mean to be getting at here is someone who is experiencing frustration and stress because of some personal reason, hence, personal frustration.
8. **a**   Only learning—bringing abut a relatively permanent change—is an adaptive response to the stressors in our lives.
9. **c**   Each of the others is at least a little bit helpful, but fixating—just doing the same thing over and over—obviously isn't working and is inefficient.
10. **c**   We have to perceive a problem. We have to think about it (a cognition). We are likely to get emotional. But stress-inducing conflicts are called "motivational conflicts" because what is conflicted are own motives, drives, desires, wishes, wants, etc.
11. **b**   Isn't this one down-right "cute"? Being all dressed up with no place to go might lead to the experience of stress, but I cannot see how it can be classified as an avoidance-avoidance conflict.
12. **a**   There seems to be no more stress-producing experience (on average) than the loss of one's spouse.
13. **b**   In fact, in Selye's GAS, the stages are alarm, resistance and exhaustion.
14. **b**   The first, third, and fourth alternatives describe the hardy personality type quite well, whereas the second alternative is unrelated.
15. **a**   Cognitive reappraisal is the only technique mentioned here that actually gets to the source and nature of one's stressor, rather than dealing with the feelings that result from stress.

True/False

1. **F**   Wouldn't it be sad if this statement were true? It would be sad because it is just not possible to "avoid stress altogether."
2. **T**   The frustration-aggression hypothesis is wrong, of course, but this is what it says.
3. **T**   This is a pretty good definition of frustration.
4. **F**   Avoidance-avoidance conflicts are nasty and unpleasant, and resolving them can be difficult at times, but surely they can be resolved.
5. **T**   Not only can something be a stressor for someone and not for someone else, but that same event may not produce stress at some other time.
6. **F**   Quite the contrary. Rushing through a tough decision just to get it over with may end up causing you even more grief. The advice is to take one's time and be as sure as possible.
7. **F**   Relaxation techniques surely can help one feel better, and there's nothing wrong with that, but relaxation is an emotion-focused strategy because it will not help minimize or eliminate the stressor underlying the stress.

TOPIC 11B: HEALTH PSYCHOLOGY

Multiple Choice

1. **c**   By definition, health psychologists are involved in the management and prevention of physical illness and disease, whether psychological disorders are involved or not.
2. **b**   The second statement may very well be true, but it certainly is not one of the basic assumptions of health psychology, where the others are.
3. **c**   Perhaps because it is so deadly, there is a lot of concern about coronary heart disease (CHD), and it is one set of physical disorders that is reasonably well correlated with psychological variables.
4. **a**   High cholesterol level is a physical measure, not a psychological one, as required to be a part of the TABP.
5. **a**   Each of these is a potential candidate for causing physical health problems, but of these, one's degree of anger or hostility seems to best predict physical health problems, CHD, in particular.
6. **a**   Again, each of these would be helpful, but none would be so significant as getting everyone to stop smoking.
7. **d**   Here I go again with what may look like trivial statistics—but these are so impressive! The best answer is that nearly three-quarters (70 percent) of the top ten causes of death in the United States are largely determined by unhealthy behaviors.
8. **b**   The second statement, about secondhand smoke, we know now, is absolutely false. Because this statement is so clearly false, I don't mind listing the others with statistics in them.
9. **d**   AIDS is very worrisome, of course, and can be deadly, but it is the least common (by far) of the sexually transmitted diseases listed.
10. **d**   It may get into the bloodstream through blood or semen, but the cause of AIDS is a virus, HIV.
11. **a**   The subgroup (and please remember how careful we must be about making any general statements about any subgroups) that has changed most is that of homosexual males—although some very recent data suggest that there may be some reversal of that phenomenon going on.

True/False

1. **F**   They may have been, but they were most likely trained as health psychologists, one of the fastest-growing areas of interest in psychology.
2. **T**   Sounds strange, and the data are a bit tentative but unlike for men, for women this observation is true.
3. **T**   This may be the saddest item on any test, simply because it is true.

EXPERIENCING PSYCHOLOGY

Make a Log of Your Stressors

As a college student—no matter what your age—you are no stranger to stress. Stress is a universal experience, and it is one that is very common among college students. Granted that stress cannot be completely avoided, perhaps some of the stressors in your life can be. A preliminary step to reducing one's stressors is to identify them honestly. The basic question of this exercise is, "What events or situations in your life, *right now*, are causing stress?

For three days in a row, keep a log of those things that you find stressful. At least one of the three days should be a class day and one should be a weekend day when you have no classes scheduled. From the minute you get up, and at one-hour intervals all day long, pause and reflect: "What aggravated you within the last hour?" "What hassles did you encounter?" "What made your blood pressure rise?" "What made you angry?" "What did you find upsetting?" "What conflicts or frustrations did you face?"

With any luck, there may be several hours in each day when the honest answer to these questions is "nothing." We may experience stress regularly, but we don't necessarily experience new stressors every hour of every day. Actually, stopping every hour to consider one's stressors can itself be quite an annoying hassle, but it will only be for three days, and it may be very revealing.

After three days of self-observation, look back over your list of stressors and hassles very carefully. Do any patterns emerge? Are there any particular situations in which you are most likely to experience stress? Are these situations avoidable? Do any particular people trigger a stress response for you? Are these people avoidable? Can you classify the stressors of your three-day log as being primarily frustrations, conflicts, or just life events? What can you change to minimize these stressors in your life?

This is an exercise that you can repeat throughout the semester. It might be interesting to compare your log with that of one of your friends. How does your log of stressors in mid-semester compare to one that you construct during finals week; or when you are at home for the holidays; or on vacation?

Chapter 12

The Psychological Disorders

STUDY TIP #12

Preparing For Exams I: The Difference Between Learning and Performance

Learning is a process that takes place inside an individual. We cannot see learning take place. We cannot plot its course. What we must do is infer that learning has taken place by measuring an individual's performance. Simply put, learning involves acquiring new information; performance involves retrieving that information when it is needed. And, justifiably or not, it is your performance that tends to be evaluated. Your performance, not your learning, earns your grades in the classroom and your raise or promotion in the workplace.

So how will this great insight help your study? If you accept my premise, it means that you need to spend time and effort learning new information—here new information about psychology. But then you also ought to spend some time practicing what is really going to be graded: your retrieval of that information. And how do you do that? In the simplest terms, you test yourself. You test yourself (practice retrieval) before your instructor comes along and tests you for real.

There are a couple of things you might consider. Once you have finished reading a section of the textbook, feel that you understand it quite well, and can adequately answer the "Before You Go On" questions there, think about how the information in that section might show up on your next classroom exam. If you had to generate three multiple-choice questions over that material, what might they be? Yes, you may "know" the information now, but will you recognize it when it appears on a test? The other thing that you can do, of course, is to work through the "Practice Tests" that we have provided for each of the Topics in the text. These questions are not likely to show up on your classroom exams, but at least they give you an idea of what sorts of questions we psychology professors can dream up. A note: Please don't rely on Practice Tests as a primary means of studying. They don't help much in the process of elaborating on new information and forming new memories. They are designed to help in improving your performance, not your original learning.

Outline ~ Chapter 12: The Psychological Disorders

TOPIC 12A: Anxiety, Somatoform, Dissociative, and Personality Disorders

I. What is "Abnormal"?
    A. **Abnormal** refers to maladaptive cognitions, affects, and/or behaviors that are at odds with social expectations and result in distress or discomfort.
    B. What may be abnormal and disordered in one culture or social situation may be viewed as normal and commonplace in another.

II. Classifying Abnormal Reactions: The DSM
    A. **Diagnosis** is the act of recognizing a disorder on the basis of a specified set of symptoms.
    B. Emil Kraepelin published the first classification scheme for "mental disturbances" in 1883.
    C. The American Psychiatric Association published its system for classifying psychological disorders, *The Diagnostic and Statistical Manual of Mental Disorders*, in 1952.
        1. The most recent edition, published in 2000, is the DSM-IV-TR (where TR stands for "text revision").
        2. The DSM-IV lists 297 different diagnostic categories.
        3. Except for known biological factors, the manual attempts to avoid reference to etiology, or causes, of disorders.
        4. The system is important for adequate communication concerning disorders.

III. Problems with Classification and Labeling
    A. The DSM-IV refers only to disordered behaviors, not to disordered people.
    B. Labels *do not explain* behavior and may stick long after the symptoms are gone.
    C. **Comorbidity** refers to the occurrence of two or more disorders in the same individual.
        1. For those suffering any disorder in his or her lifetime, nearly 80 percent will have two or more disorders.
        2. Many psychological disorders are also comorbid with physical illnesses.

IV. A Word on "Insanity"
    A. The term insanity is a legal term, not a psychological one.
    B. **Insanity** usually requires that one did not know or fully understand the consequences of his or her actions at a given time, could not discern the difference between right and wrong, and was unable to exercise control over his or her actions at the time a crime was committed.
    C. A related issue, competence, concerns whether one is in control of his or her mental and intellectual functions to understand courtroom procedures and aid in his or her own defense.

V. A Few Cautions
    A. "Abnormal" and "normal" are not two distinct categories.
    B. Abnormal does not mean dangerous.
        1. People jailed for violent crimes are no more likely to have a psychological dosorder than not jailed persons.
        2. Persons with psychological disorders are more likely than persons without such disorders to be *victims* of violent crimes.
    C. Abnormal does not mean bad.
    D. Psychological disorders may occur in mild and moderate forms.

VI. Anxiety Disorders
    A. **Anxiety** refers to a feeling of general apprehension or dread accompanied by predictable physiological changes.
        1. Anxiety disorders are the most common of all the psychological disorders, affecting 13.3 percent (19.1 million persons) in the U.S. aged 18-54.
        2. They are diagnosed two to three times more in women than in men.

B. The major symptom of **generalized anxiety disorder** is distressing, felt anxiety.
   1. Anxiety may be intense or diffuse, and can cause substantial interference.
   2. People with this disorder may be prone to drug and alcohol abuse.
C. In **panic disorder**, the major symptom is more acute—a recurrent, unpredictable, unprovoked onset of sudden, intense anxiety, or a "panic attack."
   1. Onset is usually between adolescence and the mid-twenties.
   2. A comorbid diagnosis of depression significantly increases the rate of suicide and suicide attempts.
D. The essential feature of **phobic disorders** is a persistent and excessive fear of some object, activity, or situation that consistently leads a person to avoid that object, activity, or situation.
   1. **Specific phobias** involve fear of animals; the physical environment; blood, injection or injury; or a specific situation.
   2. **Social phobias** are significant and persistent fears of social or performance situations in which embarrassment may occur.
   3. The prognosis (the prediction of the future course of a disorder) is good for phobic disorders, but few seek professional assistance.
   4. **Agoraphobia** means "fear of open places."
E. The **obsessive-compulsive disorder (OCD)** is an anxiety disorder characterized by a pattern of recurrent obsessions and compulsions.
   1. **Obsessions** are ideas or thoughts that involuntarily and constantly intrude into awareness.
   2. **Compulsions** are constantly intruding, repetitive behaviors.
   3. It seems that OCD has a biological basis, but the general prognosis is not good.
F. **Posttraumatic stress disorder (PTSD)** involves distressing symptoms that arise some time after the experience of a highly traumatic event.
   1. The person must have experienced, witnessed, or been confronted with an event that involves actual or threatened death or serious injury.
   2. The person's response involves intense fear, helplessness, or horror.
   3. Three additional clusters of symptoms include re-experiencing the event via flashbacks or nightmares, avoidance of possible reminders of the event, and increased arousal or "hyperalertness."
   4. Estimates of the lifetime prevalence of PTSD range from about two percent to eight percent of the population.
   5. PTSD is commonly associated with alcohol and substance abuse or depression.

VII. Somatoform Disorders
   A. The **somatoform disorders** involve physical, bodily symptoms or complaints with no known medical or biological cause for the symptoms.
   B. **Hypochondriasis** is the diagnosis for someone preoccupied with the fear of a serious disease.
      1. Persons with this disorder are unusually aware of every ache and pain.
      2. It affects men and women equally.
   C. **Somatization disorder** is characterized by several, recurrent, long-lasting complaints about physical symptoms for which there is no physical cause.
   D. In **conversion disorder**, there is a loss or altering of physical functioning that suggests a physical disorder, but there is no medical explanation for the symptoms.
      1. One remarkable symptom of this disorder (which occurs only in some patients) is known as *la belle indifference,* a seemingly inappropriate lack of concern over one's condition.
      2. The Greeks knew this disorder; they named it hysteria.
      3. This disorder intrigued Freud, which led him to develop a new method of therapy.

VIII. Dissociative Disorders
   A. The underlying theme of the **dissociative disorders** is that a person seeks to escape from some aspect of life or personality seen as the source of stress, discomfort, or anxiety.
   B. **Dissociative amnesia** is the inability to recall important personal information—an inability too extensive to be explained by ordinary forgetfulness.

1. What is forgotten is usually some traumatic incident and some or all of the experiences that led up to or followed it.
2. There is no medical explanation for the loss of memory.
3. These cases tend to be more common in wartime.
   - C. When amnesic forgetfulness is accompanied by a change of location, the disorder is known as **dissociative fugue.**
   - D. The major symptom of **dissociative identity disorder** is the existence within the same person of two or more distinct personalities or traits.
     1. This disorder is still commonly known as multiple personality disorder.
     2. Changes in personality are dramatic and extreme.
     3. Changes can take place without warning or provocation.
     4. Which personality will be dominant cannot be predicted or controlled by the individual.
     5. People with this disorder often have been the victim of child abuse or sexual abuse.
     6. The diagnosis is rarely made in other countries.

IX. Personality Disorders
   - A. **Personality disorders** are long-lasting patterns of perceiving, relating to, and thinking about the environment and oneself that are maladaptive and inflexible and cause either impaired functioning or distress.
   - B. The DSM-IV lists eleven personality disorders, which are clustered in three groups.
     1. Cluster I includes disorders of odd or eccentric reactions such as paranoid personality disorder or schizoid personality disorder.
     2. Cluster II includes disorders of dramatic, emotional or erratic reactions, such as histrionic and narcissistic personality disorders.
     3. Cluster III disorders involve anxiety and fearfulness such as avoidant personality disorder or dependent personality disorder.
   - C. Cluster I: Disorders of Odd or Eccentric Reactions
     1. *Paranoid personality* refers to extreme sensitivity, suspiciousness, envy, and mistrust of others.
     2. *Schizoid personality* refers to an inability to form, and an indifference to, interpersonal relationships.
   - D. Cluster II: Disorders of Dramatic, Emotional, or Erratic Reactions
     1. *Histrionic personality* disorder describes someone who is overly dramatic, reactive, and demonstrates intensely expressed behavior.
     2. *Narcissistic personality* disorder reflects a grandiose exaggeration of self-importance, a need for attention or admiration, and a tendency to set unrealistic goals.
   - E. Cluster III: Disorders Involving Anxiety and Fearfulness
     1. *Avoidant personality* disorder refers to an over-sensitivity to the possibility of being rejected by others and an unwillingness to enter into relationships for fear of being rejected.
     2. *Dependent personality* disorder describes a person who allows and seeks others to dominate and assume responsibility for action; this person has a poor self-image and lacks confidence.
   - F. The prognosis for the personality disorders is poor.
   - G. The **antisocial personality disorder** is characterized by an exceptional lack of regard for the rights and property of others, accompanied by impulsive, often criminal behaviors.
     1. Persons with the disorder used to be called "psychopaths" or "sociopaths."
     2. Symptoms include deceit and manipulation of others without guilt or regret.
     3. The disorder is more common among persons of low socioeconomic status, who live in an urban setting and have a history of symptoms dating from childhood.
     4. Although the disorder is very resistant to treatment, there is evidence of a burnout factor when these people reach their 40s.

TOPIC 12B: ALZHEIMER'S DEMENTIA, MOOD DISORDERS, AND SCHIZOPHRENIA

I.   Alzheimer's Dementia
    A.   Dementia is a condition characterized by the marked loss of intellectual abilities.
    B.   A slow deterioration of one's intellectual functioning is the most common symptom associated with **Alzheimer's disease**; personality changes also occur.
    C.   It is a physical disease caused by abnormal changes in brain tissue.
    D.   It is diagnosed with certainty at autopsy.
        1.   There will be a mass of tangles of abnormal protein fibers.
        2.   Waste materials, called plaques, are degenerated nerve fibers that wrap around a core of protein.
        3.   There will be small cavities filled with fluid and debris.
        4.   Atrophy will be evident.
    E.   It is a disorder becoming increasingly more common.
        1.   About 7 million in North America and Europe have been diagnosed.
        2.   In the year 2000 there were 4.5 million persons in the U. S. diagnosed with Alzheimer's; by the year 2050, that number is estimated to be 13.2 million.
    F.   There is a genetic predisposition for the disorder.
        1.   Obesity is a risk factor for developing Alzheimer's dementia.
        2.   Receiving a head injury or trauma is a risk factor.
        3.   Using folic acid in one's diet may reduce the chance of getting Alzheimer's.
        4.   Engaging in cognitively challenging activities may reduce the risk of Alzheimer's dementia in old age.
    G.   A number of hypotheses are being investigated for the cause and treatment of the disorder.

II. Mood Disorders
    A.   With **mood disorders**, the intensity or extreme nature of one's mood is the major symptom.
    B.   **Major depression** is the diagnosis for a constellation of symptoms that includes feeling sad, low, and hopeless, coupled with a loss of pleasure or interest in most normal activities.
    C.   **Dysthymia** is a mild case of major depression, but it tends to be more chronic, or continuous.
    D.   In **bipolar disorder**, episodes of depression are occasionally interspersed with episodes of mania.
        1.   This is still referred to as "manic depression."
        2.   **Mania** is characterized as an elevated mood with feelings of euphoria or irritability and increased levels of activity.

III. Observations on the Causes of Depression
    A.   There is evidence for a genetic, or inherited, predisposition to the bipolar mood disorder.
    B.   We suspect that there is a genetic basis for major depression as well.
    C.   The **diathesis-stress model** proposes that the expression of disordered behaviors (particularly depression) results from the interaction of an inherited predisposition and the experience of stress or trauma.
        1.   Some neurotransmitters, collectively referred to as biogenic amines, appear to influence mood.
        2.   Brain anatomy appears to be different for some of the individual disorders.
    D.   A variety of psychological factors may influence the development of depression.
        1.   These could include learning experiences, situational stress, and cognitive factors.
        2.   Freud believed that depression was a reflection of early childhood experiences that leads to anger directed inwardly.
        3.   Women are twice as likely than men to be diagnosed with mood disorders.

IV. Schizophrenia
  A. **Schizophrenia** involves a distortion of reality and a retreat from other people, accompanied by disturbances in affect, behavior, and cognition.
  B. Schizophrenia can be found around the world at the same rate: about 1 percent of the population
  C. Recent research indicates that schizophrenia has three dimensions of symptoms.
    1. **Negative symptoms** refer to emotional and social withdrawal, reduced energy and motivation, apathy and poor attention.
    2. **Positive psychotic symptoms** include hallucinations and delusions.
      a. **Hallucinations** are false perceptions.
      b. **Delusions** are false beliefs.
    3. Positive disorganized symptoms of schizophrenia include disorders of thinking and speech, bizarre behaviors, and inappropriate affect.
  D. The correlates of negative symptoms include structural abnormalities in the brain, a clearer genetic basis, more severe complications at birth, a lower educational level, poorer adjustment patterns before onset, and a poorer prognosis.
  E. Correlated with both types of positive symptoms are excesses of the neurotransmitter dopamine, relatively normal brain configuration, severe disruptions in early family life, over-activity and aggressiveness in adolescence, and a relatively good response to treatment.
  F. Not all of the data on typing schizophrenia has been supportive.
  G. The DSM-IV-TR characterizes schizophrenic subtypes as paranoid, disorganized, catatonic, and undifferentiated.

V. What Causes Schizophrenia?
  A. Schizophrenia has a genetic basis (though not as clearly so as mood disorders).
  B. Schizophrenia is a disease of the brain.
  C. The role of dopamine in excess amounts in the brain is being investigated.
  D. Another theory is that some people are genetically prone to develop the symptoms of schizophrenia when they are exposed to stressors—the diathesis-stress model, again.
  E. The consensus, however, is that schizophrenia is a complex disease of the brain, not a "disorder of living."

Practice Test Questions

TOPIC 12A: ANXIETY, SOMATOFORM, DISSOCIATIVE, AND PERSONALITY DISORDERS

Multiple Choice

1. As you read this item, which provides the best estimate of the percentage of North Americans suffering from a psychological disorder?
   ___a. 10 percent   ___c. 40 percent
   ___b. 20 percent   ___d. There is no way to make such an estimate.

2. Which words, terms, or concepts are NOT included in your textbook's definition of abnormality?
   ___a. maladaptive   ___c. distress or discomfort
   ___b. bizarre or strange   ___d. affect, behavior, and/or cognition

3. Which of the following is TRUE concerning people with psychological disorders?
   ___a. They tend to be more dangerous than others.
   ___b. They usually realize that they have some sort of problem.
   ___c. They are distinctly different from persons who are normal.
   ___d. They are people who have poor self-control or will power.

4. The "etiology" of a disorder refers to the
   ___a. cause of the disorder.   ___c. type of treatment called for.
   ___b. extent to which it is disabling.   ___d. nature of the likely outcome of the disorder.

5. Classification schemes and labels for psychological disorders, such as those found in the DSM-IV-TR, have some potential problems. Which of these is NOT one of those problems?
   ___a. Labels tend to dehumanize real human suffering.
   ___b. There is no logical or sensible rationale behind such schemes.
   ___c. They usually focus on the individual and not the larger group to which the person belongs.
   ___d. Schemes and labels may define and describe but they do not explain.

6. Tracy reports feeling anxious, nervous, and "on edge" all day long. She is tired, but cannot seem to sleep well. Sometimes she feels like crying for no reason at all. If Tracy has a disorder, the best diagnosis is probably that Tracy is experiencing a _____ disorder.
   ___a. psychogenic fugue   ___c. generalized anxiety
   ___b. obsessive-compulsive   ___d. panic

7. What two words best differentiate between panic disorder and generalized anxiety disorder?
   ___a. acute and chronic   ___c. rational and irrational
   ___b. stimulus and response   ___d. distress and discomfort

8. More than anything else, what is the difference between fear and anxiety?
   ___a. Fear is more commonly irrational; anxiety is rational.
   ___b. Fear involves the autonomic nervous system, anxiety does not.
   ___c. Fear is the symptom of a disorder; anxiety is not.
   ___d. Fear requires an object; anxiety does not.

9. Everything else being equal, which of these disorders has the best prognosis?
   ___a. schizophrenia   ___c. phobic disorder
   ___b. dissociative identity disorder   ___d. antisocial personality disorder

10. Constantly checking and rechecking to confirm that the front door is really locked may be a sign of
    ___a. a fugue state.   ___c. a conversion disorder.
    ___b. a phobia.   ___d. an obsessive-compulsive disorder.

11. Which of these is most likely to result from experiencing some real, life-threatening event?
    ___a. psychogenic fugue   ___c. posttraumatic stress disorder
    ___c. child abuse   ___d. panic attacks

12. By definition, what do the somatoform disorders have in common?
    ___a. either hallucinations or delusions   ___c. exaggerated fears and anxiety
    ___b. bodily symptoms or complaints   ___d. feelings of profound depression

13. The disorder that used to be called multiple personality disorder is
    ___a. significantly less common than it was 50 years ago.
    ___b. now one of the more common forms of schizophrenia.
    ___c. classified as a dissociative identity disorder.
    ___d. characterized by a sense of *la belle indifference.*

14. More than anything else, what do personality disorders have in common that makes them different
    from other varieties of psychological disorders?
    ___a. As a group, they are extremely rare.
    ___b. They involve significant levels of anxiety.
    ___c. They tend to begin at an early age and to be long lasting.
    ___d. They generally provide more distress for the person with the disorder than for others.

True/False

1. ____True ____False   Insanity is a term that comes form the legal profession, not from psychology or psychiatry.

2. ____True ____False   Classifying psychological disorders is a project that was begun in the 1950s and culminated in the first Diagnostic Manual in 1960.

3. ____True ____False   By definition, psychological disorders must involve one's affect, one's behaviors, or one's cognitions.

4. ____True ____False   Although comorbidity is common among the personality disorders, it rarely occurs with the anxiety disorders.

5. ____True ____False   Social phobias include the fears of eating in public and public speaking.

6. ____True ____False   Although it is classified as an anxiety disorder, there is increasing evidence that OCD has a strong biological basis.

7. ____True ____False   The phenomenon known as *la belle indifference* is best associated with conversion disorder.

8. ____True ____False   People with antisocial disorder used to be called "psychopaths" or "sociopaths."

TOPIC 12B: ALZHEIMER'S DEMENTIA, MOOD DISORDERS, AND SCHIZOPHRENIA

Multiple Choice

1. If someone experiences delusions, this symptom shows us a disorder of
   ___a. affect.   ___c. cognition.
   ___b. behavior.   ___d. affect, behavior, or cognition, depending.

2. Alzheimer's dementia
   ___a. is a physical disease of the brain and, therefore, is not listed in the DSM-IV-TR.
   ___b. cannot be diagnosed before one's death.
   ___c. occurs only in the elderly (persons over 75).
   ___d. is degenerative and deadly.

3. The collection of disorders called "mood disorders" has as its major symptom
   ___a. disorganized thinking and confusion.
   ___b. the experience of strange, unexplainable behaviors.
   ___c. disturbances of affect.
   ___d. cognitive disorientation.

4. By far, the most common form of mood disorder is
   ___a. depression.   ___c. paranoia.
   ___b. bipolar.   ___d. mania.

5. Concerning mood disorders, which of the following is FALSE?
   ___a. Depression is more common in women than in men.
   ___b. It is more common to find depression alone than mania alone.
   ___c. Depression generally occurs in a series of episodes.
   ___d. The symptoms of mania rarely recur or relapse.

6. Of these factors, which seems LEAST likely to be involved as a cause of depression?
   ___a. hormone levels   ___c. neurotranmitters
   ___b. genetic predispositions   ___d. biogenic amines

7. Which of these symptoms tends NOT to be associated with schizophrenia?
   ___a. high levels of felt anxiety
   ___b. social withdrawal and retreat from others
   ___c. flattened affect
   ___d. disturbed cognitions, including delusions

8. Which of these would be considered to be a positive symptom of schizophrenia?
   ___a. a good prognosis   ___c. hallucinations
   ___b. loss of affect   ___d. social withdrawal

9. About which statement concerning the causes of schizophrenia do we feel most certain?
   ___a. Dopamine causes schizophrenia.
   ___b. Schizophrenia results from child abuse.
   ___c. Schizophrenia runs in families.
   ___d. Parents of schizophrenic persons are cold and aloof.

True/False

1. ____True ____False   Rates of death attributed to Alzheimer's dementia have increased markedly over the past 35 years.

2. ____True ____False   By definition, patients cannot be depressed and anxious at the same time.

3. ____True ____False   Dysthymia is another (technical) term for major depressive disorder.

4. ____True ____False   Schizophrenia means "split mind"—literally, splitting of the mind into two (or more) different, yet distinct, personalities.

5. ____True ____False   About one-quarter of those diagnosed with schizophrenia will simply never get better.

Key Terms and Concepts
Topic 12A

abnormal_____

_____

diagnosis_____

_____

etiology_____

_____

comorbidity_____

_____

insanity_____

_____

anxiety_____

_____

generalized anxiety disorder_____

_____

panic disorder_____

_____

phobic disorder_____

_____

specific phobias_____

_____

social phobias_____

_____

agoraphobia_____

_____

obsessive compulsive disorder_____

_____

obsessions_____

_____

compulsions_____

_____

posttraumatic stress disorder_____

_____

somatoform disorders_____

_____

hypochondriasis_____

_____

somatization disorder_____

_____

conversion disorder_____

_____

dissociative disorders_____

_____

dissociative amnesia_____

_____

dissociative fugue_____

_____

dissociative identity disorder_____

_____

personality disorders (PDs)_____

_____

antisocial personality disorder_____

_____

Topic 12B

dementia_____

_____

Alzheimer's dementia_____

_____

mood disorders_____

_____

major depressive disorder_____

_____

dysthymia_____

_____

bipolar disorder_____

_____

mania_____

_____

diathesis-stress model_____

_____

schizophrenia_____

_____

negative symptoms of schizophrenia_____

_____

positive symptoms of schizophrenia_____

_____

delusions_____

_____

hallucinations_____

_____

Answers to Practice Test Questions

TOPIC 12A: ANXIETY, SOMATOFORM, DISSOCIATIVE, AND PERSONALITY DISORDERS

Multiple Choice

1. **b**   Granted that it's only an estimate and granted that it's a bit too conservative, but of these choices, the best bet would be to say that approximately 20 percent of the population has a psychological disorder at any point in time.
2. **b**   Yes, some reactions of persons with psychological disorders may seem strange or bizarre, but these terms are certainly not part of the definition of abnormality.
3. **b**   One of the sad realities of mental disorders is that—in virtually every case—the person with the disorder is (or at one time was) aware of the fact that something is not right. The other alternatives are simply false statements.
4. **a**   Etiology means source or cause; prognosis is the term used to describe the likely outcome of a disorder.
5. **b**   There are several problems with schemes for labeling and classifying disorders, but each of those schemes is certainly based on some logical or sensible rationale for doing so.
6. **c**   This is a pretty good description of the symptoms of generalized anxiety disorder.
7. **a**   The anxiety in panic disorder is acute—of short duration, but intense—while the anxiety of generalized anxiety disorder is chronic—of long duration.
8. **d**   Typically, fear requires an object, anxiety does not. We talk of being afraid of something, which implies an object of that fear.
9. **c**   By definition. All disorders are unpleasant and distressing, but in most cases, phobias are easily treated and have a very positive prognosis.
10. **d**   This would be a definitional symptom of obsessive-compulsive disorder.
11. **c**   Real, life-threatening events eventually can result in a wide range of disorders, but the best choice here is posttraumatic stress disorder because it virtually defines the disorder. (Again—you've got to know those definitions!)
12. **b**   Soma means "body," hence, somatoform disorders involve some bodily symptoms or complaints.
13. **c**   There is little doubt that psychologists will continue to talk about "multiple personalities" for some time, but the DSM-IV-TR correctly now names this as "dissociative identity disorder."
14. **c**   Not only is the third alternative, **c**, the correct choice, but the other alternatives are nearly the opposite of being true.

True/False

1. **T**   Insanity is a term that has been around for a long time in many different contexts. As it is used today, however, it is a legal term, not a psychological one.
2. **F**   No, systems for classifying disorders go back to at least the late 1800s—remember Kraepelin?
3. **T**   Psychological disorders impact on one's psychological functioning, and we have agreed that one's psychological functioning involves either affect, behavior, or cognition.
4. **F**   Comorbidity, remember, is the joint occurrence of two disorders in the same person at the same time. Yes, comorbidity is common among the personality disorders, but it is similarly common among the anxiety disorders as well.
5. **T**   Indeed, these would be two excellent examples of social phobias.
6. **T**   As our understanding of underlying physiological and genetic processes continues to increase, the reality of this statement will, I suspect, generalize much beyond OCD.
7. **T**   It is not one of the defining characteristics of conversion disorder, but it is commonly found in this disorder.
8. **T**   Even though the terms are not found in the DSM-IV, they are still commonly used.

Multiple Choice

1. **c**   By definition, delusions are false beliefs, and beliefs are cognitions—they may give rise to certain behaviors or affects, but they themselves are cognitions.
2. **d**   Alzheimer's disease is certainly listed in the DSM-IV. Of course it can be diagnosed. It can be found in relatively young people; and it is degenerative and deadly.
3. **c**   The only "catch" here is to recall that "affect" is related to emotion or mood.
4. **a**   This one isn't even close and the answer is depression. Also note that paranoia isn't even a mood disorder.
5. **d**   As is the case for depression, episodes of mania tend to recur and relapse. In other words, we seldom find just one isolated case of mania.
6. **a**   There is surely a genetic predisposition for depression and depression (somehow) involves the collection of neurotransmitters called biogenic amines. I know of no serious hypothesis that relates depression to hormone level.
7. **a**   There may be some anxiety associated with schizophrenia, but it is not likely, and the other symptoms virtually define the disorder.
8. **c**   A good prognosis is surely a good thing, but it is not a symptom. Loss of affect and social withdrawal are indeed losses, and, hence, are negative symptoms. The most common positive symptoms of schizophrenia are hallucinations and delusions.
9. **c**   That schizophrenia runs in families is an assertion with which most psychologists would readily agree. Saying that dopamine causes schizophrenia is an overstatement. Yes, dopamine may be involved or implicated, but we cannot say that it "causes" schizophrenia.

True/False

1. **T**   For several reasons, this statement is correct.
2. **F**   Sure they can. Depression and anxiety are not mutually exclusive. To be depressed and anxious at the same time is to provide a very difficult clinical picture, but it is possible, even common.
3. **F**   No. Dysthymia does involve depression, but it is much less severe and is less debilitating than major depression.
4. **F**   Schizophrenia does mean (literally) "splitting of the mind," but not into separate personalities. The split referred to is a split from reality as the rest of us experience it.
5. **T**   And about one-quarter will get better and stay that way, while about half seem to get better for awhile and then (for a myriad of reasons) relapse, and have their symptoms return.

EXPERIENCING PSYCHOLOGY

What Do People Believe About Psychological Disorders?

There are popular misconceptions about many areas of psychology, but in none more so than in abnormal psychology. This simple, 10-item, true-and-false survey will give you some insight to the mistaken ideas that many people have about the psychological disorders. It might be interesting to compare the responses of persons who have had a psychology class with the responses of those who have not.

___T ___F   1. Most violent crimes are committed by persons who are mentally ill.

___T ___F   2. People with psychological disorders are obvious; they act in some bizarre way.

___T ___F   3. This week, more people will be diagnosed with psychological disorders than with cancer and cardiovascular disease combined.

___T ___F   4. Except in rare cases, a clear distinction can be drawn between "normal" and "abnormal" behaviors.

___T ___F   5. Geniuses are particularly prone to psychological disorders.

___T ___F   6. Psychological disorders are more prevalent in highly technical, advanced, societies.

___T ___F   7. Most mental disorders are incurable.

___T ___F   8. People with mental illness seldom realize that they are ill.

___T ___F   9. Mental illness is about as common among children and adolescents as it is among adults.

___T ___F   10. If a person is diagnosed with one psychological disorder, he or she almost certainly will not have another, different disorder as well.

As you know, Items number 3, 6, and 9 are true, while the others are false.

Chapter 13

Treatment and Therapy for Psychological Disorders

STUDY TIP #13

Preparing For Exams II: Some Thoughts On Multiple-Choice Exams

Multiple-choice exams are the most common for students in their first psychology course. I know that you have taken hundreds of multiple-choice tests over your academic career. I also know that general "rules" have many exceptions. Nonetheless, there are some hints about taking multiple-choice exams that we can review quickly.

1. *There is no substitute for being prepared.* No matter how clever or lucky you are, the best way to prepare for an exam of any type is to study for it.
2. *Relax—be cool.* You're prepared for this exam. This is no time to panic. Take a deep breath, exhale slowly, and relax.
3. *Read the directions and give the test a quick once-over.* Yes, you probably know what to do, but take a minute to make sure that you're following the directions. Scan the whole test. Estimate time needs.
4. *Skip items of which you are unsure.* If you encounter an item for which the answer is not immediately obvious, that's okay. Skip it. Don't agonize over it. Skip it. Just don't forget to come back to it later.
5. *Be sure you know what the item is asking about.* You know that you know the material. If it's not immediately clear, you've got to find a match between what you know and what this item is asking about.
6. *Eliminate distracter alternatives.* If you don't see the best answer right away, at least mark out those that are clearly wrong, that don't fit grammatically, or that say the same thing as some other alternative.
7. *See* if *the answer to one item can be found somewhere in another item.* Imagine one question that asks: "In Hemingway's The Old Man and the Sea. . . ." followed later by a question that asks, "who wrote The Old Man and the Sea?" Believe me, it happens.
8. *Look out for double negatives.* If something is said to be "not false," then it's true. If someone is "not unintelligent," then he or she is smart.
9. *Avoid absolute statements (most of the time).* Particularly in psychology, very little is <u>always</u> or <u>never</u>, but may be <u>often</u> or <u>seldom</u>.
10. *Do not be afraid to change your answer.* No matter what you may have been told, there is no evidence that students are likely to change from correct answers to incorrect ones. Change your answers if you'd like.

Outline ~ Chapter 13: Treatment and Therapy for Psychological Disorders

TOPIC 13A: HISTORY AND BIOMEDICAL TREATMENTS

I. A Historical Perspective
- A. Ancient Greeks and Romans believed that individuals who were depressed, manic, irrational, intellectually retarded, or who had hallucinations or delusions had offended the gods.
    1. It was believed that prayer and religious rituals could aid some.
    2. Others died as a result of their treatment or were killed.
- B. Hippocrates believed that mental disorders had physical causes.
- C. During the Middle Ages (1000-1500) and well into the eighteenth century, the prevailing attitude toward the mentally ill was that they were in league with the devil or were being punished by God.
- D. The fist insane asylum opened in 1547 at St. Mary of Bethlehem Hospital in London; it is commonly referred to as "Bedlam."
- E. In Paris, Philippe Pinel (1745-1826), a French physician in charge of an asylum, ordered the chains and shackles removed from some of the inmates.
    1. The symptoms of many of the patients improved.
    2. His belief in moral treatment for the mentally ill can be seen as the beginning of a gradual enlightenment concerning mental illness.
- F. Benjamin Rush (1745-1813) was the founder of American psychiatry.
    1. He published the first text on mental disorders.
    2. His general attitudes were very humane.
- G. Dorthea Dix (1802-1887) was an American nurse who campaigned for reform in prisons, mental hospitals and asylums.
- H. Clifford Beers published a book in 1908 that is credited with being one of the factors that contributed to the "mental health movement."
- I. Since the early 1900s, progress has been uneven.
    1. World War I and the Depression reduced monies available to support institutions.
    2. Within the past 50 years, conditions have improved.
    3. There is still prejudice against persons with psychological disorders.

II. Psychosurgery
- A. **Psychosurgery** is the name we give to surgical procedures, usually directed at the brain, used to affect psychological reactions.
    1. The "split-brain" procedure can alleviate symptoms in extreme cases of epilepsy.
    2. Small surgical lesions in the limbic system have been effective in reducing or eliminating violent behaviors.
    3. A cingulotomy has been used successfully to reduce extreme anxiety and the symptoms of obsessive-compulsive disorder.
    4. Surgical techniques are being used to treat Parkinson's disease.
    5. A **lobotomy** severs the major neural connections between the prefrontal lobes and lower brain centers.
- B. Prefrontal lobotomies are not done today since psychoactive drugs can produce results with fewer side effects.

III. Electroconvulsive Therapy
- A. **Electroconvulsive therapy (ECT),** or shock treatment, involves the passing of an electric current between 70 and 150 volts across a patient's head for a fraction of a second.
    1. ECT has had a poor reputation in the past.
    2. In the United States, more than 110,000 patients receive ECT each year.
- B. The group of patients best suited for ECT are those for whom depression is a major symptom, but for whom other symptoms (such as hallucinations or delusions) are also present.
- C. No one knows exactly why ECT has the beneficial effects that it does.
- D. Because of the inherent dangers, more than 10-12 treatments in a series are seldom administered.
- E. Administering a shock to just one side of the brain, called a unilateral ECT, may be a safer yet equally effective procedure with fewer side effects.

IV. Drug Therapy
    A. **Antipsychotic drugs** alleviate or eliminate psychotic symptoms.
        1. Henri Laborit, a French neurosurgeon, used *chlorpromazine* in the early 1950s to calm his patients before surgery.
        2. The drug subsequently was used on patients with psychological disorders, and the drug revolution began.
        3. Most antipsychotic drugs work by blocking the receptor sites for the neurotransmitter dopamine.
            a. These drugs are most effective in treating the positive symptoms of schizophrenia, such as delusions, hallucinations, and bizarre behaviors.
            b. Clozapine is an exception, because it reduces negative symptoms such as social withdrawal, as well as positive ones.
        4. Antipsychotic drugs have revolutionized the care of psychotic patients, but they can have unpleasant side effects.
        5. About 30 percent of patients with schizophrenia do not respond to these drugs.
        6. Symptom-free patients who suddenly stop using their medication find that their symptoms return.
        7. If antipsychotic drugs are to be discontinued, the withdrawal must be gradual.
    B. **Antidepressant drugs** elevate the mood of persons who are feeling depressed, and there are three major classes.
        1. MAO (monoamine oxidase) inhibitors
            a. These drugs inhibit the enzyme monamine oxidase, which normally breaks down levels of serotonin, norepinephrine, and dopamine in the brain.
            b. A major drawback is that they can be toxic and interact with foods containing tyramine.
        2. Tricyclics
            a. These drugs generally are safer and more effective than the older MAO inhibitors.
            b. They affect the operation of the neurotransmitter serotonin.
        3. SSRIs (selective serotonin reuptake inhibitors)
            a. These drugs act faster to relieve symptoms and have fewer side effects.
            b. Prozac was introduced in 1987, and works by inhibiting the re-uptake (or breaking down) of serotonin; increased serotonin level elevates mood.
            c. Three other SSRI medications include Zoloft, Luvox, and Paxil.
        4. There are two classes of drugs currently being investigated for use with bipolar disorder; the newer antipsychotics, and anti-epileptic or anti-seizure medications.
        5. Antidepressant medications usually take two to four weeks to show any effect, and may take six weeks to be effective.
        6. Most of these drugs produce some kind of unpleasant side effect.
        7. Lithium salts are mood stabilizers that are most useful in controlling the manic stage of bipolar disorders.
        8. When antidepressant drugs are effective, they may actually bring about long-term cures.
        9. For patients who do not respond to drug therapy, ECT may be appropriate.
    C. **Anti-anxiety drugs** (tranquilizers) help reduce the felt aspect of anxiety.
        1. Some are muscle relaxants, such as Miltown or Equanil.
        2. The majority are benzodiazepines (e.g., Librium, Valium, and Xanax), which act directly on the CNS.
            a. These drugs are very effective and are the most commonly prescribed of all medications.
            b. Dependency and addiction can develop.
            c. These drugs are prescribed more frequently for women over age 45 than they are for men.

TOPIC 13B: THE PSYCHOTHERAPIES

I.   Who Provides Psychotherapy?
    A. People with different training and cultural experiences provide psychotherapy.
        1. A *clinical psychologist* can provide psychotherapy.
            a. This person usually has a Ph.D. in psychology, with a one-year internship, and extensive training in psychodiagnostics.
            b. A Psy.D. degree emphasizes more practical, clinical work.
        2. A *psychiatrist* is the only therapist permitted to prescribe medications.
            a. This person is a medical doctor, who completes an internship and residency in a mental hospital.
            b. Psychiatry is a specialty area in medicine.
        3. The *counseling psychologist* usually has a Ph.D. in psychology, and typically works with less disturbed patients.
        4. A *licensed professional counselor* will have a degree in counseling and will have met state requirements for licensure.
        5. A *psychoanalyst* is a label given to a psychologist or psychiatrist who has received training and certification in the methods of Freudian psychoanalysis.
        6. *Clinical social workers* may have a master's degree or Ph.D.; they traditionally have been involved in family and group therapy.
    B. People in related professions also may provide therapy.
        1. Included are those with a master's degree in psychology, occupational therapists, psychiatric nurses, and pastoral counselors.
        2. Mental health technicians typically have an associate degree in mental health technology, but seldom provide unsupervised therapy.
    C. Some therapists have special training in dealing with clients from various cultures or ethnic groups.

II. How Do I Choose the Right Therapist?
    A. Many people and agencies can serve as good resources.
    B. Check with your family physician, clergy person, local mental health center, college counseling center, psychology instructor, family and friends.
    C. Give the therapist at least three to four sessions to see if working together will be effective.
    D. If you do not feel that you are benefiting from therapy, discuss this with the therapist and be prepared to change if necessary.

III. Psychoanalytic Techniques
    A. Freud was a therapist first, and a personality theorist second.
    B. **Psychoanalysis** is based on several assumptions involving conflict and the unconscious mind.
        1. The biological, sexual, aggressive strivings of the id are often in conflict with the superego, associated with being overly cautious and experiencing guilt.
        2. The id also can be in conflict with the rational ego, which may be called upon to mediate between the id and superego.
        3. Conflicts that are unresolved are repressed into the unconscious.
        4. Freud believed that the way to rid oneself of anxiety was to identify the repressed conflict, bring it into the open, and resolve it.
        5. The goals of psychoanalysis are insight and resolution of repressed conflict.
    C. Freud's approach to psychoanalysis included some of the following ideas.
        1. The major task of the patient was to talk openly about all aspects of life, which was a time-consuming process.
        2. The method of **free association** encouraged patients to say aloud whatever entered their minds.
        3. **Resistance** refers to the unwillingness or inability to discuss freely some aspect of one's life.
        4. Dream interpretation was referred to as the "royal road" to the unconscious.
            a. Manifest content refers to dreams as they are recalled.

           b.   Latent content refers to the dream as a symbolic representation of the contents of the unconscious.
     5.   **Transference** occurs when the patient unconsciously comes to view and feel about the analyst in much the same way he or she feels about another important person in his or her life.
           a.   The relationship between the analyst and patient can become complex and emotional.
           b.   Countertransference refers to an analyst allowing his or her feelings and experiences to interfere with objective interactions with the patient.

IV.   Post-Freudian Psychoanalysis
    A.   In recent years, psychoanalysis has become less common, and strict Freudian analysis, rare.
    B.   The most significant change is the concern for shortening the length of analysis.
    C.   Today's analyst will take a more active role in therapy.
    D.   More emphasis is directed to the present rather than to childhood experiences.

V.   **Humanistic techniques** and existential therapies have a concern for self-examination, personal growth, and development.
    A.   The goal of **client-centered therapy**, founded by Carl Rogers, is to help an individual self-actualize.
     1.   The focus is on the present, not the past or childhood.
     2.   Another focus is on one's feelings or affect.
     3.   The therapist attempts to mirror the feelings of the person.
           a.   This requires that the therapist be an active listener.
           b.   The therapist also needs to be **empathic**, or able to understand and share the essence of another's feelings.
           c.   The therapist will try to express unconditional positive regard.
    B.   Gestalt therapy is associated with Fritz Perls (1893-1970).
     1.   The goal is to assist a person to integrate his or her thoughts, feelings, and actions, and increase self-awareness, acceptance, and growth.
     2.   Sessions are often convened in small group settings.

VI.   Behavioral Techniques
    A.   **Behavior therapy** is a collection of techniques founded on the principles of learning.
    B.   **Systematic desensitization** involves applying classical conditioning to alleviate feelings of anxiety, particularly those associated with phobic disorders.
    C.   Exposure and response prevention has shown promise as a treatment for OCD.
    D.   In **aversion therapy**, a stimulus that may be harmful but that produces a pleasant response is paired with an aversive, painful stimulus until the original stimulus is avoided.
    E.   **Contingency management** occurs when the therapist can manage the control of rewards and punishments to modify the behavior of a patient.
    F.   **Contingency contracting** amounts to establishing a contract with a client so that exhibiting certain behaviors will result in certain rewards.
    G.   **Modeling** involves the acquisition of an appropriate response through the imitation of a model.
     1.   For children with phobias, modeling by other children can be effective.
     2.   Modeling also is used in assertiveness training to aid individuals in expressing how they feel and think in social situations.

VII.   Cognitive Techniques
    A.   **Rational-emotive therapy** is associated with Albert Ellis.
     1.   Its premise is that psychological problems arise when people try to interpret what happens in the world on the basis of irrational beliefs.
     2.   The therapist takes a directive role in interpreting the client's system of beliefs and encourages active change.
    B.   **Cognitive restructuring therapy** is associated with Aaron Beck.
     1.   It is less confrontational and direct than RET.

2. The patient is given opportunities to test his or her beliefs, which will lead to positive outcomes.

VIII. Group Approaches
    A. Group therapy is a label applied to a variety of situations in which a number of people are involved in a therapeutic setting at the same time.
        1. A participant can realize that he or she is not the only one with problems.
        2. One can receive support from others.
        3. Helping someone else can be therapeutic.
        4. A participant can learn to present himself or herself more effectively to others.
    B. In **family therapy,** the roles, interdependence and communication skills of family members are addressed.
        1. One assumption is that each family member is a part of a system where his or her thoughts, feelings, and behavior impact other family members.
        2. A second assumption is that difficulties arise from improper methods of family communication.

IX. Evaluating Psychotherapy
    A. Evaluating psychotherapy is a difficult task.
        1. Sometimes there is a spontaneous remission of symptoms.
        2. It is difficult to agree on what is meant by recovery or cure.
    B. Two large meta-analysis studies showed positive results for psychotherapy.
    C. In general, there is no evidence that any one type of therapy is universally better than others.
        1. There is evidence that some types of therapy are better suited for some types of problems than others.
        2. Which therapy is best suited for which disorder is one of the most active areas of research in psychotherapy.
        3. There is evidence that some therapists are more effective than others.
    D. Many studies have indicated that when the primary treatment is medical, psychotherapy and medication together yield the best prognosis.
    E. Each variety of psychotherapy has its strengths and weaknesses.
    F. A recent push from many psychologists calls for **empirically supported therapies.**
        1. The implication is that only therapies with demonstrated empirical research support would be offered.
        2. There are several problems with this approach.
            a. "Cognitive therapy," for example means different things to different people.
            b. Many would rather not get into the business of "prescribing specific therapies.

Practice Test Questions

TOPIC 13A: HISTORY AND BIOMEDICAL TREATMENTS

Multiple Choice

1. We can claim that the treatment of persons with psychological disorders in humane, systematic ways was a generally accepted practice
   ___a. during the Greek and Roman empires.
   ___b. early in the Middle Ages (approximately 1200 A.D.).
   ___c. late in the seventeenth century.
   ___d. at the beginning of the twentieth century.

2. Descriptions of persons with psychological disorders can be traced as far back as
   ___a. the earliest written records of history.
   ___b. the era of Plato and Hippocrates.
   ___c. the Dark Ages and the Crusades.
   ___d. the time of the French Revolution (late 1700s).

3. Throughout history, the treatment of the psychologically disordered has been guided mostly by
   ___a. those politicians in power and wanting to remain in power.
   ___b. whatever religion happened to dominate the era.
   ___c. the profit motive—the desire of a few to profit from the grief of others.
   ___d. the contemporary view of what caused the disordered symptoms.

4. Who is credited as being one of the first to treat the mentally ill in his care humanely and with compassion, unchaining them from the shackles in the institution?
   ___a. Phillipe Pinel   ___c. Johann Malleus
   ___b. Martin Luther   ___d. Clifford Beers

5. Insane asylums
   ___a. were first found in ancient Greece.
   ___b. provided a safe haven for the mentally ill.
   ___c. had virtually disappeared by the late 1700s.
   ___d. provided asylum for the general population, not the inmates.

6. A prefrontal lobotomy
   ___a. severs connections between the cerebral cortex and lower brain centers.
   ___b. lesions or removes the corpus callosum, thus separating the two hemispheres of the brain.
   ___c. destroys the part of the limbic system (the amygdala) involved in emotionality and violent behaviors.
   ___d. involves gradually removing more and more brain tissue until the psychotic symptoms stop.

7. Prefrontal lobotomies
   ___a. were very dangerous—nearly one-quarter of lobotomized patients died.
   ___b. were discovered by accident when a patient was shot in the head and his symptoms disappeared.
   ___c. are now outlawed in the United States.
   ___d. were performed on tens of thousands of persons in the 1940s and 1950s.

8. Why does electroconvulsive therapy produce the effects that it does?
   ___a. Levels of the neurotransmitter dopamine are increased.
   ___b. Pleasure centers in the brain are stimulated.
   ___c. Unpleasant, depressing memories are destroyed.
   ___d. No one really knows for sure why it works.

9. The first antipsychotic drug used effectively was
    ___a. chlorpromazine. ___c. lithium salts.
    ___b. Valium. ___d. Prozac.

10. Anti-anxiety drugs
    ___a. have long-lasting effects.
    ___b. are classified as either MAO inhibitors or tricyclics.
    ___c. cure the symptoms of hallucinations and delusions.
    ___d. ease or alleviate the symptoms of anxiety.

True/False

1. ____True ____False "Psychosurgery" means "lobotomy."

2. ____True ____False ECT produces a seizure in the brain, very much like an epileptic seizure.

3. ____ True ____False Antipsychotic medications suppress symptoms, but rarely can they be said to cure a disorder.

TOPIC 13B: THE PSYCHOTHERAPIES

Multiple Choice

1. What makes a psychiatrist different from a psychologist is that the psychiatrist
    ___a. practices psychotherapy.
    ___b. is more knowledgeable in matters of testing and diagnostics.
    ___c. went to medical school.
    ___d. is more likely to be Freudian in orientation and practice psychoanalysis.

2. What do all of the psychotherapies have in common?
    ___a. They all involve talking and listening.
    ___b. They all are used to assist with medical treatments.
    ___c. They all seek to discover repressed conflicts.
    ___d. They all require a long-term (two-to-three year) commitment.

3. Freudian psychoanalysis is based on many assumptions, including each of the following EXCEPT that
    ___a. the patient may be truly unable to tell the analyst why he or she is experiencing anxiety.
    ___b. early childhood experiences can have an impact on the way that one feels as an adult.
    ___c. once the analyst gets the patient to act better, he or she will think and feel better.
    ___d. the true nature of the patient's problem may be revealed in the content of his or her dreams.

4. In Freudian psychoanalysis, the process of coming to feel about the analyst as one used to feel about an important or significant other person is a process called
    ___a. transference. ___c. latent analysis.
    ___b. free association. ___d. resistance.

5. One thing that psychoanalysis after Freud still holds as a basic assumption is that
    ___a. there is no good reason for anxiety to feel so negative and unpleasant.
    ___b. hypnosis can be a useful way of developing transference.
    ___c. anxiety stems from some sort of repressed conflict.
    ___d. analysis is meant to be a time-consuming process, usually lasting for years.

6. What do client-centered therapy and psychoanalysis have in common?
    ___a. the assumption of an active role by the therapist to interpret and evaluate what the person has to say

___b. an assumption that, at least at the beginning of therapy, the client may not understand the source of his or her distress

___c. the assumption that the focus of therapy should be on what the person feels and not on what the person thinks

___d. the assumption that earlier, even childhood, experiences are more important or significant than how one feels currently

7. To be an active listener and to be able to share and understand the feelings of others is to

    ___a. offer unconditional positive regard.   ___c. self-actualize.

    ___b. be existential.   ___d. be empathic.

8. Most of the techniques of behavior therapy come from

    ___a. suggestions made by previous patients.

    ___b. Freud's theories.

    ___c. the learning laboratory.

    ___d. research in education.

9. Everything else being equal, which therapy seems best suited for a client who is very dependent and not terribly intelligent?

    ___a. psychoanalysis   ___c. contingency management

    ___b. client-centered therapy   ___d. cognitive therapy

10. Which of these is based more on the principles of classical conditioning than on the principles of operant conditioning?

    ___a. systematic desensitization   ___c. token economies

    ___b. contingency management   ___d. contingency contracting

11. Which behavior therapy technique derives most clearly from the work of Albert Bandura?

    ___a. aversion therapy   ___c. implosive therapy

    ___b. contingency contracting   ___d. modeling

12. A basic premise of cognitive therapy is that people

    ___a. do not realize how they feel.

    ___b. develop irrational beliefs about themselves and the world.

    ___c. do strange things in order to be reinforced by others.

    ___d act out childhood fantasies when they become adults.

13. One type of disorder for which cognitive therapy seems particularly well suited is

    ___a. schizophrenia.   ___c. depression.

    ___b. personality disorder.   ___d. phobia.

14. Which of these techniques consistently takes a cognitive approach to psychotherapy?

    ___a. person-centered therapy   ___c. family therapy

    ___b. systematic desensitization   ___d. rational-emotive therapy

True/False

1. ___True ___False   Anybody can be a psychotherapist, but only a person with an MD can be certified as a psychoanalyst.

2. ___True ___False   All psychotherapies are designed to ultimately bring about a change in a person's affect, behavior, and/or cognition.

3. ___True ___False   As opposed to its latent content, the manifest content of a dream is the content as expressed and described by the patient.

4. ____True ____False   By definition, contingency contracting is essentially the opposite of unconditional positive regard.

5. ____True ____False   All psychotherapies are equally effective for any particular psychological disorder.

Key Terms and Concepts
Topic 13A

psychosurgery_____

_____

lobotomy_____

_____

electroconvulsive therapy_____

_____

antipsychotic drugs_____

_____

antidepressant drugs_____

_____

antianxiety drugs_____

_____

Topic 13B

psychoanalysis_____

_____

free association_____

_____

resistance_____

_____

transference_____

_____

client-centered therapy_____

_____

empathic_____

_____

behavior therapy_____

_____

systematic desensitization_____

_____

aversion therapy_____

_____

contingency management_____

_____

contingency contracting_____

_____

modeling_____

_____

cognitive therapy_____

_____

rational-emotive therapy_____

_____

cognitive restructuring therapy_____

_____

cognitive-behavior therapy (CBT)_____

_____

group therapy_____

_____

family therapy_____

_____

empirically supported therapies_____

_____

Answers to Practice Test Questions

TOPIC 13A: HISTORY AND BIOMEDICAL TREATMENTS

Multiple Choice

1. **d** Although there were those throughout history who took a humane approach to the mentally ill, a general acceptance of such treatments was really a 20th century phenomenon.

2. **a** We may be much more aware of psychological disorders today, but reports of persons with disorders can be found among the earliest records of written history.

3. **d** How anyone goes about treating psychological disorders is driven—more than anything else—by an understanding of the nature and the causes of those disorders. This is true today, and always has been.

4. **a** It was Phillipe Pinel who, late in the 18th century, discovered the effects of unchaining the insane (as they were called in those days) and treating them humanely.

5. **d** The truth of it is that the persons who experienced most of the asylum when insane asylums were in vogue were those in the general population who no longer had to confront the psychologically disordered on a daily basis. The insane, then, could be "put away."

6. **a** Regardless of the specific procedures involved, lobotomies sever connections between the controlling cerebral cortex and lower brain centers.

7. **d** None of the first three statements is true. It is true, however, that tens of thousands of these operations were performed in the mid-twentieth century.

8. **d** Yes, we do have some reasonable hypotheses, but the truth is that we still do not know with any precision why ECT has the beneficial effects that it does.

9. **a** I typically don't like to ask questions about specific drugs because there are so many of them and because new ones are being introduced continuously. However, I do think it noteworthy that chlorpromazine was the first psychoactive medication, introduced by Henri Laborit.

10. **d** This one is so easy, you may have a problem with it. Anti-anxiety medications do just what their name suggests they do: they alleviate the feelings of extreme anxiety.

True/False

1. **F** Lobotomy is a type of psychosurgery, but it is not correct to equate the two as synonyms. There are other types of psychosurgery.

2. **T** Just why this has beneficial effects is not known, as we noted in item #8 above, but as stated, this is true.

3. **T** For individuals, we can find exceptions, but by-and-large, anti-psychotic medications are more likely to suppress symptoms than to cure disorders. We make this statement on the basis that when medications are withheld, psychotic symptoms tend to reappear.

TOPIC 13B: THE PSYCHOTHERAPIES

Multiple Choice

1. **c** The only possible problem with this item is its simplicity. Both practice psychotherapy. I'd hate to make the statement in alternative **b** in a room full of psychologists, and psychoanalysts are likely to be Freudian, whether they be psychologists or psychiatrists.

2. **a** Freud correctly characterized psychotherapy as "talk therapy." The last three alternatives may be true of some forms of therapy, but are not true "generally."

3. **c** Alternative **c** is a better statement for a goal of behavior therapy than for Freudian analysis.

4. **a** This statement provides a reasonable definition of the Freudian concept of transference.

5. **c** Psychoanalysis today is significantly changed from the way that Freud practiced it, but what makes it psychoanalysis is the same basic assumption that disordered symptoms reflect repressed conflict of some sort.

6. **b**   Both types of therapist would agree that patients, or clients, may not be aware of the true source of their distress, at least at the outset of therapy.

7. **d**   Here we have a rather straightforward definition of empathy.

8. **c**   Behavior therapies in general are aimed at bringing about relatively permanent changes in one's behaviors following principles derived from the psychology of learning laboratories.

9. **c**   Alternatives **a**, **b**, and **d** presuppose an active, involved, introspective client. Only contingency management will be truly effective in this scenario.

10. **a**   The last three techniques are applications of operant conditioning procedures, while the first is a classical conditioning procedure.

11. **d**   You should know this one even without reading the chapter if you remember from our discussion of learning that Albert Bandura is associated with social learning theory and modeling.

12. **b**   Cognitive therapy deals with cognitions—in particular, irrational cognitions or beliefs about one's self and one's place in the world.

13. **c**   Yes, cognitive therapy can be—and has been—used for virtually all disorders, but of these choices, it is best suited for treating depression—often in conjunction with drug treatment.

14. **d**   By definition, rational-emotive therapy is the only one of these techniques that is specifically cognitive in orientation.

True/False

1. **F**   This one is false on two counts. Not just anybody can be a psychotherapist, and psychoanalysts can be psychologists as well as psychiatrists.

2. **T**   This is the one thing that all psychotherapies have in common—a goal of bringing about some sort of lasting change. The differences have to do with how to go about making that change.

3. **T**   Latent content is the "hidden" symbolic content of dreams, whereas manifest content is the content as the person describes it.

4. **T**   This one takes some thought. Unconditional positive regard provides reinforcement for virtually everything the client says (or does), whereas contingency management will provide conditional positive regard; one earns reinforcement only for doing what is appropriate. Hence, they are, in this way, opposites.

5. **F**   This item is simply not true. Yes, in general, all are effective, but for any particular disorder, some are more effective than are others.

EXPERIENCING PSYCHOLOGY

Designing Your Own Mental Health Directory

Given the statistics on the prevalence of the psychological disorders, it is very unlikely that any of us can go very long without the need for some sort of psychotherapy or treatment for psychological disorders—either for ourselves of for someone close to us. When the need arises, there are many options available to you. You may contact your psychology instructor, family doctor, or clergy person. You may contact the student services office on your campus, or a local community mental health facility. You may ask friends, family, or the local office of the Mental Health Association for a referral.

It will only take a few minutes now to explore the possibilities for therapy, counseling, or treatment. Look through the campus directory, or the yellow pages of the phone book for names, addresses, and phone numbers. Make a list of resources or agencies that you could call if you encounter a need for mental health services. Put the list someplace handy—in with your notes, in your address book, wherever. The need for psychotherapy seldom arises as an emergency situation, where seconds count. Nonetheless, it just makes good sense to be prepared, to have a course of action ready should the need arise.

Chapter 14

Social Psychology

STUDY TIP #14

<u>Dealing With Family And Friends</u>

Let's again step back from all this academic/study discussion for a minute and consider an issue of more personal concern that may very well impact on your study habits.

Make no mistake: Going to college is going to change you and your life. You are going to learn a great deal of information about many subjects. You also are going to meet a variety of new and different people, and you'll make new friends. You will grow—personally, socially, and professionally. As new friendships and relationships blossom, stresses and strains can be put on old ones.

Making new friends is easier for some people than it is for others. If you are one of those for whom the process is difficult, please realize that you're not alone. Also realize that you can learn to be more comfortable in social situations; like anything else, it takes practice. Respect, civility and the common decency of what used to be called "good manners" go a long way toward developing a relationship with others.

Here are a few pointers to consider when interacting with others.

1. Try to be as pleasant and cordial as possible.
2. Give others an opportunity to express themselves.
3. Try taking the position, "I would really like to understand why you did or said or think or feel as you do."
4. Listen carefully and see if you can summarize what you've heard.
5. Consider interactions to be two-way; you need to be ready to share how you feel about things.
6. Try to recognize and understand differences, not asking everyone else to change to minimize those differences.
7. Be prepared to agree to disagree if necessary.
8. Be honest with your comments and compliments.
9. Try to avoid being critical and blaming.
10. If working with others on a project, be sure to do your share.
11. Act toward others, as you would like them to act toward you.
12. Don't be afraid to apologize if you recognize that you did something wrong or said something unkind.
13. Smile whenever you can and whenever it's appropriate.

Outline ~ Chapter 14: Social Psychology

TOPIC 14A: SOCIAL COGNITIONS: ATTITUDES, ATTRIBUTIONS, AND ATTRACTIONS

I.   Preview
    A.   **Social psychology** is the field of psychology concerned with how others influence the thoughts, feelings, and behaviors of the individual.
    B.   Much of social psychology has taken on a cognitive flavor.
    C.   Social cognition involves two related questions.
        1.   What information about the social nature of the world do we have stored in memory?
        2.   How does that information influence social judgments, choices, attractions, and behaviors?

II.   The Nature of Attitudes
    A.   An **attitude** is a relatively stable evaluative disposition directed toward some object or event; it consists of feelings, behaviors, and beliefs.
        1.   Attitudes are for or against, pro or con, positive or negative, i.e., *valenced*.
        2.   There is a preparedness to respond to the object of an attitude.
        3.   Attitudes must have objects.
    B.   Attitudes have three components: affective, behavioral, and cognitive.
        1.   These three components need not be consistent.
        2.   Some have argued that attitude is a two-dimensional concept involving affect and cognition only.
        3.   Some add a component of **behavior intention,** that is, the intent to behave.

III.   Prejudice, Stereotypes, and Discrimination
    A.   Of particular interest to social psychologists are attitudes held about other people.
    B.   **Prejudice** implies an attitude that represents a biased—often negative—disposition toward groups of persons.
        1.   Negative prejudicial attitudes have real and often significant consequences for the target of such attitudes.
        2.   Racism and sexism are two common prejudicial attitudes.
    C.   A **stereotype** is a rigid set of positive or negative beliefs about a group of people.
        1.   It amounts to a rigid, over-generalized, often biased schema.
        2.   *Explicit stereotypes* are those of which one is consciously aware.
        3.   *Implicit stereotypes* are those which operate at an unconscious level of awareness.
    D.   **Discrimination** is the behavioral component of prejudice and refers to the (usually) negative behavior(s) directed at a member of a group simply because of that person's membership in the group.

IV.   Attitude formation
    A.   Most experts agree that attitudes are formed through learning.
    B.   *Observational learning* is the term used to describe those instances where one develops an attitude because he or she sees (valued) others holding the same attitude, and even being reinforced for doing so.
    C.   *Classical conditioning* uses associative techniques of pairing an otherwise neutral object with one about which strong attitudes are already held.
    D.   *Operant conditioning* predicts that whenever attitudinal behaviors are reinforced the underlying attitude will develop and strengthen.
    E.   The **mere exposure phenomenon** (associated with Zajonc) suggests that the more one is exposed to an object, the greater the likelihood that he or she will develop positive attitudes about that object.

V. Attitude Change Mechanisms
    A. Leon Festinger's theory of **cognitive dissonance** proposes that a negative motivational state arises when our attitudes, thoughts, and behaviors are out of balance or inconsistent.
        1. Dissonance theory can help people understand behaviors that are seemingly incomprehensible.
        2. Negative situations are more likely to arouse dissonance than positive ones.
        3. **Postdecisional dissonance** is the cognitive dissonance experienced after making a decision between two mutually exclusive, equally attractive, different alternatives.
    B. As an alternative to cognitive dissonance theory, Daryl Bem proposed **self-perception theory**, that says we keenly observe behavior, including our own, and look for an explanation for that behavior.
    C. **Persuasion** is the application of rational and/or emotional arguments to convince others to change their attitudes and behaviors.
        1. The **Yale communication model**, the most widely accepted model of persuasion, considers the influence of the source of a message, the structure of a message, and the audience for a message.
        2. Persuasion depends on the source of the communication.
            a. **Credibility**, the believability of the communicator involving expertise and trustworthiness, increases persuasion.
            b. There are other factors that influence persuasion, including vocal pleasantness, facial expressiveness, attractiveness of the communicator, etc.

VI. Attitude Change by Persuasion
    A. Persuasion amounts to applying arguments meant to deliberately convince others to change their attitudes.
    B. Successful persuasion depends on the nature of the message and the audience.
        1. In a rational appeal, one uses facts and figures to persuade an audience.
        2. Emotional appeals can be even more effective.
        3. Fear appeals must arouse fear, convince listeners that dire consequences could happen, and include instructions on how to avoid the dire consequences.
        4. The **elaboration likelihood model** is a model of persuasion stating that there are two routes to persuasion: the central route and the peripheral route.

VII. Attribution Processes
    A. An **internal attribution** explains the source of a person's behavior in terms of a characteristic of the person (a trait or disposition).
    B. An **external attribution** explains the source of a person's behavior in terms of the situation or context outside the individual.
    C. When forming attributions, distinctiveness, consensus, and consistency are important determiners.
    D. Whether one uses internal or external attributions often depends upon a trait inference process (What kind of person is he?) or a situational inference process (What kind of party is this?).
    E. The **fundamental attribution error** is the tendency to favor internal attributions rather than external situational explanations.
    F. The **just world hypothesis** is a bias in which people come to believe that good things only happen to good people and bad things only happen to bad people.
    G. With the **self-serving bias**, success or positive outcomes are attributed to personal, internal sources, and failures or negative outcomes are attributed to situational or external sources.
    H. With the **actor-observer bias** one tends to use external attributions for his or her behaviors and internal attributions for the behaviors of others.

VIII. Interpersonal Attraction
    A. **Interpersonal attraction** can be seen as a favorable and powerful attitude toward another person.
    B. Several theories explain interpersonal attraction.
        1. The reinforcement-affect model claims that people are attracted to others who provide rewarding experiences.

2. The social exchange model argues that what matters most is a comparison of the costs and benefits of establishing a relationship.
3. Equity theory extends the social exchange model to add the appraisal of rewards and costs for both parties in a relationship.
4. Attachment theory is based on feelings or affect more than cognitions, and suggests that people develop relationship styles that they maintain throughout their life span.

C. Regardless of underlying theory, there are several factors that affect interpersonal attraction.
1. Reciprocity says that a person tends to value and like others who like and value him or her.
2. Proximity suggests that simple physical closeness yields attraction
3. The **mere exposure phenomenon** claims that liking increases with repeated exposure.
4. Physical attractiveness is related to interpersonal attraction.
   a. Among college students, it may be the most important factor in interpersonal relationships.
   b. In this context, the **matching phenomenon** suggests that one is often attracted to someone else of the same level of physical attractiveness and social status.
5. Considerable research supports the assertion that the more similar two people are, the more likely they will be attracted to each other.
   a. One tends o be repelled or put-off by those perceived as dissimilar.
   b. Opposites may attract, but similarity is more powerful over time.

TOPIC 14B: SOCIAL INFLUENCE

I. Conformity
A. Modifying behavior under perceived pressure to do so, so that it is consistent with the behavior of others, is **conformity.**
B. Solomon Asch found people susceptible to social pressure when in an ambiguous situation.
1. Any social support for one's position minimizes conformity.
2. This is known as the **true partner effect.**
C. Several factors impact the degree of conformity.
1. The more competent the majority, the greater the conformity.
2. The more ambiguous the situation, the greater the conformity.
3. There are small gender differences, with women conforming more than men in some circumstances.

II. Obedience to Authority
A. Obedience results when one yields to the pressure of perceived authority.
B. Obedience was demonstrated in the laboratory by Stanley Milgram.
1. "Teachers" were asked to shock "learners" in a task presented as a learning experiment.
   a. In fact, no one was really shocked.
   b. The person acting as the "learner" was a confederate of Milgram.
2. Even when "learners" yelled in protest, many participants continued to deliver "shocks" when asked to by the experimenter.
   a. 65% of participants (men and women) obeyed fully with the experimenter.
   b. All of the participants reported feeling badly about what they had done, but they did it anyway.
C. Milgram fully debriefed his subjects, but was severely criticized for placing people in such a stressful situation.

III. Bystander Intervention
A. The social psychology of bystander intervention deals with conditions under which observers (bystanders) will come to the aid of someone perceived to be in trouble.

B. Latané and Darley's cognitive model suggested that a series of cognitive events must occur before a bystander will intervene.
    1. First, the bystander must notice what is happening.
    2. The bystander must label the situation as an emergency.
    3. The bystander must decide that it is his or her responsibility to do something.
    4. The bystander must implement his or her decision
C. There are several factors that account for the **bystander effect**, or social inhibition of helping.
    1. **Audience inhibition** is the tendency to be hesitant to do anything in front of others, especially strangers.
    2. **Pluralistic ignorance** is one's tendency to believe that only he or she is confused and does not know what to do in an emergency, whereas everyone else is standing around doing nothing for some good reason.
    3. The principle of **diffusion of responsibility** states that the greater the number of other people present, the smaller is each individual's perceived obligation to intervene.
    4. The **empathy-altruism hypothesis** is a hypothesis stating that empathy is one reason for helping those in need.
    5. **Egoism** is a motive for helping someone in need to avoid personal distress for not helping.
    6. A person is more likely to help when he or she is alone rather than in a group.

IV. Social Loafing and Facilitation
  A. **Social loafing** is the tendency to work less (decrease individual effort) as the size of the group in which one is working becomes larger.
    1. Loafing increases to the extent that the individual performance cannot be identified.
    2. Degrees of loafing vary significantly across cultures.
  B. When the presence of others improves an individual's performance, there is evidence of **social facilitation.**
  C. **Social interference** occurs when the presence of others leads to poor performance.

V. Decision Making in Groups
  A. Groups can, and often do, outperform individuals in problem solving.
    1. Groups tend to recognize answers faster.
    2. Groups with high-quality members perform better than groups with low-quality members.
    3. Groups bring more resources to problem-solving tasks.
    4. Interpersonal cohesiveness and task-based cohesiveness increase productivity.
  B. The risky shift phenomenon occurs when groups make decisions that are riskier than those made by individuals.
  C. The **group polarization effect** claims that group participation will make any individual's reactions more extreme or polarized.
  D. **Groupthink** is an excessive concern for reaching a consensus in group decision-making to the extent that critical evaluations are withheld, and involves eight symptoms.
    1. An illusion of invulnerability
    2. Rationalization
    3. Unquestioned belief in the group's inherent morality
    4. Stereotyped views of the enemy
    5. Conformity pressures
    6. Self-censorship
    7. An illusion of unanimity
    8. Emergence of self-appointed "mindguards"

Practice Test Questions

TOPIC 14A: SOCIAL COGNITIONS: ATTITUDES, ATTRIBUTIONS, AND ATTRACTIONS

Multiple Choice

1. Most psychologists believe that attitudes are made up of a number of different components or aspects. The one component that seems most central to an attitude is
   ___a. some attitudinal object.   ___c. a tendency to behave in a certain way.
   ___b. a belief or cognition.   ___d. an evaluative (+ or -) feeling.

2. When advertisers try to change your attitudes about their products or services, in which component of your attitude are they really most interested?
   ___a. cognitive   ___c. affective
   ___b. evaluative   ___d. behavioral

3. Advertisers who try to change attitudes about their product by showing satisfied customers providing testimonials about how wonderful that product is are using _____ as a technique for attitude change.
   ___a. classical conditioning   ___c. observational learning
   ___b. stereotype development   ___d. operant conditioning

4. If I can get you to do something that is contrary to an attitude you currently hold, you may change that attitude. If I am successful, I have changed your attitude using
   ___a. cognitive dissonance.   ___c. coercive persuasion.
   ___b. classical conditioning.   ___d. cognitive response theory.

5. A communicator is trying to persuade others to change their attitudes. Which characteristic of that communicator is LEAST important in predicting if the communication will be successful?
   ___a. credibility   ___c. expertise
   ___b. celebrity   ___d. trustworthiness

6. Attributions are typically made in terms of each of the following EXCEPT
   ___a. internal vs. external factors.   ___c. learned vs. inherited factors.
   ___b. dispositional vs. situational factors.   ___d. intrinsic vs. extrinsic factors.

7. When we overemphasize personal reasons in our explanations of another's behaviors and overlook the forces of the environment, we are
   ___a. making a fundamental attribution error.
   ___b. demonstrating a belief in the just world hypothesis.
   ___c. employing a self-serving bias in our judgment.
   ___d. failing to take into account the actor-observer bias.

8. Basically, attribution theory deals with
   ___a. different techniques for changing the attitudes of others.
   ___b. how we tend to explain the behaviors of ourselves and others in social situations.
   ___c. factors and processes that lead to interpersonal attractions.
   ___d. forming expectations about how we should behave in social situations.

9. Which of these is NOT a theory or model used to explain the basis of interpersonal attraction?
   ___a. equity model   ___c. dissonance model
   ___b. social exchange model   ___d. reinforcement model

10. One of the aspects of attachment theory suggests that
    ___a. everybody relates to others in essentially the same way.
    ___b. the style with which one forms attachments as a child predicts how one will do so as an adult.
    ___c. women tend to form interpersonal attachments that are different from those of men.
    ___d. how one goes about forming attachments to others depends more upon the situation than on the people involved.

11. With regard to interpersonal attraction, which statement is FALSE?
    ___a. The "mere exposure" phenomenon tells us that familiarity breeds contempt.
    ___b. We tend to like and value those who like and value us.
    ___c. Physical attractiveness is correlated with attraction.
    ___d. People tend to be attracted to those who have similar attitudes.

12. Which is likely to have the LEAST impact on attraction?
    ___a. physical proximity   ___c. attitudinal similarity
    ___b. physical attractiveness   ___d. perceived sexuality

True/False

1. ___True ___False   Social cognitions include those behaviors in which we engage when we are in groups, both large and small.

2. ___True ___False   Attitudes have three components: personal, social, and environmental.

3. ___True ___False   Attitude change can begin by bringing about a change in one's affect, behavior, or cognitions.

4. ___True ___False   Most people attribute their own success to dispositional factors and their own failures to situational factors.

5. ___True ___False   Even if someone likes us now, if they did NOT like us originally, we probably will not value them as a friend.

TOPIC 14B: SOCIAL INFLUENCE

Multiple Choice

1. When Solomon Asch studied conformity, he found each of the following EXCEPT that
    ___a. even participants' perceptual judgments could be influenced by group pressure.
    ___b. most of his participants (more than 75%) conformed at least once.
    ___c. the least amount of social support was sufficient to help a person resist group pressure.
    ___d. most of the participants continued to conform even after they knew that the group's members were confederates of the experimenter.

2. In an Asch conformity situation, when will conformity to group pressure be the greatest? When the other participants in the study group are presented as being
    ___a. friends and classmates.   ___c. social psychologists.
    ___b. architects and draftsmen.   ___d. apathetic conformists.

3. The major difference between conformity and obedience is
    ___a. peer pressure.
    ___b. the presence of an authority figure.
    ___c. the nature of the task involved.
    ___d. the person's perception that there is social pressure.

4. Which result does NOT follow from Milgram's studies of obedience?

    ___a. Personality characteristics of the subjects allowed Milgram to predict who would obey and who would not.

    ___b. When told about the experiment, virtually no one believed that he or she would have delivered the shocks.

    ___c. No participants in the experiment stopped delivering shocks before the 300-volt level, when the "learner" began protesting.

    ___d. More than half of the participants delivered the highest level of shock to the "learner."

5. Which conclusion from Milgram's research is justified?

    ___a. Persons of some nationalities are more likely to obey than are others.

    ___b. When told to harm others, few people felt guilty about it.

    ___c. The perception of authority is a powerful force in conformity.

    ___d. Women are more likely to conform than are men.

6. What is the major reason why some have criticized Milgram's study of obedience as being unethical?

    ___a. He made a fundamental attribution error.

    ___b. He shocked people without their consent.

    ___c. He allowed participants to believe that they were hurting someone.

    ___d. He failed to adequately debrief his participants.

7. Which of the following is NOT taken to be a necessary step in considering whether to intervene in an emergency?

    ___a. One must notice or perceive the situation as an emergency.

    ___b. One must interpret the situation as an emergency.

    ___c. One must know or care about the victim.

    ___d. One must decide to take responsibility to do something.

8. Which of these best characterizes pluralistic ignorance?

    ___a. the feeling that one does not know what to do in an emergency

    ___b. the perception that there is a good reason why others are not acting

    ___c. the decision that there is nothing that can be done to help

    ___d. the belief that intervention will cause more harm than good

9. What the concept of "diffusion of responsibility" tells us is that if you were in need of assistance, you would most likely receive that assistance if

    ___a. there were only a few people around at the time.

    ___b. the persons who see you are women, not men.

    ___c. you happen to be in a small town, not a big city.

    ___d. there happens to be a large crowd nearby.

10. Based on his observations of bicycle riders in competition, Norman Triplett performed one of the first experiments in social psychology (in 1898) on the phenomenon called

    ___a. bystander apathy.   ___c. audience inhibition.

    ___b. cognitive dissonance.   ___d. social facilitation.

11. Zajonc and others suggest that the presence of others is likely to improve or facilitate one's performance if

    ___a. the task at hand is easy and well learned.

    ___b. those others act in a supportive, approving fashion.

    ___c. the task is difficult or complicated.

    ___d. those others act in a hostile, disapproving fashion.

12. Janis's concept of "groupthink" tells us that

    ___a. groups strive to reach consensus, right or wrong.

___b. individuals are more likely to express divergent opinions in a group than when they are alone.

___c. members of a group prefer that others in the group do most of the work.

___d. group decisions tend to be conservative and unoriginal.

True/False

1. ____True ____False   By definition, people are more likely to obey than to conform.

2. ____True ____False   Asch found that some people will conform most of the time, no matter what their perception of the nature of the group applying pressure to conform.

3. ____True ____False   Up to a point, the more people who express the same judgment, the more likely an individual will yield or conform to that judgment.

4. ____True ____False   Even Milgram was surprised by the results of his experiments.

5. ____True ____False   Social interference and social loafing are more common phenomena than is social facilitation.

Key Terms and Concepts
Topic 14A

social psychology_____

_____

attitude_____

_____

behavior intention_____

_____

prejudice_____

_____

stereotype_____

_____

explicit stereotype_____

_____

implicit stereotype_____

_____

discrimination_____

_____

modern racism_____

_____

mere exposure phenomenon_____

_____

cognitive dissonance_____

_____

post-decisional dissonance_____

_____

self-perception theory_____

_____

persuasion_____

_____

Yale communication model_____

_____

credibility_____

_____

elaboration likelihood model_____

_____

attribution theory_____

_____

internal attribution_____

_____

external attribution_____

_____

fundamental attribution error_____

_____

just world hypothesis_____

_____

self-serving bias_____

_____

actor-observer bias_____

_____

interpersonal attraction_____

_____

matching phenomenon_____

_____

Topic 14B

conformity_____

_____

true partner effect_____

_____

obedience_____

_____

bystander effect_____

_____

audience inhibition_____

_____

pluralistic ignorance_____

_____

diffusion of responsibility_____

_____

empathy_____

_____

empathy-altruism hypothesis_____

_____

egoism_____

_____

social loafing_____

_____

social facilitation_____

_____

social interference_____

_____

group polarization effect_____

_____

groupthink_____

_____

Answers to Practice Test Questions

TOPIC 14A: SOCIAL COGNITIONS: ATTITUDES, ATTRIBUTIONS, AND ATTRACTIONS

Multiple Choice

1. **d** As you know, there is considerable disagreement on how best to characterize the structure of attitudes, but the one thing that all characterizations have in common is that attitudes involve some degree of evaluation of something.

2. **d** I like this one. What matters most is the behavioral component. The advertiser wants you to do something: buy the product or service.

3. **c** As the text suggests, this approach is based on Bandura's social learning theory—learning through observation and vicarious reinforcement—a sort of, "Well, it seemed to work for them, so maybe it'll work for me, too."

4. **a** If I can get you to act contrary to your attitude, I will have established cognitive dissonance. This will then motivate you to do something, perhaps change your attitude.

5. **b** It may be helpful to have a communicator who is a celebrity, just to get people's attention, but if that celebrity is not perceived as credible, expert and trustworthy, it will do little good.

6. **c** Actually, alternatives **a**, **b**, and **d** are just different ways of saying exactly the same thing. I cannot imagine how learned vs. inherited factors fit into a discussion of attribution.

7. **a** These actions provide a good definition of the fundamental attribution error.

8. **b** Social psychologists are interested in each of these, of course, but attribution theory specifically concerns how one goes about explaining the behaviors of others and oneself.

9. **c** I suppose that it would not be too difficult to imagine a theory of interpersonal attraction based on cognitive dissonance (a very powerful notion). But, as far as I know, we'd have to imagine it, whereas each of the others is a well-known model.

10. **b** One of the appealing aspects of attachment theory is that it views the formation of interpersonal relationships as a life-long process and suggests that there is evidence that styles remain quite consistent.

11. **a** The first statement is, in fact, quite the opposite of reality. If anything, familiarity breeds attraction. (And please don't forget: As always, we're talking "in general." There are exceptions.)

12. **d** Sexuality is an important component of attraction for some, but compared to the others, it would be rated last, or least important.

True/False

1. **F** I hope I didn't get you on this one. Cognitions are beliefs, thoughts, ideas, etc. How can cognitions be behaviors—behaviors of any sort?

2. **F** Yes, attitudes are often said to have three components (although there is not total agreement on what they are), but they are usually the familiar affect, behavior, and cognition, not these.

3. **F** The logic is that if one (any one) component of an attitude changes, others will change as well.

4. **T** Here is a true piece of social psychology that may not conform to common sense.

5. **F** Actually, we are probably going to like someone who likes us now but didn't originally, even better than we might like someone who has liked us from the start—which is quite a mouthful, but makes sense if you go over it a couple of times.

TOPIC 14B: SOCIAL INFLUENCE

Multiple Choice

1. **d**   The last alternative is the best choice here because IF Asch's participants knew that the others in the "group" were confederates of Asch, the project would not have worked at all.

2. **b**   Here you are, judging lines, surrounded by people you do not know, believing them to be architects and draftsmen—who work with lines all day long. Isn't it likely that you would defer to their judgment—no matter what your eyes were telling you?

3. **b**   What makes obedience obedience is that it is conformity to the demands or wishes of an authority figure, real or perceived.

4. **a**   The last three statements are quite true, although perhaps a bit picky, but there is no indication that the first is true.

5. **c**   Of these choices, the only truly justified conclusion is that the perception of authority is a strong force in conformity.

6. **c**   None of the other alternatives are at all true, but Milgram did put people through considerable stress when he led them to believe that they were actually delivering a shock to another person.

7. **c**   We must notice, interpret, and take responsibility. It matters little whether the victim is known to us.

8. **b**   Alternative **b** is a good statement of pluralistic ignorance. Again, as we have seen many times earlier, a lot of learning in introductory psychology is a matter of developing vocabulary.

9. **a**   Alternatives **b** and **c** are basically irrelevant. Diffusion of responsibility tells us that you are less likely to be helped if you are in a large crowd.

10. **d**   Triplett was interested in social facilitation, and he demonstrated it by having children reel in fishing line, either alone or in groups.

11. **a**   When we are performing "in public," the main thing that happens is that arousal levels go up, which is okay so long as we know what we are doing, and that what we are doing is simple and well rehearsed.

12. **a**   The problem with groupthink is not that it is pressure to reach a consensus, but that it is pressure to reach a consensus no matter what, right or wrong.

True/False

1. **F**   I'm not sure that I even know what this statement means! If anything, we are more likely to conform than to be in situations where obedience is even an issue.

2. **F**   Yes, there are individual differences in the likelihood to conform, but group composition issues are significantly more important. As it is stated, this is not an accurate statement.

3. **T**   This is precisely what Asch found in his experiments.

4. **T**   He sure was.

5. **T**   There is an unsettling, unpleasant side to this statement, which as put forward here is true. We are more likely, it seems, to be hindered by group membership than stimulated by it.

EXPERIENCING PSYCHOLOGY

Norms and Compliance

We live in a social world in which we all have formed expectations about the acceptability of behaviors in given situations. That is, we have learned how one is "expected to act," or is "supposed to act," in a social context. These expectations are called *norms*. This exercise asks you to see what happens when you violate those social norms. Can you get anyone else to change his or her behaviors just by violating a few simple social norms?

Please be very careful. Some people can become very upset when social norms are violated. Try these activities in good humor but **be sensitive to the feelings of others**, quickly explaining what you are doing at the sign of any discomfort.

- While others watch you, try eating a banana by peeling back only a part of the peel, and then eating it as you would an ear of corn. Or eat a chocolate bar with a knife and fork, cutting it into small, bite-sized pieces. (This violation of social norms became a running gag on the *Seinfeld* television comedy series for weeks.)
- Dress in a manner that is significantly different from how you usually do when you go to classes. How long does it take for your friends and acquaintances to comment on your choice of clothes?
- Note the reactions you get if you simply walk across campus holding hands with a friend of the same sex.
- Here's a classic (from the old television program *Candid Camera*). Enter an elevator and ride up and down for a while facing the rear wall of the elevator compartment. Does anyone enter and join in facing the rear? Now try the same thing with some friends. What is the reaction of someone entering the elevator to find four of you facing the rear?
- (You'll need the permission of one of your instructors for this one.) Arrive at class a bit early, go to your seat, but simply stand there—do not sit down, even as the class begins. Try the same thing with the aid of two or three classmates—and the permission of the instructor. How do people react when they come to a classroom and find you standing there? A simple variation is to just stand at some open location on campus with a few friends, all of you staring up into space, as if there were really something interesting up there. How many others do the same, or stop to ask you just what in the world you are looking at?

Chapter 15

Industrial/Organizational, Environmental, and Sport Psychology

STUDY TIP #15

"What About The SQ3R Method?"

Nearly 50 years ago, a teacher named Francis Robinson described a strategy for studying that he called the SQ3R Method. It is recommended for two reasons: 1) it is simple, and 2) it works. You only need to know what the letters stand for.

S = Survey. The idea is to anticipate what you are about to study by looking ahead, reading the chapter outline and glancing through the chapter. What lies ahead?

Q = Question. Continually and actively ask yourself about what you are reading. If nothing else, from time to time just stop and ask yourself what I call the universal study question: "Whaaa?—in the sense of "What did I just read about?" (Again, we have our "Before You Go On" Questions in the text to help you out on this one.)

R1 = Read. Once you've surveyed and questioned, the time has come to get to it and read the text. Remember to space or distribute your practice (your reading).

R2 = Recite. In this instance, we don't really mean to perform "out loud." The basic idea is to "talk to yourself" about what you're reading. Keep your questions in mind and "recite" the answers to them as they are encountered.

R3 = Review. Sounds like we've been through this before, doesn't it? By review, Robinson meant what I meant when I cautioned you to schedule time to go back over your classroom notes, plan to read your text more than once, and reevaluate your study strategy after every quiz or exam.

Outline ~ Chapter 15: Industrial/Organizational, Environmental, and Sport Psychology

TOPIC 15A: INDUSTRIAL/ORGANIZATIONAL PSYCHOLOGY

I. **Industrial/organizational (I/O) psychologists** specialize in the scientific study of affect, behavior, and cognition in work settings.
   A. I/O psychology is one of the fastest growing areas of specialization in psychology.
   B. Fitting the person to the job and the job to the person are two important considerations.

II. Defining "Good Work": The Job Analysis

   A. Issues relevant to I/O psychology include personnel selection, training, and motivation.
   B. One must begin with a **job analysis**, which involves a study of the tasks, duties, and responsibilities of a job and the abilities needed to perform it.
      1. Someone who is presently in the job or a supervisor of that position may write a job analysis.
      2. Writing a complete job analysis is a two-step process.
         a. One must compile a complete description of the behaviors required for a person in that job.
         b. The **performance criteria**, or measurable personal characteristics required to do the job well, must also be specified.
         c. Both hard (objective) and soft (subjective) criteria may be considered.

III. Selecting People Who Can Do Good Work
   A. A job application form can serve three useful functions.
      1. It can be used as a rough screening device.
      2. It can supplement or provide cues for interviewing.
      3. It provides biographical data (biodata) that may be useful in making predictions about a candidate's potential.
   B. The employment interview is an integral part of personnel selection procedures.
      1. Structured interviews are more valid than unstructured interviews.
         2. They consist of a prescribed series of questions asked of all applicants in the same order.
   C. Personnel selection often involves the administration and interpretation of psychological tests.
      1. Although personnel selection usually focuses on measures of cognitive ability, personality inventories, both general and specific, have proven to be useful in making decisions.
      2. Situational testing refers to giving applicants the opportunity to role-play the task they may be hired to do.
      3. It is important that tests demonstrate validity.

IV. Training People to Do Good Work
   A. Training is a systematic process of changing the behavior of employees to contribute to organizational effectiveness.
   B. To design and implement a training program, the following steps are useful.
      1. Assess training needs, and specific behavioral objectives.
         a. Is a training program really needed?
         b. What will it be designed to do?
         c. How will it be evaluated when it is over?
         d. General statements may be okay at first, but specific statements of specific goals are needed.
      2. Decide on the most effective training techniques to use.
         a. There are many training methods and trainers need to fight getting into a rut.
         b. Which technique to use depends upon factors such as the behaviors being trained, the nature of the trainees, the resources available, and the like.
         c. By and large, in general, hands-on, participation techniques tend to be effective

3. Measure the training effectiveness.
   a. One can evaluate affect, or behaviors, or cognitions when training is over.
   b. Effectiveness may be measured in the short-term, but also should be measured in the long-term.
   c. The more effort put into a training program from the beginning, the easier will it be to evaluate effectiveness.

V. Motivating People to Do Good Work
   A. There are three interrelated processes for motivating employees.
      1. The worker must be *aroused* to do a task.
      2. He or she must be *directed* to do the task.
      3. *Sustaining* the worker to remain on task is also important.
   B. The expectancy theory says that workers behave rationally and logically, making work-related decisions based on their beliefs, judgments, and expectations.
      1. Vroom's theory suggests that workers are motivated if they expect rewards to be contingent on levels of performance and if they value the rewards being offered.
      2. Workers must understand the relationship between their behaviors and outcomes.
   C. Equity theory, associated with J. Stacy Adams, claims that what matters most to workers is their perception of the extent to which they are being treated fairly compared to fellow workers in similar work situations.
      1. The perception of equity is what matters here.
      2. If there is a perceived inequity, changes can be predicted.
   D. Goal setting is the approach to motivating workers that is currently receiving the most research interest.
      1. Difficult but achievable goals tend to increase productivity more than easy goals.
      2. Specific, focused goals are better than general ones.
      3. Immediate feedback, which informs workers of their progress, is important in maintaining motivated behaviors.
      4. Employees must be aware of specific goals and accept those goals as reasonable. It is important to be sensitive to cultural issues.
   E. Other approaches to motivation include the importance of workers' needs and an approach called organizational behavior management, which uses operant conditioning and attends to the consequences of behavior.

VI. Job Satisfaction
   A. Job satisfaction refers to the attitude one holds toward one's work.
   B. Satisfaction can vary considerably for various aspects of a job.
   C. Research has looked for relationships between job satisfaction and characteristics of workers.
      1. There is a positive correlation between global job satisfaction and age.
      2. Gender differences are virtually nonexistent when pay, tenure, and education are controlled.
      3. Racial differences in job satisfaction in the U.S. have been small.
      4. Satisfaction is positively related to the perceived level or status of one's job.
      5. There do appear to be cultural differences in job satisfaction.

VII. Job Satisfaction and Work Behaviors
   A. Research often refutes the contention that increased performance necessarily results from increased satisfaction.
   B. Increased performance on the job may. In fact, promote job satisfaction.
   C. Job satisfaction measures can be used to aid the prediction of which workers are likely to be absent from work and which are likely to quit.
   D. *Job burnout* is a prolonged reaction to stressors in the workplace and predicts absenteeism and leaving the job altogether.

VIII. Worker Safety
  A. Safety in the workplace is an important concern and costs billions of dollars each year.
      1. As well as industrial accidents, interpersonal violence is also a growing concern.
      2. Women are often victims of workplace violence-teachers and nurses, in particular.
  B. Finding characteristics that might represent being "accident prone" has proven futile.
  C. Employers must see to it that workers are trained in safe ways to do their jobs and that safe behaviors are valued.
  D. Landy's (1989) *engineering approach* attempts to reduce accidents by designing safer equipment and implementing safer procedures.

TOPIC 15B: ENVIRONMENTAL AND SPORT PSYCHOLOGY

I.   Psychology and the Environment
  A. **Environmental psychology** is the study of how the general environment affects the behavior and mental processes of those living in it, and how people affect their environments.
  B. Environmental psychologists recognize that what may influence behavior most is one's perception of the physical environment.

II. Space and Territory
  A. **Personal space** is a mobile, imaginary bubble that surrounds a person and into which others may enter comfortably by invitation only.
  B. Hall (1966) claimed that personal space can be subdivided into four different distances, relevant for Western cultures.
      1. *Intimate distance* is defined as being between actual contact and about 18 inches.
      2. *Personal distance* is reserved for day-to-day interactions, and is from 18 inches to approximately four feet.
      3. Four to twelve feet is defined as *social distance*.
      4. *Public distance* is between 12 and 25 feet.
  C. **Territoriality** refers to setting off and marking a piece of geographical location as one's own.
      1. *Primary territories* are defined and claimed for the long term to maintain a sense of privacy and a sense of identity.
      2. *Secondary territories* are more flexible and less well-defined.
      3. *Public territories* are those one occupies for only a short time.
  D. When space and territory are violated, we can predict negative outcomes such as anxiety, distress, and sometimes aggression.

III. Life in the City: An Example
  A. By the year 2030, more than 80 percent of the population of North America, Latin America, Europe, and Oceana will live in cities.
  B. In 1962, Calhoun published his study on the overcrowding of rats, and researchers wanted to know if his observations would apply to humans.
  C. **Population density** refers to the number of people (or animals) per unit of area.
  D. **Crowding**, a psychological concept, is a subjective feeling of discomfort produced by a perceived lack of space.
      1. Crowding is a negative reaction.
      2. The negativity of crowding is largely related to one's sense of control over one's life and the situation at hand.
  E. There are advantages and disadvantages to cit life; crowding may be off set by the availability of valued resources..

IV. Noise, Temperature, and Environmental Toxins
  A. Noise is defined as an intrusive, unwanted, or excessive experience of sound.
      1. Noise levels have predictable effects on the performance of cognitive tasks.

2. More than ten million American school children are exposed to adverse levels of noise on a daily basis.
B. Extremes of temperature can have adverse effects on behavior.
   1. Riots are more likely to occur when the outside temperature is between 75 and 90 degrees.
   2. When temperatures are above 90 degrees, rioting is less likely to occur.
   3. Human sexual behaviors also decline during the very hot summer months.
C. Psychologists are engaged in research on neurotoxins, which have poisonous effects on the human nervous system.
   1. Even in small doses, some neurotoxins can cause behavioral and emotional changes in people.
   2. Exposure to these dangerous chemicals may be more readily diagnosed through behavioral or psychological means than through medical diagnosis.

V. Changing Behaviors That Impact on the Environment
   A. Psychologists have been active in establishing programs aimed at changing the behaviors of people to benefit the environment.
   B. **Applied behavior analysis (ABA)** is derived from the work of Skinner and the procedures of operant conditioning.
      1. ABA attempts to operationally define some target behavior to be modified.

      2. The next step is to determine the environmental conditions that prompt the behavior.
      3. The third step is to determine the consequences that increase, decrease, or maintain the targeted behavior.
   C. Behaviors will change and be maintained to the extent that those behaviors produce certain consequences.

VI. Psychology and Sport
   A. **Sport psychology** involves the application of psychological principles to sports and physical activities at all levels of skill development.
   B. Athletes usually score higher than non-athletes do on tests of assertion, dominance, aggression, and need for achievement; they score lower on anxiety, depression, and fatigue.

VII. Maximizing Athletic Performance
   A. One area of interest focuses on manipulating the arousal level necessary for the task.
   B. Pocket billiards is different from other sports, and is susceptible to streaks of performance or "hot hands."
      1. This is due to the lack of time between shooting, and that the opponent can do nothing to effect outcome.
      2. These factors can enable a billiards player to win more games.
   C. Psychologists try to enable athletes to give their best, or peak performance.
   D. Mental imagery combined with physical practice has proven beneficial.
      1. It is helpful to mentally rehearse a particular behavior pattern.
      2. It is important to reduce negative thoughts that may interfere with performance.
      3. It is recommended that one rehearse one's role in a team sport.
      4. One should set realistic goals.

Practice Test Questions

TOPIC 15A: INDUSTRIAL/ORGANIZATIONAL PSYCHOLOGY

Multiple Choice

1. There are several things an employer can do to improve the quality of the work force. Which of these is LEAST important?
   __ a. Find good people to start with.
   __ b. Work to improve employee satisfaction.
   __ c. Train the present work force to work well.
   __ d. Motivate employees td do their best.

2. Typically, an employee selection program begins with
   __ a. a listing of required or desired characteristics provided by management.
   __ b. an inventory of available tests and assessment techniques.
   __ c. an appraisal of current employees.
   __ d. a complete job analysis.

3. A job analysis may include each of these, but to be useful, it should include performance criteria, or
   __ a. a full listing of salaries, wages, and benefits.
   __ b. a listing of situations in which the job is to be performed.
   __ c. a list of characteristics needed for someone to do the job well.
   __ d. a listing of input from everyone else regarding what the duties of the job are.

4. In a job analysis, when Smith differentiates between "hard" and "soft" criteria, she is really differentiating between
   __ a. physical labor jobs and mental labor jobs.
   __ b. objective data and subjective judgments.
   __ c. blue-collar and white-collar positions.
   __ d. professionally gathered data and general impressions.

5. Of the following techniques for gathering information about prospective employees, which tends to provide the LEAST useful information?
   __ a. psychological tests   __ c. assessment centers
   __ b. unstructured interviews   __ d. application forms

6. In devising a training program for employees, what is the first question that an I/O psychologist should ask?
   __ a. Who is going to receive this training?
   __ b. What techniques will be used to get information across to the trainees?
   __ c. How will the outcome of the training be evaluated?
   __ d. Is this training really necessary?

7. By far, the approach that employers most often use in attempting to increase productivity is
   __ a. employee training.
   __ b. motivational seminars.
   __ c. improving morale.
   __ d. finding new and different employees.

8. In general, training programs are usually evaluated in terms of
   __ a. job analyses.   __ c. employee's needs.
   __ b. training objectives.   __ d. trainee satisfaction.

9. Although clearly there are exceptions, which approach to employee training in general is the most effective?

    __ a. one that involves hands-on experience

    __ b. one that uses classroom instruction by an expert

    __ c. one that uses as many media as possible

    __ d. one that involves repeated demonstrations

10. Which level of evaluation of a training program is likely to be of LEAST interest to the employer?

    __ a. amount of information acquired

    __ b. extent to which actual behaviors have been changed

    __ c. how participants feel about the training received

    __ d. extent to which profitability has been increased

11. Which of the following is seldom a goal of any program to motivate employees?

    __ a. getting the worker to do any task

    __ b. getting the worker to do the task we want done

    __ c. getting the worker to enjoy the task being done

    __ d. getting the worker to keep at the task

12. Equity theory claims that what matters most to employees is the extent to which

    __ a. they are making more money than employees in similar positions.

    __ b. they understand the goals they are trying to reach.

    __ c. they perceive that they are being treated fairly compared to others.

    __ d. they expect to be rewarded for what they value.

13. Job satisfaction

    __ a. is positively correlated with overall productivity.

    __ b. levels are pretty much the same in all known cultures.

    __ c. is a good predictor of absenteeism and employee turnover.

    __ d. causes increased performance on the job.

True/False

1. ___True ___False   In the United States and in other industrialized nations, worker safety issues are no longer viewed as a significant problem.

2. ___True ___False   Psychological testing and other assessment techniques can identify accident-prone individuals.

3. ___True ___False   Application forms provide a good source of biodata

4. ___True ___False   Structured interviews are more valid than unstructured interviews.

5. ___True ___False   Vroom's 1964 Expectancy Theory is mostly cognitive in its approach to employee motivation.

TOPIC 15B: ENVIRONMENTAL AND SPORT PSYCHOLOGY

Multiple Choice

1. In what way are environmental psychology and sport psychology alike?

    __ a. They both derive from Skinnerian behaviorism.

__ b. They both are fields of applied psychology.
__ c. They both are more concerned with cognitions than with affect or behavior.
__ d. They both began during World War II.

2. Psychologists have identified many types of space or territory. That with the smallest area is called
    __ a. intimate space.   __ c. social space.
    __ b. personal space.   __ d. public space.

3. What is likely to be the response made to an invasion of one's personal space?
    __ a. stress   __ c. anxiety
    __ b. physical aggression   __ d. withdrawal

4. If you are taking an exam in a classroom, you are occupying
    __ a. someone's social space.   __ c. a public territory.
    __ b. a primary territory.   __ d. someone's secondary space.

5. The difference between "population density" and "overcrowding" is mostly a difference in
    __ a. one's previous experience.
    __ b. the types of organisms involved.
    __ c. feelings of distress or discomfort.
    __ d. the number of organisms per unit of area.

6. Each of the following is likely to be a stressor associated with life in a big city EXCEPT
    __ a. airborne toxins.   __ c. noise pollution.
    __ b. available resources.   __ d. crime rates.

7. What aspect of noise can make it particularly stressful when one is attempting a cognitive task?
    __ a. its predictability   __ c. its loudness
    __ b. its tone or pitch   __ d. its melody

8. At which temperature are riots most likely to occur?
    __ a. 36 degrees F   __ c. 86 degrees F
    __ b. 66 degrees F   __ d. 106 degrees F

9. Applied behavior analysis, as used by environmental psychologists among others, is based on the work of
    __ a. Sigmund Freud.   __ c. B.F. Skinner.
    __ b. Jean Piaget.   __ d. Rachel Carson.

10. To the extent that there is such a thing as "getting a hot hand," or "being in a groove or zone" in sports, the sport for which the supportive evidence is best is
    __ a. tennis.   __ c. pocket billiards.
    __ b. golf.   __ d. professional basketball.

11. When is frenzied, excessive fan support most likely to have a negative or adverse effect on the home team's performance?
    __ a. early in the season when the team is on defense
    __ b. early in the season when the team is on offense
    __ c. in a championship game when the team is on defense
    __ d. in a championship game when the team is on offense

True/False

1. ___True ___False   Primary territories are those spaces we think of as ours and no one else's.

2. ___True ___False   In both India and the United States, the stress of city life is significantly reduced if one believes that one has the freedom to leave the city if one really wants to.

3. ___True ___False   If we want to reward someone for engaging in an appropriate, complex pattern of behavior, applied behavior analysis tells us that we should hold off on giving a reward until the entire behavior pattern has been repeated several times.

4. ___True ___False   Hockey and football players have a higher tolerance for pain than do bowlers and golfers.

5. ___True ___False   Mental imagery or mental practice can help an athlete reach his or her peak performance.

Key Terms and Concepts
Topic 15A

industrial/organizational (I/O) psychology_____

_____

job analysis_____

_____

performance criteria_____

_____

training_____

_____

expectancy theory_____

_____

equity theory_____

_____

job satisfaction_____

_____

Topic 15B

environmental psychology_____

_____

personal space_____

_____

territoriality_____

_____

population density_____

_____

crowding_____

_____

noise_____

_____

neurotoxins_____

_____

applied behavior analysis_____

_____

sport psychology_____

_____

Answers to Practice Test Questions

TOPIC I5A: INDUSTRIAL/ORGANIZATION PSYCHOLOGY

Multiple Choice

1. **b.** Well-intended employers might take steps to see that their employees were happy or satisfied with their jobs, but the truth is that employee satisfaction is the least important of these factors.

2. **d.** Any of the first three statements might describe actions you would like to take, but to get things going, one first does a complete job analysis.

3. **c.** Again, if you were an employer looking to hire people, you might be concerned with each of these things, but it would be critical to have decided on performance criteria which, by definition, are those characteristics an employee will need to do the job well.

4. **b.** Hard criteria are objective and can be measured, while soft criteria are more subjective and call for opinions or judgments.

5. **b.** Unstructured interviews are notoriously poor in terms of validity as an assessment technique (which is not to say that interviews have no place in the process, particularly if they are structured interviews).

6. **d.** I think that this is quite insightful. The very first thing that must be asked—and too often is not—is whether any sort of training program is needed in the first place.

7. **a.** The data are clear on this one. In terms of money and time invested, employers are most likely going to go with training to try to increase productivity.

8. **b.** Training programs are evaluated in terms of specific behavioral goals which are specified in the program's training objectives.

9. **a.** As is the case for virtually all types of training and education, the more the trainee is actively involved in a hands-on experience, the better the training will be.

10. **c.** We could probably debate this one, but I would think that employers would be least concerned about how the participants felt about their training, and most concerned with bottom-line profitability issues. The real answer, of course, will depend on the original goals of the training.

11. **c.** Again, I think the best argument is that one would be least interested in whether the employee enjoyed what he or she was doing, so long as he or she did it well.

12. **c.** By definition, equity theory deals with the workers' perception of fair treatment compared to other workers at the same level within the organization.

13. **c.** Although job satisfaction is not a good predictor of job productivity (and it certainly does not cause increased performance), it is a good predictor of absenteeism and turnover.

True/False

1. **F** Issues of worker safety are very important indeed. Over $100 billion is lost each year in the U.S. to industrial accidents. Did you note how these first two items are "out of order?"

2. **F** Unfortunately, they cannot. There does not seem to be any constellation of personality traits that can lead us to predict whether a person is likely to be accident-prone.

3. **T** Again, this is so simple, it may have given you pause to think. Biodata are types of information about oneself-exactly the sorts of things asked for on application forms.

4. **T** Definitely. In fact, structured devices of any sort are more valid than unstructured ones.

5. **T** Vroom believed that workers behaved rationally and logically and on that basis, constructed a cognitive model of worker motivation.

TOPIC 15B: ENVIRONMENTAL AND SPORT PSYCHOLOGY

Multiple Choice

1. **b.** They are related only in the sense that they are both varieties of applied psychology. The other alternatives are flat wrong.

2. **a.** These labels for psychological space judgments are listed in order from smallest to largest.

3. **a.** How one responds to that stress remains to be seen, but the invasion of one's's personal space is a stressor, producing stress.

4. **c.** All this space and territory labeling does get confusing, but I believe the only relevant alternative here is the third one.

5. **c.** The main issue here (as it often is) is one's perception, one's feeling of distress and discomfort that accompanies overcrowding.

6. **b.** Indeed, one of the advantages of city life, not one of its stressors, is that there generally are many more resources available to its population.

7. **a.** I'm not sure I know what the "melody" of a noise would be; tone and loudness do matter, but what matters most is the predictability of noise.

8. **c.** This may appear to be a picky item, but I don't think that it is. The answer is 86 degrees—not 106 degrees, where the temperature is so high as to debilitate everyone, i.e., it's too hot to riot.

9. **c.** Applied behavior analysis, even as practiced today, is a nearly literal translation of the work of B.F. Skinner to the real world.

10. **c.** The answer is pocket billiards, at least at the professional level. One critical thing is that once one player begins to shoot, there's nothing that the other player can do about it.

11. **d.** This is a two-part question. First, it's clear that fan support will have more of an effect (positive or negative) in a championship game. Then, the negative effect occurs more commonly when the team is on offense, trying to execute a variety of maneuvers that become difficult with very high levels of arousal. This is true, by the way, for virtually any team sport.

True/False

1. **T**   This isn't a bad definition of a primary territory.

2. **T**   The sense of being in control of one's fate reduces stress from nearly every source. Just the belief that one can escape overcrowding makes that overcrowding more bearable.

3. **F**   The more you think about this, the sillier it should sound. If reinforcers are to be effective, they need to be administered as soon as possible after the appropriate behavior.

4. **T**   This one makes sense, doesn't it? What's not clear is which is cause and which is effect, but this is a true statement.

5. **T**   There is considerable evidence that mental practice and imaging can be beneficial in athletic training.

EXPERIENCING PSYCHOLOGY

Manager for a Day

Jack Farwell is plant manager for Acme Flange Fabrication, Inc., a manufacturing company in the Midwest that is experiencing several problems. Pressured by foreign imports and a reduced demand for the high-quality flanges that AFF makes have reduced profits considerably.

Jack sees the need for increased productivity as an opportunity to introduce some changes at AFF. He wants to use some of the new technology that has revolutionized flange manufacturing. He also realizes that to return Acme Flange to its highly respected position in the industry, management will have to take a new look at techniques to motivate a group of talented but discouraged factory workers.

Installing new equipment and restructuring the organization means retraining at all levels of the company. In some cases, retraining will be directed at the acquisition of new skills; in others, it will mean fostering changes in attitudes and communication styles. To complicate matters, contract negotiations with the local union begin soon. Farwell wants to be sure that the changes he is proposing can be implemented while enhancing job satisfaction among AFF employees. He will have to address concerns about day care, flexible time schedules, and pregnancy leaves.

Now, being as specific and brief as possible, see what sort of advice you can offer Mr. Farwell, based on your reading of this chapter. Here are a few specific "issues"—

1. Jack needs to hire an assistant plant manager. What is one of the first things that Jack has to do?

2. In selecting a new assistant manager form a list of candidates, what are some of the sources of information that Jack can use in his effort to find the best person for the job?

3. If Jack sent his current supervisors to an I/O psychologist in hopes of finding a potential assistant manager from that group, what sorts of assessments might these supervisors encounter?

4. Once Jack hires a new assistant, he feels that the supervisors and sales people will need training in order to effectively deal with new production techniques and newly developed products. What are some of the questions that Jack needs to ask with regard to his plans for a training program?

5. Jack wants to motivate his employees to do their best work. For each of the following approaches to worker motivation, what issues will Jack have to address? (a) expectancy theory (b) equity theory (c) goal setting

6. No matter what, Jack has to improve productivity at the plant. To what extent does Jack need to concern himself with issues of worker satisfaction?